IRON
DIVISION

KT-458-840

I had the great honour to command the 3rd Division in the early days of the World War II. During those days the Division gained for itself a very fine reputation; it never failed to achieve what was required from it; it always stood firm as a rock in battle.

This reputation was maintained in the campaign in North-West Europe from Normandy to the Baltic: right up to the end of the war.

Now we are at peace.

The 3rd Division is a Regular Division of the British Army. I am confident that it will continue to maintain in times of peace the splendid reputation it gained on the battlefields of World War II.

Montgomery of Alamein
Field Marshal

4-10-46

Above: The original draft by Field Marshal Viscount Montgomery of a Special Order of the Day issued on his visit to 3rd Division in the Suez Canal Zone on 4 October 1946./*Lady Whistler*

Below: A rifle section of the 2nd Battalion East Yorkshire Regiment, forming up under fire for the assault on Venrai, October 1944.
/Imperial War Museum

IRON DIVISION

The History of the 3rd Division

Robin McNish

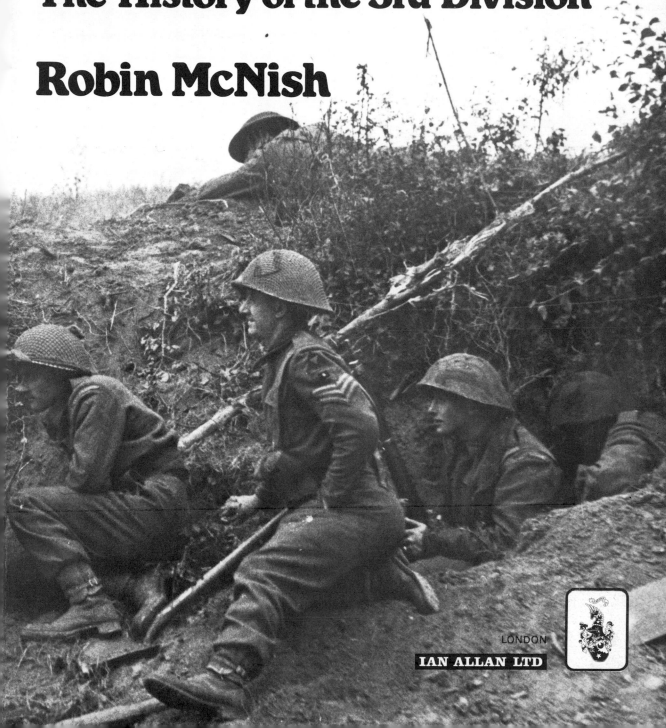

LONDON

IAN ALLAN LTD

First published 1978

ISBN 0 7110 0837 X

All rights reserved. No part of this book may be
reproduced or transmitted in any form or by any
means, electronic or mechanical, including photo-
copying, recording or by any information storage
and retrieval system, without permission from the
Publisher in writing

Design by Anthony Wirkus LSIAD

© Crown Copyright 1978
Published with the permission of the
Controller of Her Majesty's Stationery Office

Published by Ian Allan Ltd, Shepperton, Surrey,
and printed in the United Kingdom by
Ian Allan Printing Ltd

Contents

Chapters 10 and 11 include Sections on 38 Group
Royal Air Force, with whom 3rd Division was
closely associated from 1960 to 1977.

The sketches on the title pages of each Chapter were
drawn by David O'Driscoll.

HERTFORDSHIRE
COUNTY LIBRARY

356·110

8794148

Left: Bivouac area of the 3rd Division at Vila Velha during the
Peninsular War. Today's soldiers will recognise many aspects of
bivouac life ranging from Security of Weapons to Maintenance of
Transport./*National Army Musuem*

The Divisional Sign

Formation signs were first introduced during World War I. The sign adopted by 3rd Division was that shown on the left — a St Andrews Cross over a circle, in yellow or sometimes white. It was taken from the Arms of Major-General Aylmer Haldane, GOC from 1914 to 1916. It was used as a means of readily identifying transport, and there is no confirmation that it was ever worn on uniform.

Formation signs lapsed between the wars but were reintroduced early in 1940, patterns again being decided by GOCs. Major-General Bernard Montgomery chose the well-known sign, shown on the right, of three black triangles surrounding an inverted red triangle. The 'pattern of three' represented the Third Division, composed of three infantry brigades, each of three battalions. Initially the sign was used only on vehicles, but after Dunkirk it became standard wear on battle dress. The triangles sign has been in use ever since and continues to be the sign used by 3rd Armoured Division.

Brigade and Unit Identifications

In 1944 and 1945, brigades were identified by the wearing of horizontal red strips under the Divisional sign. 8 Brigade (the senior) wore one strip, 9 Brigade wore two, and 185 Brigade wore three strips. By this time Regimental shoulder titles had also been adopted and these were worn above the Triangles; previously units had been identified by coloured flashes worn below the Triangles, eg the East Yorkshires wore a Red-White-Black strip, and the Royal Ulster Rifles a Dark Green and Black quartered square. On the reformation of 3rd Division in 1951, brigades continued to wear the Divisional sign. However after 1957 brigades frequently moved between divisions, and they therefore adopted their own brigade signs. These are illustrated in the back end paper.

Foreword
Field Marshal Lord Carver, GCB, CBE, DSO, MC

I am delighted to have been asked to write a foreword for this history of the 3rd Division, which I had the honour to command from 1962 to 1964.

Lieutenant-Colonel McNish, in these pages of text and illustration, has brought to life a great story of which all those who have served in the division have reason to be proud. Although the division's exploits form only a small proportion of the whole history of the British Army, they illustrate vividly what life and fighting has been like for the average British soldier since Wellington's day, when the army has been involved in major wars. Between them, and especially in the minor campaigns which have continued throughout the army's history, the soldier's loyalty is focused on smaller organisations, his unit, his regiment or brigade.

3rd Division, being a regular division has had no particular territorial link nor permanent affiliation. Nevertheless it has generally had a particularly English flavour about it, although Scottish, Irish and Welsh units have often been included and at Waterloo itself two of its three brigades were foreign in origin.

Normally fated to suffer disbandment between major wars, the division's identity has been preserved. However, for the last twenty years it has formed part of the army's strategic reserve and in that rôle pioneered the skills of rapid movement by air, both strategically and tactically. Now it turns, for the first time in its history, to the rôle of an armoured division, taking with it a fine reputation to which these pages pay eloquent tribute.

Michael Carver

FM

Introduction

When General Michael Walsh tasked me with writing this book my mind was invaded by a host of questions, the foremost of these being at what level to pitch the Division's history, ranging from 1809 to 1977, bearing in mind the limitations of space and time. But when I considered the aim given me — to produce a book which would interest and inspire present and future members of the Division — this question quickly resolved itself. Other than to explain the immediate background to 3rd Division's activities, this book contains the minimum of strategy and politics. Instead it endeavours, by using personal accounts wherever possible, to show how the Division and its members have fared in success and adversity over 168 years of war and turbulent peace. Events and accounts have been selected with a view to producing a balanced story, but inevitably many units, individuals and events, with an equal claim to mention, will have been omitted. All I can do is apologise with humility, and say that they are here in spirit if not in name.

Readers will note that there were long periods in the 19th Century when no 3rd Division existed, and may therefore question 1809 as the starting point. My answer would be that while it is true that no continuous thread runs from the 3rd Division of the Peninsular War to the 3rd Division of the 1970s, what matters is that men will always draw strength and inspiration from the achievments of those who have borne the same unit or formation title in the past. Aylmer Haldane, who commanded 3rd Division from 1914 to 1916 knew this well when he wrote:

'The 3rd Division was the lineal descendant of the division of that number which Sir Arthur Wellesley, on 18 June 1809, had formed in Portugal. The commander whose name will always remain most intimately associated with the 3rd Division was Sir Thomas Picton, under whom it earned the soubriquet of "The Fighting Division". While under my command it lost none of its laurels, and became widely known as "The Iron Division".

'That the 3rd Division maintained so great a name was attributable to the enforcement of discipline and a strong sense of duty, supplemented by the existence of divisional espirit de corps, which I did everything in my power to create and foster. Soon after I got command I compiled a pamphlet which embodies that history and it was issued to all ranks serving in it and to reinforcements.'

Haldane's policy continues to this day, for any soldier entering the Headquarters of 3rd Division reads in prominent gold lettering that Major-General MacKenzie was the first Divisional Commander, and that Talavera and Bussaco are its first Battle Honours.

The existence of Divisional espirit de corps which Haldane highlighted invites comment on a further subject — the relationship between the Division and its component Regiments. Regimental espirit de corps has been, and will always be, one of the singular strengths of the British Army, but in the intensive fighting of 1914-18 and 1944-45, reinforcements were often drafted to units regardless of parent regiment. In these circumstances the title 'Iron Division' or the wearing of the three black triangles provided an instant corporate fighting spirit, and in postwar times a common standard of training and operational readiness has continued to foster this same spirit among the units of many different arms and services that compose the Division.

It is hoped that readers of this book will find interest and entertainment and some will no doubt look for lessons to learn. While I am certain they will find a goodly number, in my opinion the lesson that stands out is that success in war depends not only on leadership in battle but also on preparation beforehand. Sufficient resources, equipment and time must be made available to enable the units of a formation to train together realistically in peacetime, and if any of these elements is missing, success in operations cannot be assured.   RRM

Left: A Sergeant of the 2nd Battalion, Royal Warwickshire Regiment, 185 Infantry Brigade, in 1944./*Imperial War Museum*

Acknowledgements

Major-General Walsh has asked me to start by expressing his thanks to the Trustees of the Army Central Fund and the Trustees of the Robert Ogilby Trust for their generous financial assistance, without which the publication of this history would not have been possible.

Producing the book has brought me in contact with very many charming, helpful people, and it is difficult to do full justice to the quality of their assistance, but nonetheless I will try.

First, I must acknowledge the help of those experts who took the trouble to read through and comment on specific chapters; in Chapter 1, Major George Ward's advice on the formation and development of Divisions in the Peninsular War was invaluable and I must also thank him for drawing my attention to the Hawley Letters, which were edited by him, and used in Chapter 3; while Major Freddie Myatt of the Weapons Museum, Warminster, gave me the greatest possible help concerning Infantry weapons and battle tactics in the Peninsular War and later campaigns. In writing Chapter 2, I found that Lt-Col Joe Bell, RAChD, had made a detailed study of the Waterloo campaign, and I am most grateful for his assistance. For commenting on Chapters dealing with the World Wars, I must thank the following officers who fought with the 3rd Division during those years: In Chapter 5, Brigadier E. K. Page, late 130 Howitzer Battery, RFA; Chapter 6, Brigadier D. R. Wilson, late Royal Lincolns; Lt-Col H. W. Faure Walker, late Coldstream, and Lt-Col M. R. R. Turner, late East Yorkshires; and in Chapters 7 and 8, General Sir Richard Goodwin, late CO 1st Suffolk, Major-General C. L. Firbank, late CO 2nd Lincolns, and Brigadier G. G. Mears, late CRA 3rd Division.

My thanks are particularly due to Lady Whistler, and Mrs H. E. Richardson, the widow of General Rennie, for granting me access to their late husbands' documents and photographs. I am also very grateful to Mrs Doris Pullan, the widow of Hugh Gunning, 3rd Division's Press Officer 1944-1945, for allowing me to examine her late husband's papers and despatches.

The Section on CANLOAN in Chapter 7 was prepared from material kindly supplied by Lieutenant Lorne Ballance, President of the Association, and by Lt-Col Rex Fendick.

I must thank Flight Lieutenant Jim Ashton for writing the sections on 38 Group Royal Air Force in Chapters 10 and 11 and for selecting the aircraft photographs; and Squadron Leader David Bates for co-ordinating all aspects of the 38 Group contribution.

The history of a Division is entwined with the histories of units that have formed part of it. I particularly wish to thank the following members of Regimental Headquarters and Associations who have helped in many different ways: Major H. W. Schofield, HQ Household Division; Colonel J. A. C. G. Eyre, RHQ The Household Cavalry; Major C. W. J. Lewis, The Blues and Royals Association; Major B. O. Simmonds, Home HQ, 15th/19th Kings Royal Hussars; Lt-Col G. B. Eastwood and Major R. G. Bartelot, The Royal Artillery Institution; Major P. H. Cordle, RHQ The Grenadier Guards; Colonel B. A. Fargus, RHQ The Royal Scots; Lt-Col R. K. May and Major A. E. S. Jackson, RHQ The Kings Own Royal Border Regiment; Lt-Col W. W. M. Chard, RHQ The Royal Regiment of Fusiliers; Lt-Col R. M. Pratt, The Royal Northumberland Fusiliers Association; Lt-Col M. Ryan, The Royal Warwickshire Regimental Museum; Lt-Col A. W. J. Turnbull, Royal Norfolk Regiment Association; Lt-Col H. S. R. Case, The Suffolk Regiment Association; Captain A. R. Smith, RHQ Royal Anglian Regiment (Lincolnshire), Major T. A. Girdwood, Royal Anglian (Bedfordshire & Hertfordshire), and Major T. R. Stead, Royal Anglian (Essex); Lt-Col J. K. Windeatt, RHQ The Devonshire and Dorset Regiment; Lt-Col A. C. M. Urwick, Light Infantry Office (Taunton); Colonel G. M. Thornycroft, Light Infantry (Shropshire & Hereford); Lt-Col R. B. Humphreys, Light Infantry (Durham); Lt-Col C. J. Robinson, East Yorkshire Regiment Association; Lt-Col W. M. B. Dunn, RHQ Kings Own Scottish Borderers; Lt-Col W. R. H. Charley, RHQ The Royal Irish Rangers; Lt-Col J. D. Ricketts, RHQ The Worcestershire and Sherwood Foresters Regiment; Major M. K. Beedle, RHQ The Staffordshire Regiment; Major A. D. Parsons and Major T. J. Cooper, RHQ Duke of Edinburgh's Royal Regiment; Lt-Col G. P. Wood, RHQ The Argyll and Sutherland Highlanders; Colonel J. R. Baker and Major H. P. Patterson, RHQ, Royal Green Jackets; Lt-Col G. C. E. Crew, RAChD Museum; Major-General A. Maclennan, The RAMC Museum; Major R. T. R. Whistler, RHQ The Royal Military Police; Lt-Col W. W. Leary, HQ The Intelligence Corps; and Lt-Col P. Massey, HQ The Honourable Artillery Company. I must also thank those units that contributed photographs for Chapters 10 and 11.

I am indebted to the many individuals who have provided me with personal accounts, documents, photographs, and background information, and have helped in many other ways; I apologise for any inadvertent omissions from this list: Major R. W. Acworth, Lt-Col K. St B. Adams, Major J. F. Ainsworth, Captain M. J. Ball, Lt W. Banks, Mr R. Barnard, Mr G. E. Bayley, Brigadier F. A. Bibra, General Sir Cecil Blacker, Mr Charles Blackwood, Major Gregory Blaxland, Major B. N. G. Bleackley, General Sir Robert Bray, Maj-Gen H. E. N. Bredin, Miss Ena Brown, Brigadier G. D. Browne, Major H. W. Bruce, Major M. D. Burroughes, Maj-Gen R. M. Carnegie, Field Marshal Lord Carver, Lt-Col R. H. Chappell, Maj-Gen J. B. Churcher, Mr Tom Coyne, Brigadier J. C. Cunningham, Brigadier B. W. Davis, Maj-Gen A. J. Deane-Drummond, Rt Hon Edmund Dell MP, Major George Duckett, Captain A. C. Duckworth RN (Rctd),

Lt-Col C. C. Dunphie, Captain Richard East, Maj-Gen D. B. Egerton, Mr T. J. Fairbank, Brigadier G. R. Flood, Captain R. D. Franks RN (Retd), Brigadier F. W. E. Fursdon, Major R. J. M. Garrett, Major J. W. Gibson, Captain A. A. Gilbert, Maj-Gen G. C. A. Gilbert, Lt-Gen Sir George Gordon-Lennox, Rear Admiral E. F. Gueritz, Mr M. L. B. Hall, General Sir Charles Harington, Major C. J. D. Haswell, Colonel W. A. Heal, Captain D. Hewlett, Lt-Col C. A. S. Hinton, Captain R. L. Hislop, Capt A. H. Hopkins, Brigadier H. C. Illing, Major Michael Jackson, Brigadier R. M. Jerram, Lt-Col E. Jones, Brigadier E. H. P. Lassen, Maj-Gen A. R. Leakey, Major G. E. Lewis, Major J. F. Lister, Lt-Col B. C. Mallinson, Lt-Col R. M. S. Maude, Major B. S. McCombe, Lt-Gen Sir Terence McMeekin, Lt L. A. Neal, Dr I. D. Paterson, Maj-Gen J. H. Penrose, Captain D. J. Perry, Mr Paul Phillips, Major H. B. Pirie, General Sir Nigel Poett, Capt C. J. L. Puxley, Major I. H. K. Rae, Colonel J. D. W. Renison, Major A. J. Rennie, Lt-Col A. J. Robertson, Major M. J. C. Robertson, Brigadier D. Rossiter, Major A. R. Rouse, Mr Norman Scarfe, Lt-Col N. G. Scotter, Colonel R. H. Senior, Lt-Col John Stubbs, Major A. D. Slyfield, Lt R. J. S. Smith, Colonel A. C. L. Sperling, Mr E. J. Spinks, General Sir Hugh Stockwell, Maj-Gen Sir Nigel Tapp, Maj-Gen P. A. M. Tighe, Brigadier W. D. Tighe-Wood, Colonel J. W. Tomes, Brigadier A. J. Trythall, Brigadier G. A. Viner, Major J. A. Waring, Lt-Col J. K. Warner, Mr Rashleigh Williams, Maj-Gen Sir John Willoughby, Brigadier H. Wood and Lt-Gen Sir Richard Worsley.

I must acknowledge the kind permission of Publishers, Authors and their Heirs to quote from the following books:

Sir C. W. C. Oman: *Adventures with the Connaught Rangers*; Mr Charles Oman.

John Selby; *Thomas Morris: The Napoleonic Wars*; Longman Group Ltd.

Christopher Hibbert: *The Wheatley Diary*; Longman Group Ltd.

The Queens Lancashire Regiment: *Historical Records of the XXX Regiment*.

Lieutenant Brooksbank: *Letters from the Crimea*; The Staffordshire Regiment.

Nicholas Bentley: *Russell's Despatches from the Crimea*; Andre Deutsch Ltd.

Sir Aylmer Haldane: *A Soldier's Saga*; William Blackwood & Sons Ltd.

Siegfried Sassoon: Poem 'The General'; Mr G. T. Sassoon.

Cyril Falls: *The First World War*; Curtis Brown Ltd.

Brigadier-General J. E. Edmunds: *History of the Great War*; HMSO.

Major-General Simpson: *The History of the Lincolnshire Regiment*, 1914-18; RHQ Royal Anglian Regiment (Lincolnshire).

The Memoirs of Field Marshal Montgomery; Wm. Collins Sons & Co Ltd.

Donald Lewin: *Montgomery as a Military Commander*; B. T. Batsford Ltd.

Gregory Blaxland: *Destination Dunkirk*; William Kimber & Co Ltd.

Norman Scarfe: *Assault Division*; Wm. Collins Sons & Co Ltd.

Charles Graves: *The Royal Ulster Rifles*; RUR Regimental Committee.

Brigadier Maurice Tugwell: *The Unquiet Peace*; Allan Wingate Ltd.

I am most grateful to Sir John Smyth VC for his permission to quote from his book *Bolo Whistler — the Life of General Sir Lashmer Whistler*, of which I have taken full advantage.

My thanks are due to the following for their untiring help with my research: The Trustees of the Army Museums Ogilby Trust for permission to quote from the Hawley Letters, and to the Secretary, Colonel Pip Newton, for assistance in gathering material for Chapters 1 and 2; Lt-Col Ben Neave-Hill and Miss Alex Ward of the Army Historical Branch; Mr David Smurthwaite and Mr Borris Mollo of the National Army Museum; Mr Robert Crawford and Mr Michael Willis of the Imperial War Museum; Mrs Kathleen Twyman-Musgrave of the Public Record Office; Lt-Col Douglas Johnson of the Defence Press Office; Mr Arthur Davey and Mrs Catherine Oates of the Army Record Centre; Mr John Andrews and Mr Charles Potts of the MOD Library; the staff of the MOD Reprographic Services, and Mrs Marion Hughes of the Bulford Garrison Library.

For providing the medals which are reproduced at the start of each chapter I must thank Major Harold Barnsley of the Army Medal Office, and the Trustees of the Rifle Brigade Museum. I must also thank Sergeant George Moffat RAOC and Corporal Kevin Ingledew RAOC for photographing the medals and for patiently carrying out many other photographic tasks.

The maps were drawn by Corporal Allan Cathro, Royal Engineers, and I much appreciate his patient and skilful work.

I have been supported throughout by the staff of Headquarters 3rd Division and I particularly wish to thank the DAAG, Major David Younger, and the A Branch Clerks, Sergeant Michael Turner-Sterling and Corporal Jim Gould; while my very special thanks (and sympathy) go to the members of the typing pool — Mrs Stella Stock, Mrs Shirley Carter, Miss Ann Morell, Miss Julie Doris and Miss Susan Parritt — who laboured long and cheerfully over barely legible manuscipts.

The draft of every chapter was painstakingly read by Brigadier Ronnie Stonham, whose detailed comments on style and content have made a major contribution to the final product, and I am most grateful to him.

Finally my thanks are due to my Commander, Major-General Michael Walsh, whose clear directions and encouragement have been of the greatest help throughout.

We are very grateful to the Trustees of the Imperial War Museum and National Army Museum with whose kind permission many of the photographs in this book are reproduced.

1.
The Peninsular War

The Formation of Divisions

Lieutenant-General Thomas Picton

The Peninsular Soldier

Bussaco

The Storming of Badajoz

Salamanca

Victory in the Peninsula

Right: Military General Service Medal 1793-1844, issued retrospectively in 1848.

Badajoz — the Hour approaches
The 88th (Connaught Rangers)
6th April, 1812.

(70)

than one night, must take immediate and effectual measures to ascertain the number of ovens in the neighbour-
hood; and if they should be insufficient to supply the
troops to which he is attached with bread, he will take
care that a sufficient number are built forthwith.

" 8. No man of the brigades in huts must be allowed
to quit the lines of his regiment without being dressed
with his side arms, according to the orders of his regiment."

G. O.　ADJUTANT GENERAL'S OFFICE.
　　　　　Abrantes, 18th June, 1809.

1. WHEN the Commissary issues English hay, the
ration is to be 10 lbs. for each horse or mule; when he
issues straw, or any other forage of the country, it is to
be 14 lbs.

2. The Commander of the Forces is concerned, from
reports which have been lately made to him of the practice of some of the regiments in the army, to be obliged
to desire the Captains of companies to inspect the arms,
ammunition, and flints, in possession of the soldiers of
their companies at every parade with arms, and particularly on the march, which takes place on the morning of
a march.

3. Colonel Low, of the King's German Legion, is
appointed to act as Brigadier General till his Majesty's
pleasure is known, and is to command the brigade of the
Legion, consisting of the 5th and 7th battalions of the
line.

　　　　　　　　　　　　　Brigadier

(71)

Brigadier General Low will be pleased to recommend
an Officer as his Brigade Major.

4. As the weather will now admit of the troops hutting, and they can therefore move together in large bodies,
brigades are to be formed into divisions as follows :

Guards . . . . }
Brig. Gen. Cameron's Brigade . . . } 1st Division.
Hanoverian Legion . . . . }
Major Gen. Hill's Brigade . . . . . }
Brig. Gen. R. Stewart's ditto . . . } 2d Division.
Major Gen. M'Kenzie's Brigade . . . }
Colonel Donkin's ditto . . . . . . } 3d Division.
Brig. Gen. A. Campbell's Brigade . . }
Colonel Peacocke's ditto . . . . . } 4th Division.

Lieutenant General Sherbrooke will take the command
of the 1st division; the senior General Officers of brigades will respectively take the command of the division
in which their brigades are placed, till the other Lieutenant Generals will join the army.

The brigades in divisions are to be formed from the
right, as placed in this order:

The divisions will stand in one or more lines, in respect
to each other, as will be ordered at the time.

An Assistant Adjutant General will be attached to the
Officer commanding the division; an Assistant Provost
will also be attached to each division.

Assistant Adjutant Generals are attached as follows :
Lieutenant Colonel Lord Aylmer, 1st Division.
Captain Cotton . . . . . . 2d ditto.
Major Williamson . . . . . 3d ditto.
Captain Cooke . . . . . . 4th ditto.

F 4　　　　　　　　　　　5. The

Left: The General Order of 18 June 1809 which ordered the formation of Divisions. The staff officer who drafted it clearly had firm ideas of priorities, placing Forage, Arms Inspections, and Officers' Appointments above Order Number 4./*Ogilby Trust*

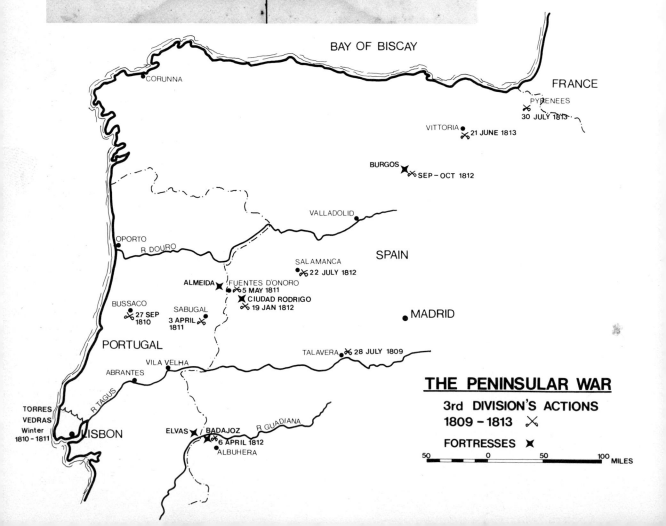

BAY OF BISCAY

FRANCE

CORUNNA

PYRENEES
30 JULY 1813

VITTORIA
21 JUNE 1813

BURGOS
SEP – OCT 1812

VALLADOLID

OPORTO
R. DOURO

SALAMANCA
22 JULY 1812

SPAIN

ALMEIDA　FUENTES D'ONORO
5 MAY 1811
CIUDAD RODRIGO
19 JAN 1812

MADRID

BUSSACO
27 SEP
1810

SABUGAL
3 APRIL
1811

PORTUGAL

VILA VELHA

TALAVERA　28 JULY 1809

ABRANTES

TORRES
VEDRAS
Winter
1810 – 1811

R. TAGUS

LISBON

ELVAS　BADAJOZ
6 APRIL 1812
R. GUADIANA

ALBUHERA

THE PENINSULAR WAR
3rd DIVISION'S ACTIONS
1809 – 1813

FORTRESSES

50　0　50　100 MILES

'As the weather will now admit of the troops hutting, and they can therefore move together in large bodies, brigades are to be formed into divisions . . .' These simple words appeared in General Order Number 4 of 18 June 1809, and were to mark the beginning of the long and eventful history of the 3rd Division of the British Army.

The early Summer of 1809 was as hot and dry as any in Portugal, and the soldiers of Wellington's army in bivouac at Abrantes and Vila Velha were resting and reorganising after their successful Oporto campaign of May. Soon they would be on the march again, this time into Spain towards Talavera and Madrid. The troops of this army belonged to many famous regiments and these were grouped into brigades, each identified by its commander's name. The brigade had been the standard formation in the British army for many years, but the system had weaknesses of which Wellington was well aware. Since landing at Lisbon in April he had been considering ways of improving it, with the result that on 18 June he issued the General Order quoted above. It is interesting to note that in the French army, the division had become a commonplace feature by 1809, and had contributed greatly to its successes in the Revolutionary Wars. In the British service however, although tentatively and partially adopted by Cathcart in Denmark in 1807 and by Moore at Corunna in 1808, the division was a novelty, and Wellington was the first British commander to develop its full potential.

Wellington's operational tasks in the Peninsula were formidable. Initially he had to defend Lisbon and secure the frontiers of Portugal, and in the long term expel the French from the Peninsula altogether, in cooperation with Spanish revolutionary armies of doubtful quality. Such tasks required a commander of exceptional qualities, and fortunately Wellington was a painstaking organiser and administrator was well as a brilliant battlefield commander. He had many problems to tackle — supply in the field and discipline, for example — but one of the most fundamental concerned the command and grouping of his army, which contained 3,000 Hanoverian and 16,000 Portuguese troops, as well as 20,000 British. The brigades into which the infantry were organised numbered nine in all — the Guards, seven Anglo-Portuguese, and one Hanoverian. The Anglo-Portuguese brigades each contained two British and one Portuguese battalion, with companies of the 60th Rifles attached; the 60th were equipped with the Baker rifle and specially trained as a skirmishing force.

Wellington considered this organisation in the light of the dispersed campaigning that lay ahead in the sierras and plains of the Peninsula, and decided not only to group brigades into divisions, but also to give each division its integral supporting arms, staff and services. As he saw it, this divisional grouping would allow him a manageable number of subordinates to whom he could delegate tactical sectors of the battlefield — the term 'Span of Command' will be familiar to many present-day soldiers, particularly those concerned with the restructuring of British Forces in Germany — and also the flexibility to be able to detach properly balanced formations from his main army to operate on the long frontier between Portugal and Spain. Furthermore it would provide the opportunity for the components of the

divisions to train and fight together permanently, thus fostering team spirit and interdivisional rivalry; the adoption of divisional nicknames as the war progressed was to illustrate this well, and by the winter of 1811 the 3rd was generally known as the 'Fighting Division'. Lieutenant-Generals were to be appointed to divisions, but until their arrival each division was to be commanded by the senior brigadier, who also continued for the time being to command his own brigade. The process of attaching staff, supporting arms and services to divisions progressed steadily. From 18 June 1809, each division was given staff officers from the Adjutant-General's and Quartermaster-General's departments, and Provost-Marshals. On 1 August divisional Commissaries were appointed, and in 1810 each division received its own Medical Officer, train of ambulances and Engineer Officer; (at that time the Corps of Royal Engineers consisted of Officers and Artificer NCOs only; field work was carried out by infantry or civil labour under engineer supervision). In the winter of 1810-11 divisions were given their own mule transport and, in January 1814, detachments of semaphore signallers under infantry subalterns. So by the end of the war the concept of the self-contained divisional team was well established.

Brigades first formed up tactically into their divisions when they reached the frontier on 2 July 1809, ready for the expedition into Spain that led to Wellington's victory at Talavera on 27/28 July. In this battle 3rd Division's first commander, Major-General Mackenzie, was killed, gallantly leading his brigade into action at a critical moment. He was succeeded by Major-General Robert Crawfurd, commanding the Light Brigade, which joined the army and 3rd Division the day after the battle. 'Black Bob' Crawfurd remained in command until 22 February 1810, when the Light Division was formed, his place being taken by Lieutenant-General Thomas Picton, newly arrived from England.

Lieutenant-General Thomas Picton

When Picton assumed command of 3rd Division he had already been in the army for 39 years, having been commissioned in the 12th Regiment of Foot at the age of 13. He was a tough, energetic, hard-drinking professional soldier, and first made a reputation for himself when a Captain in the 75th Regiment in 1783. His biography in the 'Military panorama for 1812' states that 'by an intrepidity of conduct and daring resolution of mind . . . he quelled a mutiny which broke out in that Regiment and which, from the complexion that it assumed, promised the most disastrous consequences'. The disturbance had been sparked off by an order disbanding the battalion at the end of the American War of Independence. Picton, the senior officer present, dashed in amongst the mutineers sword in hand, collared the ring-leader and hauled him off to the guardroom, whereupon the mutiny collapsed. However later in his career it was alleged that when Governor of Trinidad he allowed a woman to be tortured to extract a confession of theft; his arrival as Commander 3rd Division was therefore viewed with mixed feelings. Ensign William Grattan of the 88th Regiment (Connaught Rangers) recorded that when Picton inspected the Division for the first time 'every eye was turned towards him and . . . his

Above: Lieutenant-General Thomas Picton, from the painting by
M. A. Shee RA. General Picton commanded the 3rd Division in the
Peninsula from 1810 to 1814. At Waterloo he commanded the
5th Division, and during the battle he was killed by a bullet in the
head./*National Army Museum*

During the autumn and winter of 1809 adjustments to
divisional organisations took place, but by April 1810 3rd
Division's composition was:
Two British brigades, one of three line battalions, the
other of two line battalions and three companies of the
60th Rifles.
One Portuguese brigade of four line battalions and a
Caçadore (Rifle) battalion.
One Artillery battery of six 6-pounder cannon;
and this composition altered little for the rest of the war.

The Peninsular Soldier

To appreciate Wellington's successes it is necessary to
understand the character and battle-tactics of the soldiers
that were the raw material of his divisions. Until the early
1800s the army had been largely recruited from the
lowest levels of society — drunks, convicts and wasters
— together with many Irish peasants escaping from
abject poverty at home. Then in 1806 the Government
authorised and encouraged the voluntary transfer to the
regular army of the better recruits who had completed a
minimum of a year's training in the militia, and these men
constituted over half the Peninsular army. Furthermore,
by 1809 the standard of the direct entry recruit had risen
with many young men volunteering for the commendable
reasons of patriotism and love of adventure. The army
still contained a hard core, perhaps 10 per cent, of
drunkards, potential deserters and plunderers, but most of
these men were hardy and brave enough in battle.

The strength of Wellington's army lay in his infantry.
Each line battalion consisting of between 600 and 1,000
men organised into eight 'battalion' companies, a
grenadier company and a light company. The grenadiers,
generally the most experienced soldiers in the battalion
carried out particularly demanding tasks, and the light
company men, nicknamed 'Light Bobs', were used for
skirmishing and observation. Whenever possible
battalions fought in line two ranks deep, allowing every
man to fire his muzzle-loading 'Tower Musket' in a single
volley, and, as the French generally attacked in narrow
columns, the hail of one ounce musket balls, enveloping
both the flanks and the front of the columns, had a
shattering effect. The musket's effective fighting range
was only 100 yards, so the British infantry waited
patiently in line until the French columns were at close
range. To protect his troops from artillery covering fire
Wellington often posted them on the reverse slope and
ordered them to lie down until the enemy were within
range. To stand up again and face the enemy who were
then almost upon them was a movement requiring
considerable courage and discipline.

Reloading the musket after the first volley was a
complicated procedure but a well trained battalion would
be ready to fire again in 20 seconds, by which time the
enemy would barely have recovered from the havoc of the
first volley. Further fire might be necessary but generally
a bayonet charge would throw the enemy back in
confusion.

Before the main encounter, fierce battles between
skirmishers on both sides took place, for in front of their
columns the French would throw a swarm of *Tirailleurs*
(sharp-shooters) and *Voltigeurs* (light infantry) whose
object was to soften up and demoralise their opponents.

demeanour and appearance closely observed' . . . but,
Grattan continues, 'I never saw a more perfect specimen
of a splendid-looking soldier. In vain did those who had
set him down in their minds as a cruel tyrant seek to find
out such a delineation in his countenance . . . on the
contrary there was a manly open frankness in his
appearance that gave a flat contradiction to the slander,
and in truth Picton was *not* a tyrant, nor did he ever act
as such during the many years he commanded 3rd
Division'. Unfortunately in his subsequent address to
McKinnon's Brigade, Picton exasperated the 88th by
referring to them, by reputation, as the 'Connaught
Footpads'. After representations by Colonel Wallace, the
commanding officer and Brigadier-General McKinnon,
Picton made a handsome retraction of his remark at a
dinner party attended by all the senior officers in the
division. He was to command 3rd Division until the end
of the war, being absent only while recovering from
wounds received at Badajoz in 1812. He was a first class
divisional commander; courageous, skilful and energetic.
Under his leadership the soldiers of the 'Fighting
Division' brimmed over with self confidence, and
although they never exactly loved him, they were full of
admiration and respect for him and generally forgave his
rough and hasty tongue.

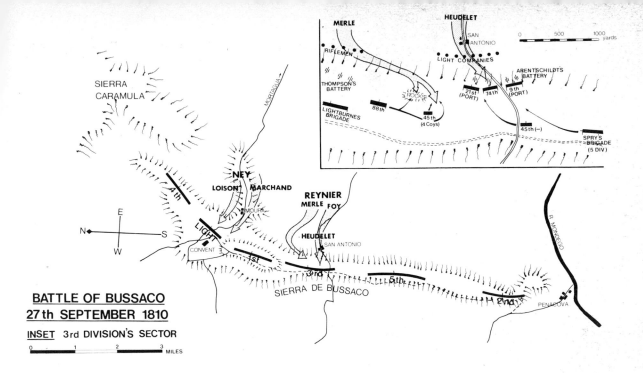

BATTLE OF BUSSACO
27th SEPTEMBER 1810

INSET 3rd DIVISION'S SECTOR

0   1   2   3
MILES

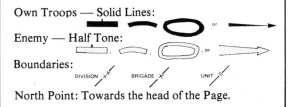

Notes on Maps

Unless otherwise stated, the following method of map-marking has been used throughout:

Own Troops — Solid Lines:

Enemy — Half Tone:

Boundaries:

DIVISION   BRIGADE   UNIT

North Point: Towards the head of the Page.

The British reply was to advance a protective screen of riflemen from the companies of the 60th Rifles attached to each division, and whose muzzle-loading Baker rifles were accurate at 250 yards. The screen of riflemen would be augmented as necessary by the light companies of line battalions.

3rd Division played a leading part in the majority of Peninsular battles and sieges, but space does not permit them all to be described in detail. Attention will therefore be focussed on three actions in which the division played a decisive part — Bussaco, the Storming of Badajoz, and Salamanca.

Excellent descriptions of these battles are given by William Grattan of the 88th Regiment, whose comments on Picton have already been quoted. Grattan served continuously with 3rd Division from late 1809 to Spring 1813 and, like Picton, was off duty only after being wounded to Badajoz. He was intensely proud of his Regiment — 'The most Irish of all Irish regiments, the boys that took the world "aisy" ... as strange a set to manage as ever tried an officer's temper!' ... but throughout his account he reiterates his equal pride in being a member of the 3rd Division. Although there is

little doubt that the Connaught Rangers set a standard of battle-fighting second to none, the other 3 Div units were also tough, brave and experienced, and we can accept that the Connaught Rangers' actions illustrate the mettle of the whole Division.

The Battle of Bussaco, 27 September 1810

Apart from a brief foray into Spain in July 1809 which resulted in the somewhat barren victory of Talavera (and which opened Wellington's eyes to the shortcomings of his Spanish allies), the Anglo-Portuguese army saw little action until the middle of 1810. Wellington anticipated that by then the French would concentrate great force in the Peninsula with which to invade Portugal, and he made good use of the intervening time by constructing the famous Lines of Torres Vedras to cover Lisbon.

When Massena launched the expected offensive Wellington withdrew from the frontier leaving the fortress of Almeida to delay the enemy, but disconcertingly its magazine accidentally exploded on 27 August and the governor was obliged to surrender. Following the loss of the fortress Wellington needed an action to restore British and Portuguese public confidence; he also wished to give his Portuguese troops battle-confidence, now that their training and integration with British divisions were complete. He looked for a position which would give him the opportunity to inflict a decisive defeat on the French who were following up his withdrawal to the Lines of Torres Vedras. He found his answer in the long hogsback of the Sierra de Bussaco which lay astride Massena's advance. This feature suited Wellington's purpose well, the flanks of the position being secured in the south by the river Mondego, and in the north by the forbidding mountains of the Sierra Caramula. The eastern face of the Sierra de Bussaco was steep and broken, presenting a formidable obstacle and an exhausting climb to assaulting troops. There were only two roads providing an easier ascent, one in the centre winding up through the San Antonio pass and the other at Moura, following a more gradual slope to the Convent situated on the highest point of the Sierra.

The eight miles of ridge extended Wellington's 32,000 men, but he had the advantage of being able to conceal his positions on the reverse slope below the skyline and to switch troops quickly to any critical point by using the lateral track behind the crest. The Allied army occupied the position by the afternoon of 26 September but the French did not attack immediately, reputedly because Massena was 'resting' his mistress (who was the wife of one of his staff officers and always travelled in ADC's uniform) in the village of Mortagua. At nightfall the Allied divisions were firmly in position behind the ridge, with their picquets of riflemen and light infantry in the woods at the foot of the forward slope. They bivouaced in complete darkness whereas the French army could be picked out by the thousands of camp fires which twinkled all over the plain below.

3rd Division held the right centre of the Allied line covering one of the likely assault routes — the San Antonio pass. Its order of battle was:

McKinnon's Brigade: 1st Bn, 45th Regt; 1st Bn, 74th Regt; 1st Bn, 88th Regt.
Lightburne's Brigade: 2nd Bn, 5th Fusiliers; 2nd Bn, 58th Regt; HQ and three companies, 5th Bn, 60th Rifles.
Champalimaud's Portuguese Brigade: 1st and 2nd Bns,

9th Line Regt; 1st and 2nd Bns, 21st Line Regt; 11th Caçadores (Rifles).
Artillery:
Arentschildt's Portuguese Battery: six 6-pounders.
Thompson's Battery: (in support) six 6-pounders.

Picton concentrated over half his Division — the Portuguese Brigade, half of McKinnon's Brigade, the light companies of all battalions (today's soldiers will note that there is nothing new in grouping for special tasks) and Arentschildt's battery — to cover the pass and took personal command of this force. Northwards towards 1st Division the ridge was sparsely held by the remainder of McKinnon's Brigade — the 88th and half the 45th — and Lightburne's Brigade.

At dawn on the 27 September Massena, believing the ridge to be lightly held — he had been unable to observe the dead ground below the crest — launched Reynier's Corps of three divisions straight up the axis of the San

Below: Bussaco — the critical moment. The 88th and 45th Regiments under Colonel Wallace assault and throw back Merle's Division, while in the left foreground riflemen of the 60th, having withdrawn before the enemy's advance, now harass him with enfilade fire.
/National Army Museum

Antonio road. Heudelet's division followed the road itself, heading straight for the point Picton had foreseen, while Merle's division moved up the steep slope towards Lightburne's brigade, and Foy's brigade followed in reserve.

It was a misty morning and from the crest it was impossible to see the enemy columns as they pounded up the slope, their *tirailleurs* driving in the British and Portuguese light infantry picquets. However Picton was ready for Heudelet's division and as it reached the summit and came into view, Arentschildt's gunners blasted it with grape. Picton then ordered forward Champalimaud's Portuguese and the 74th Regiment, and having advanced to the crest in line, all five battalions fired a shattering volley into the closely packed column, driving it back down the hill. The survivors clung to the rocky slope, but made no further attempt to attack.

On the left, Merle's division presented a more serious threat. Pressing on up the slope towards Lightburne's brigade they lost direction in the mist and rocks, and veered to their left, straight towards 3rd Division's weakest point — a gap of 1,000 yards held only by four companies of the 45th. The 88th under Colonel Wallace were on the extreme left of the gap, isolated in the mist and Grattan takes up the story:
'Wallace and his regiment now had to act for themselves. The Colonel sent his Captain of Grenadiers (Dunne) to ascertain how matters stood ... in a few minutes Dunne returned almost breathless; he said the rocks were filling fast with Frenchmen, that a heavy column was coming up the hill beyond the rocks, and that the four companies of the 45th were about to be attacked. Wallace asked if half the 88th would be able to do the business. "You will need every man" was the reply.

'Wallace with a steady but cheerful countenance turned to his men, and looking them full in the face, said "Now Connaught Rangers, mind what you are going to do. Pay attention to what I have so often told you, and when I bring you face to face with the French rascals, drive them down the hill — don't give them a false touch, but push home to the muzzle" ... This address went home to the hearts of us all, but there was no cheering; a steady determined calm had taken the place of any lighter feeling, and it seemed as if the men had made up their minds to go to their work unruffled and not too much excited.

'Wallace then threw the battalion from line into column ... on reaching the rocks he soon found out that Dunne's report was not exaggerated. A number of Frenchmen were in possession ... our column was raked from front to rear. The moment was critical, but Wallace, without being the least taken aback, filed out the Grenadiers and the first battalion company and ordered them to storm the rocks ... this done Wallace placed himself at the head of the remainder of the 88th and pressed on to meet the French column. At this moment the four companies of the 45th, commanded by Major Gwynne commenced their fire, but it in no way arrested the French column ... Wallace threw himself from his horse, and placing himself at the head of the 45th and 88th ran forward at a charging pace into the midst of the terrible flame — all was now confusion and uproar; smoke, fire and bullets; officers and soldiers; French

drummers and French drums knocked down in every direction — while in the midst of all was to be seen Wallace fighting at the head of his devoted followers, and calling out to his soldiers to "press forward". Never was defeat more complete and it was a proud moment for Wallace and Gwynne whan they saw their gallant comrades breaking down and trampling under their feet this splendid division composed of some of the best troops the world can boast of. The leading regiment, the 36th, one of Napoleon's favourite battalions, was nearly destroyed'.

Wallace and his men pursued the French down the hill, and when the 88th reformed they found they had lost 9 officers and 135 soldiers killed and wounded. After the battle the regiment was visited by Wellington and Picton who both congratulated them warmly, and Grattan concludes his account:
'They rode away, and we were once more left to ourselves, the arms were piled, the wounded of all nations collected and carried to the rear, and in a short time the dead were left without a stitch of clothes ... all firing had ceased ... the picquets were placed in front, and a double allowance of spirits was served out to Wallace's men.'

After the repulse of Heudelet's and Merle's divisions, Reynier made a further thrust with Foy's brigade, which advanced on the left of the road, heading for the gap between 3rd and 5th Divisions, which had been made even wider by the involvement of Champalimaud's Portuguese with Heudelet. By this time however, the warm sun had dispersed the mist and Wellington, noticing the threat, ordered the 5th Division to fill the gap. Leith moved Spry's brigade rapidly northwards along the lateral track. As the French columns reached the crest Spry's leading battalions, the 9th and 38th, forming into line fired a crashing volley at 100 yards and followed up with the bayonet. Meanwhile as Reynier's Corps threatened the San Antonio pass, Massena launched Ney's divisions up the road to the convent. They were met and thrown back by the Light Division, whose Portuguese brigade won its spurs with steadiness and accuracy of fire worthy of British troops. The battle of Bussaco ended with the French suffering 4,000 casualties against 626 British and an equal number of Portuguese. Wellington had given the public at home their victory and the Portuguese soldiers their self-confidence.

After withdrawing to Torres Vedras for the winter, Wellington pursued Massena out of Portugal in March 1811. That year 3rd Division took part in the victories of Sabugal and Fuentes de Onoro, and by 1812 Wellington's army was sufficiently large and well trained to start offensive operations in Spain, but first he had to secure the fortresses of Ciudad Rodrigo and Badajoz which dominated the frontier. The former fell on 19 January when Major-General McKinnon's Brigade of 3rd Division together with the Light Division, stormed the main breach, McKinnon being killed when a magazine exploded on the ramparts. The release of tension when the storming parties broke into the town generated an orgy of plunder and sack which continued for hours, despite Picton's personal appeal to his soldiers, as 'Men and Englishmen — not savages', to desist.

Marche forcée

14 degrés de froid!

Sentinelle avancée

36 degrés de chaleur!

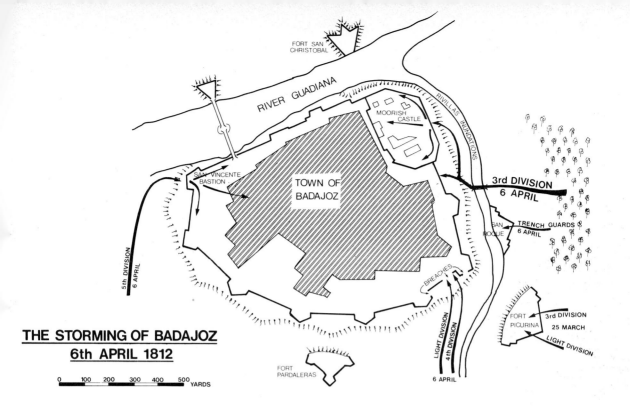

FORT SAN
CHRISTOBAL

RIVER GUADIANA

MOORISH
CASTLE

RIVILLAS INUNDATIONS

SAN VINCENTE
BASTION

TOWN OF
BADAJOZ

3rd DIVISION
6 APRIL

SAN
ROQUE

TRENCH GUARDS
6 APRIL

5th DIVISION
6 APRIL

BREACHES

FORT
PICURINA

3rd DIVISION
25 MARCH

LIGHT DIVISION

THE STORMING OF BADAJOZ
6th APRIL 1812

LIGHT DIVISION
4th DIVISION
6 APRIL

FORT
PARDALERAS

0   100   200   300   400   500
YARDS

The Storming of Badajoz, 6 April 1812

With Ciudad Rodrigo secure, Wellington marched his army south to reduce the key fortress of Badajoz, lost to the French a year earlier by Spanish incompetence and treachery; the citizens were constant collaborators with the enemy, and 4,000 of them had joined the French garrison. Badajoz presented the attacker with a daunting succession of fortifications and obstacles. A ring of detached forts, which included the Picurina, prevented the approach of siege batteries; to the north and east approach on foot was limited by the Guardiana and the inundations of the Rivillas; and finally there were the ramparts themselves, towering 30ft above a series of deep ditches and scarps, with jutting bastions every 200 yards to enfilade the attacker. Dominating the city at the north east corner was the old Moorish castle, its frowning walls perched above an almost sheer 40-foot scarp.

The Allies had besieged Badajoz twice before during the previous year. On both occasions Wellington possessed inadequate siege artillery and insufficient trained engineers, and he had been obliged to abandon operations on the approach of enemy field armies. By March 1812 he had obtained iron siege cannon heavy enough to breach the stone ramparts, but he was still short of sappers, and infantry volunteers were required to dig and revet the trenches that would enable the batteries to be brought within effective distance of the walls. It was long drawn out, exhausting, and dangerous work.

Left: The rigours of campaigning in the Peninsula were shared by French and Allied soldiers alike. A French cartoon of the period./*National Army Museum*

Wellington directed his main effort against the south east corner, and on 16 March the first of a series of works was opened, approaching the forts of San Roque and Picurina. In dismal wet weather the infantry-sappers toiled in the trenches, under constant cannon fire and up to their knees in mud. After two previous attempts to take Badajoz, the capture of the city had assumed a special meaning for the soldiers, and Grattan this time noticed a terrible hardening of their attitude; they were determined to succeed at any cost — and, in the language of soldiers of a later age, to 'take the place apart'. By the 24 March the weather had cleared sufficiently for an assault to be made on Fort Picurina. The following night 15 officers and 500 volunteer soldiers from the 3rd Division and the Light Division rushed the fort. The sappers leading the attack leapt into the ditch and placed their ladders against the wall, only to find them too short, and the storming parties that followed were showered with bullets, grenades and fire-balls, two thirds of them being killed or wounded. Grattan describes what happened next:

'Oates of the 88th was the only unwounded officer. It occurred to him that although the ladders were too short to mount the wall, they were long enough to cross the ditch. He at once formed the desperate resolution of throwing three of them over the fosse by which a sort of bridge was constructed. He led the way, followed by a few of his brave soldiers who were unhurt and forcing his way through an embrasure carried the point allotted to him. Sixty Grenadiers of the Italian Guard supplicated for mercy, but either by accident or design one of them discharged his firelock and the ball struck Oates in the thigh, he fell, and his men became furious... every man of the Italian Guard was put to death on the spot...'

The success was exploited and with Picurina secure, the batteries were brought forward to pound the main defences of the fortress. By 6 April the walls had been breached in three places, and Wellington decided to attack that night. Phillipon, the Governor of Badajoz, was ready. After the slaughter of Picurina, he had impressed on his garrison the dreadful things the British would do to them if captured, and there was to be no surrender. He was an expert in the art of defence, and every possible device of metal, stone and gunpowder had been prepared — hedgehogs of sharpened sword blades, mines, fireballs and grenades. The ditches were flooded and behind breaches hastily blocked with sandbags and masonry, the garrison waited.

3rd Division did not feature in Wellington's original plan which was for the 4th and Light Divisions to assault the breaches while 5th Division created a diversion at the north-west corner of the town. However at Picton's request Wellington allowed him to attempt the capture of the incredibly strong Moorish Castle. There were no breaches in the castle walls, and assault would have to be by ladder, a seemingly hopeless task. Perhaps Wellington never expected this attack to succeed, but nonetheless thought it might provide another useful diversion from the main assault. By late afternoon orders had been issued, the troops receiving them with quiet determination though they knew they were in for a night of terrible carnage. That evening as the sun set behind the distant hills of Portugal, the assault divisions assembled and formed up in attack formation. Commanding officers allowed their battalions to pile arms, fall out and relax until zero hour, in no doubt that their soldiers would all be present in their ranks at the appointed time, such was the spirit and self-discipline of the Peninsular Army. Grattan captures the atmosphere of the waiting period in unforgettable words:

'There is a solemnity of feeling which accompanies the expectation of every great event in our lives and the man who can be altogether dead to such feeling is little, if anything, better than a brute. The present moment was one that was well calculated to fill every bosom throughout the army; for mixed with expectation, hope and suspense it was rendered still more touching to the heart by the music of some regiments, which played at the head of each battalion as the soldiers sauntered about to beguile the last hour many of them were destined to live ... All was now in readiness. It was twenty-five past nine; the soldiers, unencumbered by their knapsacks — their stocks off — their shirt collars unbuttoned — their trousers tucked up to the knee, their tattered jackets so worn out as to render the regiment they belonged to barely recognisable — their huge whiskers and bronzed faces, which several hard fought campaigns had changed from natural hue — but above all, their self confidence, devoid of boast or bravado, gave them the appearance of what they in reality were — an invincible host.

'The Division now moved forward in one solid mass — the 45th leading followed by the 88th and 74th*, the brigade of Portuguese (9th and 21st Regiments) next, while the 5th, 77th, 83rd and 94th under Colonel Campbell brought up the rear. Their advance was undisturbed until they reached the Rivillas; at this spot some fire-balls, which the enemy threw out, caused a great light and 3rd Division, 4,000 strong, was to be seen

* The late General McKinnon's brigade, now commanded by General Kempt.

from the ramparts... the soldiers, finding they were discovered, raised a shout of defiance (which was responded to by the garrison), and in a moment every gun that could be brought to bear was in action; but in no way daunted by the havoc made in the ranks, Picton forded the Rivillas knee-deep and soon gained the foot of the castle wall.'

Grattan was clearly unable to witness every detail of the battle for in fact Picton was wounded, though not seriously, while crossing the Rivillas. Kempt assumed command (until he too was wounded) and in the confusion led his brigade in error against the curtain wall immediately south of the castle, the intended objective being the castle wall itself. Grattan continues:
'A host of veterans crowned the wall, all armed in a manner as imposing as novel; each man had beside him eight loaded firelocks, while at intervals were pikes of enormous length. The top of the wall was covered with rocks of a ponderous size, only requiring a slight push to hurl them upon the heads of our soldiers, and there was a sufficiency of hand grenades and small shell to destroy

the entire besieging army; while on the flanks of each curtain, batteries charged to the muzzle with grape and case shot, either swept away entire sections or disorganised the ladders as they were in place...'

For an hour the indomitable soldiers of Kempt's brigade fought to the top of the ladders, only to be smashed to the ground. Recklessly they replaced the ladders trampling over their dead and dying comrades, but made no impression. Similarly at the breaches the 4th and Light Divisions were heaping their dead in a ditch that 'vomited fire'. The news reaching Wellington from all points of assault became worse and at midnight he ordered the 4th and Light Divisions to desist from their hopeless task, and sent a message to Picton telling him that he must try to succeed at the Castle. By this time Picton had recovered sufficiently from his wound to rejoin his troops, and had withdrawn the remnants of the Kempt's brigade from the curtain wall. He, like Wellington, was becoming doubtful of success, but his indomitable spirit, and that of his men, prevailed. He directed Campbell's brigade to assault the centre of the main castle wall, where there were no flanking bastions, and the gallant attacks of the 4th and Light Divisions having drained off defenders from this section of the wall, 3rd Division's fresh attack looked more hopeful.

The 5th Fusiliers were to open the assault, and their CO, Lt-Col Ridge, called on Ensign Canch of the Grenadier company to lead. Writing in the *United Service Journal* in 1833, Canch described what happened next:
'I immediately attempted to ascend the ladder, but desisted at the urgent request of an officer of Engineers, to have the ladder placed more perpendicular,... this caused

Below left: 3rd Division storm the Moorish Castle of Badajoz. Ensign Canch, Lt-Col Ridge, and Fusiliers of the 'Fighting Fifth' gain a footing on the ramparts./*National Army Museum*

Below: Badajoz — the morning after. Wellington examines the breaches, and sees the obstacles faced by the assault divisions. The group of soldiers on the right is somewhat fanciful, with representatives of many different British and Imperial Regiments. They include a French grenadier (bearskin cap) and *voltigeur* (white facings). /*National Army Museum*

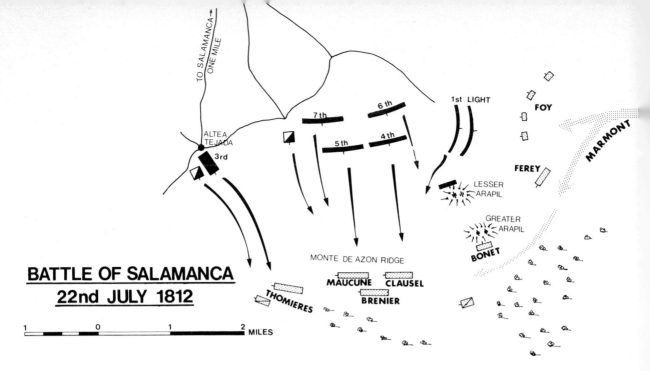

BATTLE OF SALAMANCA
22nd JULY 1812

a momentary delay, in consequence of which the Lt-Col again called out 'Canch, won't you lead the 5th Regiment?" I then immediately ascended the ladder, and succeeded in gaining the ramparts, where I was soon joined by Lt-Col Ridge'.

Amid cheers, more soldiers flew up the ladders behind them and very quickly seized the castle walls, taking few prisoners in a release of pent up frustration, and then rushed to the main gate into the town only to find it bricked up. Meanwhile Phillipon, the Governor, reacted quickly to the Division's success. He sent a French regiment (coincidentally their 88th) led by an English-speaking officer to a small wicket gate, where the officer shouted out that they were English and had come to reinforce 3rd Division. Campbell's men detected the ruse and fired a volley through the gate as it was opened. The French were thrown back but when the British tried to follow, they found their way barred by a further barricade and Colonel Ridge was killed by a French volley. Picton decided to consolidate his position and await events, knowing that with the castle in British hands the fall of Badajoz was now certain.

As the buglers of 3rd Division's battalions sounded the rally, they were answered by the faint but unmistakable blare of other British infantry bugles on the Bastion of San Vincente on the far side of the town. 5th Division's diversionary attack had achieved success where the defenders had been thinned out to reinforce the breaches, and Leith's men were already fighting their way down into the streets. The enemy heard the bugles too — on both sides of them — and their resistance crumbled. Badajoz quickly fell, and two days of rampage and looting followed. Though terrible, these extremes were in accordance with the customs of war, which allowed a fortress to be sacked if it did not surrender after the ramparts had been breached. But whatever horrors took place after Badajoz fell, the outstanding determination

and bravery of the soldiers of 3rd Division during the assault itself can be remembered with pride.

Salamanca, 22 July 1812

With the frontier fortresses in his hands, Wellington struck north-east on the axis Ciudad Rodrigo — Burgos, intending to defeat Marmont's army near Salamanca and cut the lines of communication of Soult's army in southern Spain. 3rd Division marched early in June with Sir Edward Pakenham temporarily in command and with Wallace of the 88th commanding Kempt's brigade; Picton and Kempt were both convalescing from their Badajoz wounds.

After liberating Salamanca on 17 June Wellington confronted the French some 40 miles to the north. In a series of rapid manoeuvres Marmont endeavoured to outflank the Allied army which withdrew by 22 July to the open rolling country to the south-east of Salamanca. This area is not unlike Salisbury Plain, with numerous re-entrants and areas of dead ground where a skilful commander can post and deploy his forces undetected. As Marmont advanced, all he could see were the 1st and Light Divisions drawn up on high ground and a dust cloud behind them. Thinking that Wellington was again withdrawing, the French commander launched his army in a swift flanking march to the left to cut off the divisions facing him; in fact the dust cloud he had seen was the 3rd Division marching to a concealed position at Aldeatejada.

Marmont's first objective was a pair of flat topped but dominating hills — the Greater and Lesser Arapils. He seized the Greater but Wellington beat him to the Lesser, and a long range artillery duel followed. Protected by the Greater Arapil, Marmont then flung his divisions westward in succession along the ridge of Monte de Azon, unaware of the Allied army assembled on his right flank. The French infantry pressed swiftly on in the eagerness of pursuit, and inevitably their formation became extended, with intervals between divisions increasing. Wellington, snatching a snack lunch in a farm yard, watched them calmly through his telescope. His chance had come — he would launch his army in a concentrated attack against the flank of an over-extended enemy. 3rd Division in particular could isolate and destroy the leading French division under Thomieres. In a flash he galloped off to Aldeatejada to give orders personally to his brother-in-law, 'Ned' Pakenham. Pointing at the head of Thomieres' troops just visible two miles way on the skyline Wellington told Pakenham to throw his division at them in column, and 'drive them to the devil'. The order was acknowledged with a quick hand shake, and Wellington was off to direct his 4th, 5th, 6th and 7th Divisions at the French centre.

The reaction in 3rd Division was instantaneous. The echo of the bugles had scarcely died away before the Division was marching swiftly in column of brigades up the valley leading south-east from Aldeatejada, with D'Urban's brigade of Portuguese Dragoons trotting on its flank. As the Division pounded out of the valley and up the slope towards the French, it deployed into open formation with battalions abreast in column of companies and the enemy came into view moving across the front from left to right. The enemy promptly threw forward sharpshooters and brought six cannon into

action, and 3rd Division's battery replied by unlimbering in rear and opening overhead covering fire. When only 250 yards from the French, Pakenham gave the order for battalions to form line. The French *tirailleurs* now anticipated a chance to riddle the Division when halting to deploy, but they were foiled, for Pakenham's men performed a manoeuvre only possible if practiced thoroughly in training — deployment on the move. Without pausing, each battalion made a quarter turn to the left, each company quickly moving forward to extend the frontage, and brigades now approached the enemy in line. Leading was Wallace with the 45th, 74th and 88th Regiments; Champalimaud's four Portuguese battalions followed; and in reserve came Campbell's four battalions — two of the 5th Fusiliers, and the 83rd and 94th. At 150 yards the leading French companies opened fire, causing casualties to Wallace's men who advanced without pause. Confusion grew in the French ranks, and firing became ragged. Their officers tried to steady them, and one, grabbing a musket, fired at Major Murphy, acting CO of the 88th, who fell from his horse mortally wounded. The terrified animal dragged Murphy's body by the stirrup along the front of his Regiment, which grew frantic with rage. 'Let them loose' shouted Pakenham to Wallace, and the brigade hurled itself forward, sweeping Thomieres'

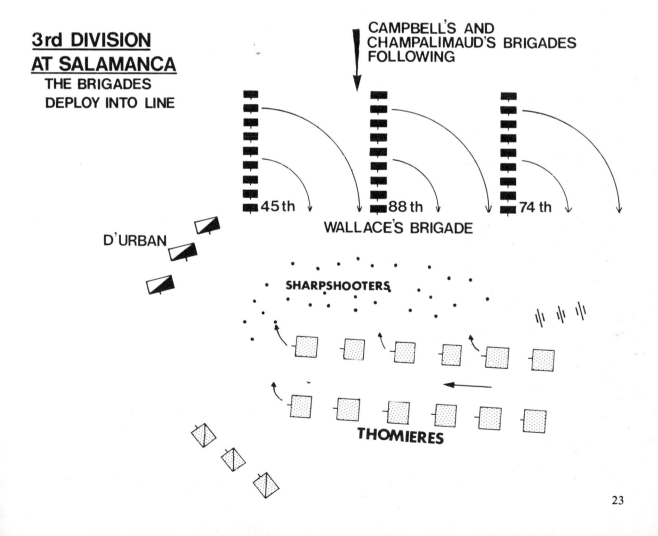

3rd DIVISION
AT SALAMANCA
THE BRIGADES
DEPLOY INTO LINE

CAMPBELL'S AND
CHAMPALIMAUD'S BRIGADES
FOLLOWING

45th   88th   74th

WALLACE'S BRIGADE

D'URBAN

SHARPSHOOTERS

THOMIERES

division back half a mile to the woods with D'Urban's Dragoons completing the rout. Thomieres himself was killed, half his division became casualties and all his guns were captured.

In the centre, Wellington concluded the destruction initiated by 3rd Division. The 4th and 5th Divisions assaulted the flanks of Maucune's and Brenier's divisions, which hastily formed square. These were broken by the volleys and bayonets of the British infantry, the destruction being completed by a savage charge of Le Marchant's brigade of cavalry. Further east the French power of recovery asserted itself when Clausel's and Bonet's divisions counter-attacked the flank of 4th Division, but Wellington's 6th Division, suddenly appearing in line from dead ground, shattered the enemy and put them to flight. The battle drew to a close in the twilight as Ferey's division fought a gallant rearguard

Below: Salamanca — the 5th Fusiliers, part of Campbell's Brigade, pursue the broken remnants of Thomiere's Division. One of the two Ensigns was killed shortly after and Ensign Bolton, the survivor, carried both colours in the final charge. Such was his exuberance that he had to be personally restrained by Pakenham from advancing too fast.
/Royal Northumberland Fusiliers

action to cover the escape of the remnants of the French Army through the forest to the south-east. Marmont himself had been badly wounded earlier by a cannon shot that shattered his arm and ribs, and his army suffered 15,000 casualties, 7,000 of them prisoners, against the Allies' 5,000.

Besides the fact of the victory itself, Salamanca established a new reputation for Wellington. Previously he had been recognised as a prudent commander in situations of static defence and set-piece attack; now he had shown himself to be a master of opportunity and manoeuvre — a second Marlborough.

Picton reassumed command of 3rd Division in January 1813, and was knighted the following month. Under him the Division continued to share in the victories of the Peninsular Army until Napoleon's abdication and exile to Elba in April 1814. The three actions described in this chapter illustrate the characteristics that contributed to the Division's great fighting reputation — steadiness and initiative at Bussaco, bravery and determination at Badajoz, swiftness and flexibility at Salamanca. 100 years were to pass before the 'Fighting Division' earned, in the most costly conflict ever, the better known nickname of the 'Iron Division'.

2.
The Waterloo Campaign

The Allied Armies assemble in Belgium

5 Brigade at Quatre Bras

Waterloo: The Position

The Defence of La Haye Sainte

Ney's Cavalry Attack

Napoleon's Final Throw — The Imperial Guard

Right: The Waterloo Medal, 1815.

Mont St. Jean - dawn, 18th June, 1815.
The 33rd (Duke of Wellington's) Regiment.

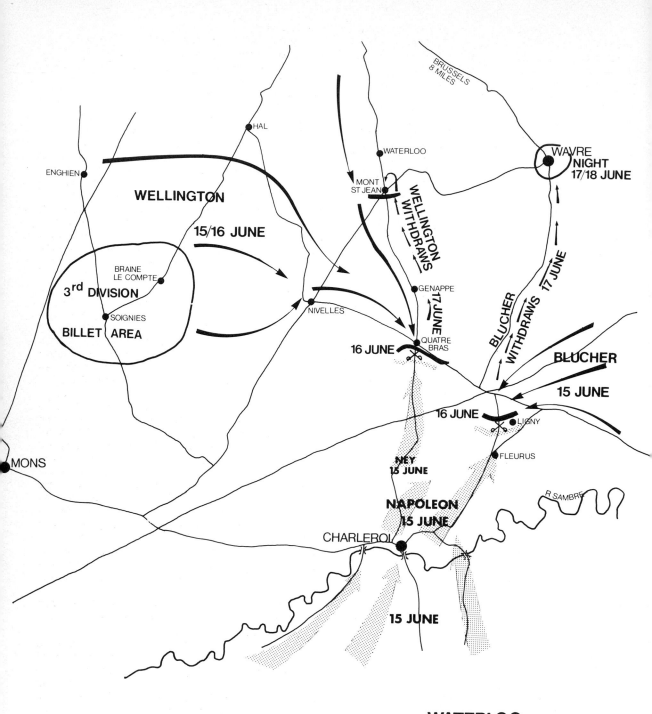

BRUSSELS
8 MILES

HAL

ENGHIEN

WELLINGTON

15/16 JUNE

BRAINE
LE COMPTE

3rd DIVISION

SOIGNIES

BILLET AREA

WATERLOO

MONT
ST JEAN

WELLINGTON
WITHDRAWS

WAVRE
NIGHT
17/18 JUNE

17 JUNE

BLUCHER
WITHDRAWS

GENAPPE

17 JUNE

NIVELLES

QUATRE
BRAS

16 JUNE

BLUCHER

15 JUNE

16 JUNE

LIGNY

MONS

NEY
15 JUNE

FLEURUS

NAPOLEON
15 JUNE

R SAMBRE

CHARLEROI

15 JUNE

WATERLOO :
THE OPENING MOVES,
15 – 17 JUNE

0 1 2 3 4 5 6 7 8 9 10 MILES

The Allied forces assembling in Belgium in May 1815 in preparation for an advance on Paris were very different from those commanded by Wellington in Spain and Portugal. After Napoleon's exile the battle-hardened Peninsular divisions were disbanded, many battalions being sent across the Atlantic to fight in the war against the USA which had broken out in 1812. Consequently when Napoleon escaped from Elba in Feburary 1815 and re-established himself as Emperor of France, the Allies were obliged to put together whatever units were immediately available. In the case of the British, many of these were the inexperienced and under-strength second battalions of regiments, who unlike their first battalions had not seen service in the Peninsula. For example Sergeant Thomas Morris of the 2nd Bn, 73rd Regiment commented that his company commander, a 60-year old Captain, had never been in action before! Fortunately there was in Belgium a scattering of officers, NCO's and units with Peninsula experience.

The Allies had been able to muster two armies. One, under Blücher, was entirely Prussian while the other, commanded by Wellington with the young Prince of Orange as his second-in-command, was drawn from a variety of nations, and was composed of 21,000 British, 5,000 King's German Legion (the KGL formed part of the British Army), 11,000 Hanoverians, 5,500 Brunswickers, 3,000 Nassauers and 17,000 Dutch/Belgians. The inexperience of the British has already been mentioned, and the quality of the remainder was as varied as their nationality. Among the Brunswick and Dutch/Belgian contingents there was a considerable number of hastily embodied militia battalions, and many other soldiers were conscripts with little training and even less enthusiasm for the war.

In view of these disparities Wellington organised his divisions so that each contained a blend of nationality and experience, and he relied on the British or KGL to stiffen the other contingents. 3rd Division's organisation which is given below reflected this policy. Its main strength undoubtedly lay in the veteran KGL Brigade, and the Division was commanded by a KGL officer, General Sir Charles Alten, KCB. Sir Thomas Picton had been given command of the 5th Division.

5th British Brigade
(Major-General Sir Colin Halkett KCB)

2nd Bn 30th Regt (615)	1st Bn 33rd Regt (561)
2nd Bn 69th Regt (516)	2nd Bn 73rd Regt (562)

2nd KGL Brigade
(Colonel Baron Ompteda)

1st Light Bn (423)	2nd Light Bn (337)
5th Line Bn (379)	8th Line Bn (388)

1st Hanoverian Brigade
(Major-General Count Kielmansegge)

Bremen Bn (512)	Verden Bn (533)
York Bn (607)	Luneberg Bn (595)
Grubenhagen Bn (621)	Jaeger Bn (Rifles) (321)

Artillery
Major Lloyd's British Field Battery (6 Guns);
Captain Cleeve's KGL Field Battery (6 Guns).
TOTAL: 6,970 Infantry, 12 Guns.

Quatre Bras
Napoleon's reaction to the assembly of the Allied armies was characteristically swift. Having reconstituted the Imperial Army he moved it to the Belgian frontier, intending to defeat the Allies before they could concentrate. By mid-June the Emperor's troops were ready and at dawn on 15 June, the 124,000-strong army struck across the frontier and over the River Sambre at Charleroi, catching Wellington and Blücher off-balance with their armies spread over 130 miles of front. Napoleon's first target was Blücher, who reacted by ordering his army to assemble at Ligny, a position that was too far forward. Napoleon saw his chance to destroy the Prussians the following day, by advancing on them before they had properly formed up, and he ordered a frontal attack from Fleurus and a left flank attack from Quatre Bras. Possession of the Quatre Bras crossroads was vital to the Emperor, not only for mounting the flank attack, but also to prevent Wellington making contact with Blücher, and he therefore detached Ney with 43,000 men to seize it.

By the afternoon of 15 June Wellington had received sufficient information on which to gauge Napoleon's intentions. Realising the importance of the crossroads he despatched ADCs and orderlies from village to village, ordering his troops to assemble and march on Quatre Bras without delay. 3rd Division at the time was dispersed in billets around Soignies and Braine-Le Compte. Ensign McCready of the Light Company of the 30th was chatting with some other officers in Soignies square when at about 4pm General Halkett rode up and called 'Any Light Infantry officers among you?' 'Yes, sir' said McCready. 'Parade your company in ten minutes' time on this spot', Halkett shouted, wheeled his horse and galloped away. This was the start of 30 hours precipitate activity for the Division; by 9pm brigades were concentrating and receiving 24 hours rations, and by midnight they were marching hard along the dark Belgian lanes. In the haste to concentrate, conflicting orders were issued and during the night many units lost their way. Divisions arrived at Quatre Bras piecemeal throughout the 16 June, but Wellington was there, personally directing units into battle positions with coolness and skill.

Until mid-afternoon when Kielmansegge's Hanoverian Brigade and Halkett's 5 Brigade reached the crossroads, Picton's 5th Division together with brigades of Dutch and Brunswickers had been bearing the brunt of the fighting. At this time British fortunes were at their lowest, many of 5 Div's battalions holding the centre being reduced to two-thirds strength and short of ammunition. Wellington took Kielmansegge's brigade and personally placed it on the left in skirmishing order to support the 95th Rifles, and he authorised Picton to use Halkett's brigade to reinforce the centre. Picton placed the 69th to the east of the Charleroi road to screen Quatre Bras itself, and the remainder of 5 Brigade was echeloned to the west of the road towards Bossu wood.

At this moment the Prince of Orange seriously influenced 3 Div's activities. He instructed the 69th to deploy from square into line, and then rode across to Halkett and despite protests ordered the remaining battalions into line also. The French cavalry attack by

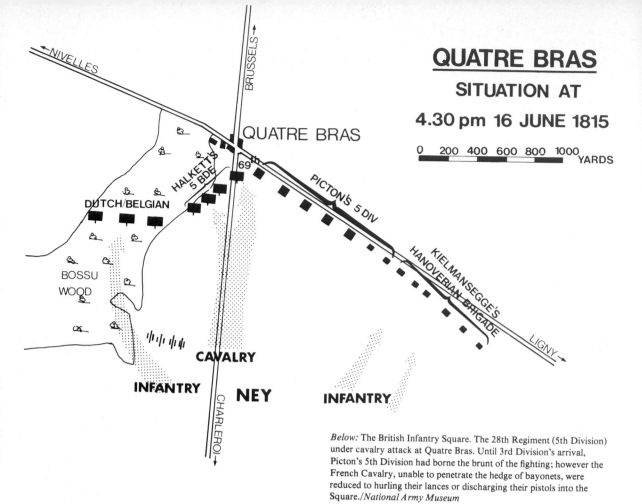

QUATRE BRAS
SITUATION AT
4.30 pm 16 JUNE 1815

0 200 400 600 800 1000 YARDS

NIVELLES

BRUSSELS

QUATRE BRAS

HALKETT'S 5 BDE

69

DUTCH/BELGIAN

PICTON'S 5 DIV

KIELMANSEGGE'S HANOVERIAN BRIGADE

LIGNY

BOSSU WOOD

CAVALRY

INFANTRY

NEY

CHARLEROI

INFANTRY

Below: The British Infantry Square. The 28th Regiment (5th Division) under cavalry attack at Quatre Bras. Until 3rd Division's arrival, Picton's 5th Division had borne the brunt of the fighting; however the French Cavalry, unable to penetrate the hedge of bayonets, were reduced to hurling their lances or discharging their pistols into the Square./*National Army Museum*

900 cuirassiers that followed resulted in near disaster for 5 Brigade. Halkett saw it coming and hastily ordered his battalions back into square, but they were slow to do so due to inexperience, conflicting orders, and an inability to see the cavalry through the head-high corn. The 69th were overrun and their colour captured, the survivors taking refuge in the square of Picton's 42nd and 44th Regiments. The 30th managed to form square and beat off the cavalry, but the 33rd and 73rd were scattered and took cover in Bossu Wood. Returning from the left flank Wellington found Halkett's brigade in very poor shape. The 69th were no longer an effective fighting force, but Wellington personally rallied his own regiment, the 33rd, and restored order in the other two battalions. Other than in the 69th Regiment 5 Brigade's casualties had not been heavy, but its rough handling was valuable experience for the sterner test it was to face two days later at Waterloo. With the arrival of fresh units at Quatre Bras Wellington gained the initiative and during the evening the reformed 5 Brigade was able to take part in a general advance to recover the ground lost during the day.

Meanwhile at Ligny, Blücher had suffered a sharp but not crippling defeat. Napoleon had failed in his aim to drive him north-east and thus separate him from Wellington. Instead Blücher retreated northwards to Wavre, thus remaining within half a day's march and supporting distance of Wellington. The latter ordered a withdrawal from Quatre Bras to Mont St Jean, previously selected by him as the best position covering Brussels. He was confident he could defeat Napoleon there, provided Blücher operated against the French flank from Wavre.

On 17 June, the Allies withdrew in oppressive heat which developed into a violent thunderstorm, and heavy rain fell throughout the late afternoon and all night. Wellington's army, mud splattered and soaking wet, reached the Mont St Jean position that evening. Sergeant

Tom Morris of the 73rd describes the scene as units were directed into position:

'As the storm continued, without any signs of abatement, and the night was settling in, orders were given to pile arms, but no man on any account to quit his position. Under such circumstances our prospect of a night's lodging was anything but cheering; the only provision we had being the remnant of the salt provision, served out on the 16th. Having disposed of that, we began to consider in what way to pass the night, to lie down was out of the question, and to stand up all night was almost equally so. We endeavoured to light some fires, but the rain soon put them out, and the only plan we could adopt was to gather arms-full of standing corn and, rolling it together, made a sort of mat, on which we placed the knapsack; and sitting on that, each man holding his blanket over his head to keep off the rain, which was almost needless, as we were so thoroughly drenched — however, this was the plan generally adopted and maintained during the night . . '

The French were equally uncomfortable. To avoid the mud, many of their cavalry slept in the saddle thus half-exhausting their horses before the morrow's battle had even started.

Waterloo: the Position
At dawn on the 18 June the rain subsided, and the stiff and shivering soldiers of 3rd Division were able to cook breakfast, clean their weapons, and examine their position, which was on the right centre, between Picton's 5th Division and the Guards of 1st Division. 3 Div was responsible for about 900 yards of front, including the farm of La Haye Sainte which jutted out like a bastion towards the French. Alten placed Ompteda's KGL Brigade on the left with the Light battalions holding the farm, Kielmansegge's Hanoverian Brigade in the centre,

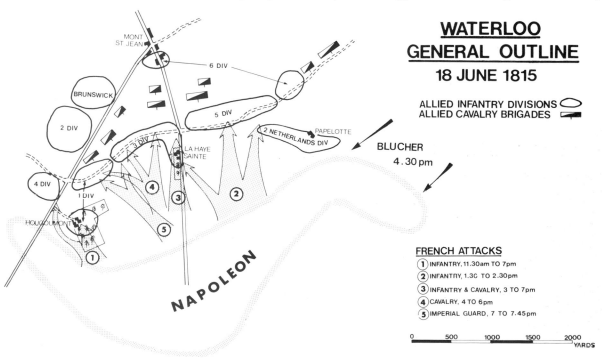

WATERLOO
GENERAL OUTLINE
18 JUNE 1815

ALLIED INFANTRY DIVISIONS
ALLIED CAVALRY BRIGADES

BLUCHER
4.30 pm

FRENCH ATTACKS
1 INFANTRY, 11.30am TO 7pm
2 INFANTRY, 1.30 TO 2.30pm
3 INFANTRY & CAVALRY, 3 TO 7pm
4 CAVALRY, 4 TO 6pm
5 IMPERIAL GUARD, 7 TO 7.45pm

0   500   1000   1500   2000
                                YARDS

and Halkett's Brigade on the right. Units were drawn up on the reverse slop giving them some protection from cannon fire. The only troops of 3 Div visible to the enemy were the Light companies deployed in skirmishing order across the valley, and the two batteries on the skyline. The understrength battalions of 5 Brigade, weakened further at Quatre Bras and averaging only 500 bayonets each, were grouped in pairs, the 30th with the 73rd and the 33rd with the 69th.

Wellington's battle plan was necessarily simple. His troops were of such mixed quality that he could not hope to fight a battle of manoeuvre like Salamanca. He would rely on his infantry to stand firm, and trust that Blücher would arrive in time to turn the enemy's right flank. Napoleon himself was to oblige Wellington by discarding skill and manoeuvre, and instead based his effort on massive frontal blows by infantry and cavalry, interspersed with sharp artillery bombardments.

Napoleon commenced operations in the centre at midday with a cannonade of 80 guns, and until the Emperor's rout at 8pm there was hardly a moment when some part of 3rd Division was not under heavy pressure. The story of that day is best told by following the fortunes of its brigades:

Below: The defence of La Haye Sainte. On the right, riflemen of the KGL Light Battalions beat off a French Cavalry attack. In the left foreground is a square of the 5th Division, and on the skyline, behind French infantry, is Napoleon's lookout tower. The inter-divisional boundary ran from bottom right towards the tower, with La Haye Sainte inclusive to 3rd Division./*National Army Museum*

Ompteda's 2nd KGL Brigade

From 1.30pm the French mounted a series of infantry attacks of divisional strength against La Haye Sainte, held by the 1st and 2nd Light battalions KGL. The riflemen of these units conducted a most gallant defence. They were eventually forced to abandon the orchard, but held on to the farm house for 5½ hours, being reinforced during the afternoon by the Jaeger battalion from Kielmansegge's brigade. By 6pm their rifle ammunition was expended, and replenishment was impossible due to the loss of their reserve ammunition wagon. Major Baring and 40 of his men withdrew to the main position leaving behind 320 dead and wounded in the area of the farm.

The Prince of Orange then took a further hand in 3rd Division's affairs and ordered Ompteda to deploy the 5th KGL Battalion in line and advance to counter-attack the enemy infantry who had occupied the farm. Ompteda could see French cavalry hovering on the flanks. He objected to the order and requested permission to remain 'in square'. Orange insisted that the cavalry were not French but Dutch, and repeated his order to the 5th KGL to advance in line. Ompteda complied by personally leading the battalion forward into the attack.

Edmund Wheatley was an English Lieutenant serving with the 5th KGL's Grenadier Company. In his diary he recorded:
'Colonel Ompteda ordered us instantly into line to charge, with a strong injunction to "walk" forward, until he gave the word. When within sixty yards he cried "Charge", we ran forward hussaing. The trumpet sounded and no one but a soldier can describe the thrill one instantly feels in such an awful moment. At the bugle sound the French

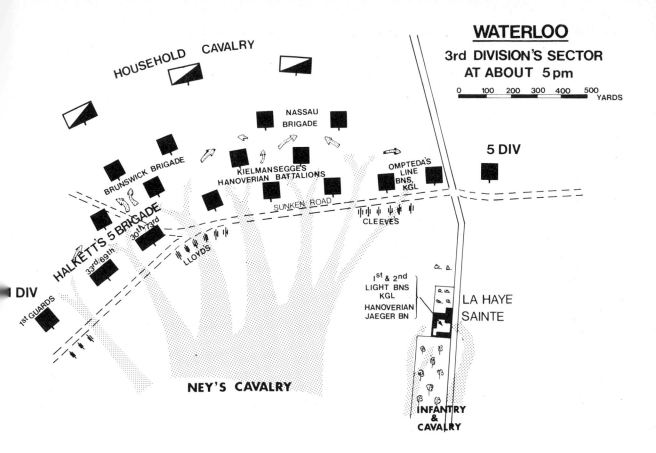

Map: WATERLOO — 3rd DIVISION'S SECTOR AT ABOUT 5pm

Labels on map: HOUSEHOLD CAVALRY · NASSAU BRIGADE · BRUNSWICK BRIGADE · KIELMANSEGGE'S HANOVERIAN BATTALIONS · OMPTEDA'S LINE BNS, KGL · 5 DIV · SUNKEN ROAD · CLEEVES · HALKETT'S 5 BRIGADE · 30th/73rd · 33rd/69th · LLOYDS · 3 DIV · 1st GUARDS · 1st & 2nd LIGHT BNS KGL / HANOVERIAN JAEGER BN · LA HAYE SAINTE · NEY'S CAVALRY · INFANTRY & CAVALRY · 0 100 200 300 400 500 YARDS

stood until we just reached them. I ran by Colonel Ompteda who cried out "That's right, Wheatley".

'I found myself in contact with a French officer but ere we could decide, he fell by an unknown hand. I then ran at a drummer, but he leaped over a ditch through a hedge in which he stuck fast. I heard a cry of "The Cavalry, the Cavalry". But so eager was I that I did not mind it at the moment, and when on the eve of dragging the Frenchman back (his iron-bound hat having saved him from a cut), I recollect no more. On recovering my senses, I looked up and found myself, bareheaded, in a clay ditch with a violent headache. Close by me lay Colonel Ompteda on his back, his head stretched back with his mouth open, and a hole in his throat.'

The 5th KGL had been cut to pieces by cavalry that had assailed them in the flank and rear, just as Ompteda had foreseen. Wheatley was taken prisoner, and marched to the rear. After enduring harsh treatment and much pain he escaped the following night, and rejoined his battalion on 29 June having undergone a remarkable succession of hardships and adventures.

The enemy remained in possession of La Haye Sainte until 8pm and from it their cannon brought a continuous and galling fire to bear on 3rd Division.

Kielmansegge's and Halkett's Brigades

Having assisted in the defence of La Haye Sainte, the Hanoverians' greatest test started at 4pm when together with Halkett's Brigade, they faced two hours of massed cavalry attacks.

Half an hour earlier there had been considerable movement towards the Allied rear of wounded, prisoners, and certain units no longer able to face the enemy's cannon fire. Ney noticed this movement and, mistaking it for a general withdrawal, ordered up 5,000 cavalry to attack Wellington's right centre and turn the withdrawal into a rout. When Wellington saw the squadrons trotting down the slope opposite, he ordered his divisions to form battalion squares; in 5 Brigade each pair of battalions formed an 'oblong'. To give greater depth to the position, he moved up a Brunswick and a Nassau brigade in rear of 3rd Division, and thus the enemy cavalry would face a chequerboard pattern of squares and oblongs.

In the two hours that followed Ney launched six massive but futile attacks against the 3rd and 1st Divisions, employing 9,000 horsemen in all, and the pattern of action was repeated time after time. The British and KGL gunners would blast the closely packed cavalry with grapeshot, intentionally leaving their guns at the last moment to take cover in the infantry squares.* The

* The original order laid down that gunners were to immobilise their cannon by removing a wheel from each and trundling it into the nearest square. This would prove difficult in the heat and contact of battle, and there is no evidence that the order was carried out. The French cavalry brought no spiking equipment with them and surprisingly did not even remove or break the sponging rods, let along try to drag the guns away.

Above: Looking right from 5 Brigade's position at 5pm. In the foreground, Ney's cavalry attack the Guards of 1st Division. In the background, Hougoumont burns but is held by the Guards throughout the battle./*National Army Museum*

cavalry that reached the summit, exhausted and disorganised, could achieve little against the bayonets and controlled musket-fire of the infantry, and were reduced to walking their horses round the squares, inflicting a few casualties with pistol-fire, to be eventually shot down or forced to withdraw by the British Household Cavalry waiting in rear.

In the intervals between these attacks the Allied infantry suffered cruelly, presenting closely packed targets for cannon, the squares not daring to deploy while enemy cavalry was at hand. Sergeant Tom Morris of the 73rd describes the third cavalry attack:

'On their next advance they brought some artillery men, turned the cannon in our front upon us, and fired into us with grape-shot, making complete lanes through, and then the horsemen came up to dash in at the opening. But before they reached, we had closed our files, throwing the dead outside and taking the wounded inside the square; and they again were forced to retire. They did not, however, go further than the pieces of cannon — waiting there to try the effect of some more grape-shot. We saw the match applied and again it came as thick as hail upon us ... Our situation, now, was truly awful; our men falling by dozens every fire. About this time, also, a large shell fell just in front of us, and while the fuse was burning out, we were wondering how many of us it would destroy. When it burst, about seventeen men were either killed or wounded by it; the portion which came to my share was a piece of rough cast-iron, about the size of a horse-bean, which took up its lodging in my left cheek; the blood ran copiously down the inside of my clothes, and made me rather uncomfortable. Our poor old captain was horribly frightened; and several times came to for a drop of something to keep his spirits up. (Sergeant Morris was in charge of the company's spirit ration). Towards the close of the day he was cut in two by a cannon shot.'

After the next cavalry attack, Wellington visited Morris's square: 'Well Halkett, how do you get on?' he enquired; 'My Lord, we are dreadfully cut up; can you relieve us for a little while?' Halkett replied. 'Impossible' said the Duke. 'Very well, my Lord', said Halkett, 'we will stand till the last man falls'. The brigade continued to suffer dreadful

Above: Colonel Harris of the 73rd Regiment personally fills the gap in the left-hand square of 5 Brigade. The brigade suffered severely from British cannon turned against them by the French cavalry.
/National Army Museum

losses. When a shot tore a gaping hole in the 73rd, Colonel William Harris noticed that his men were slow in filling the gap. Placing himself on his horse lengthwise across the space, he said 'Well my lads, if you won't, I must'. At once his horse was led back and the space filled. The 33rd and 69th suffered equally, and their square seemed likely to collapse. Halkett rode over to them, and seizing a colour, waved it over his head and rallied both battalions.

By 6.30pm 3rd Division's situation was critical. Both the Hanoverian and KGL Brigades were on the point of disintegration, and 5 Brigade had only 800 men left out of 2,000 at the start of the day. Although Ney's cavalry had been repulsed, it needed perhaps only one more concerted attack by infantry, properly supported, to break the Allies. Napoleon realised this and launched the flower of his army, the Imperial Guard, at Wellington's right. The Guard was a force of all arms — chasseurs, grenadiers, cavalry and artillery — and at 7pm their infantry columns accompanied by horse artillery moved in a blue mass across the valley, heading for the Guards Division and 5 Brigade. Ensign MacCready recorded the collision that followed:
'The Imperial Guard were seen ascending our position in as correct order as at a review. As they rose step by step before us, their red epaulettes and cross-belts over their blue greatcoats gave them a gigantic appearance, which

was increased by their high hairy caps and long red feathers, which waved with the nod of their heads as they kept time to a drum in the centre of the column. "Now for a clawing" I muttered, and I confess, when I saw the imposing advance of these men, . . . I looked for nothing but a bayonet in my body . . . Halkett, as well as the noise permitted them to hear him, said "My boys, you have done everything I could have wished, and more than I could expect, but much remains to be done; at this moment we have nothing for it but a charge". Our brave fellows replied by three cheers. The enemy halted, carried arms about 40 paces from us and fired a volley. We returned it, and giving our "Hurrah" brought down the bayonets. Our surprise was inexpressible when, pushing through the clearing smoke, we saw the backs of the Imperial Grenadiers; we halted and stared at each other as if mistrusting our eyesight. Some 9-pounders from the rear of our right poured the grape amongst them, and the slaughter was dreadful'.

The enemy's reverse was temporary; unlimbering his horse artillery he showered grape and shot on 5 Brigade, forcing it to withdraw behind the crest. The withdrawal became a panic, with groups of men rushing back to shelter in the sunken road. However the Grenadier and Light companies were quickly deployed to cover the brigade, somebody cheered, others joined in, and in a short time battalions had rallied and reformed. The French did likewise, and both sides fired away at each other at a distance of 250 yards. At this point Alten and Halkett were wounded, but the Imperial Guard were about to break before the fire of the Guards and a flank attack by the 52nd Light Infantry who swept across the Allied front from right to left. It was now 7.45pm, Wellington ordered his cavalry to advance, the French were thrown back, and 3rd Division's eight hours' of bloody torment came to an end. MacCready's final comments on the battle sum up well the feeling of utter exhaustion, shock and disbelief of the soldiers of 3rd Division who fought that day:

'Soon after we piled our arms and lay down to rest; I remember as long as I remained awake I was thinking of the work, and considering whether it would be called an action or a battle. I certainly considered we had "spilt blood enough to make our title good" to the latter honour, but I fancied that, so far as we were concerned, some grand bayoneting charge, some concluding "coup de theatre" . . . was wanting to entitle us to it. I had no idea, till I awoke in the morning, that the victory was so complete. I congratulated myself in having had the honour of serving on this memorable day with the 30th Regiment.'

This regiment ended the battle with 160 fit men only, and MacCready's Light company mustered one officer, two NCOs and eight privates:

'When we formed four deep and the poor Light Bobs could only muster a front of two men, I really did not know whether I should laugh or cry . . . My remaining eight "lights" stole me a capital breakfast, after which, about 10 o'clock, we left this glorious spot encumbered with thousands of the dead . . . they were our friends and fellow soldiers, but they died the death that every soldier looks for, and they fell by gallant foemen. "Peace to the souls of the heroes, their deeds were great in battle".'

Above: 7.45pm and the moment of triumph; Wellington waves his hat, gallopers speed down the line, and the Allied army advances.
/*National Army Museum*

3.
The Crimea

The Allies land in the Crimea
The Alma, Balaclava and Inkerman
The Siege of Sebastopol
The Assault on the Cemeteries
The Fall of Sebastopol

Right: The Crimean War Medal, 1854-1856.

Before Sebastapol, Winter 1854. The 44th (Essex) Regt.

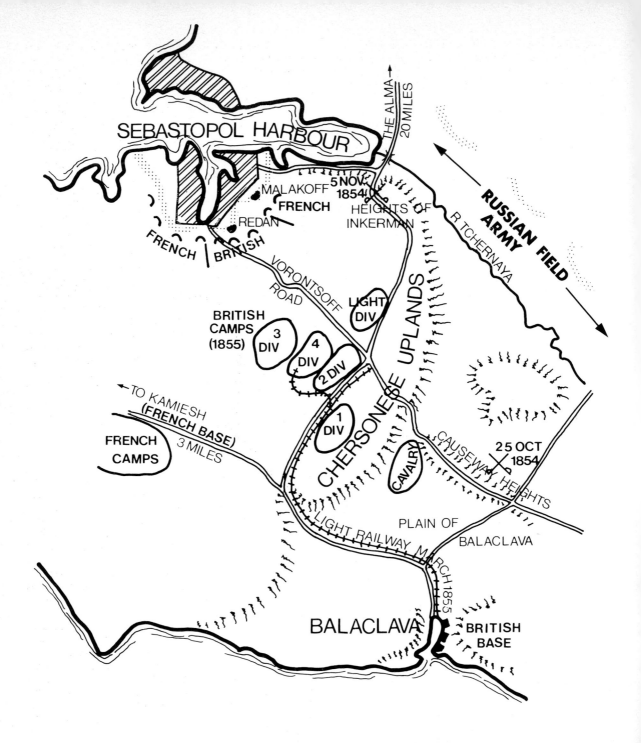

SEBASTOPOL HARBOUR

THE ALMA
20 MILES

RUSSIAN FIELD ARMY

5 NOV. 1854

MALAKOFF

FRENCH

HEIGHTS OF INKERMAN

R. TCHERNAYA

REDAN

FRENCH | BRITISH

VORONTSOFF ROAD

LIGHT DIV

BRITISH CAMPS (1855)

3 DIV

4 DIV

2 DIV

CHERSONESE UPLANDS

TO KAMIESH
(FRENCH BASE)
3 MILES

FRENCH CAMPS

1 DIV

CAVALRY

CAUSEWAY HEIGHTS

25 OCT 1854

LIGHT RAILWAY MARCH 1855

PLAIN OF BALACLAVA

BALACLAVA

BRITISH BASE

THE CRIMEA 1854 – 1855

OPERATIONS AGAINST SEBASTOPOL

0   1   2   3   MILES

Napoleon's defeat at Waterloo was followed by 39 years of European peace, during which the British army was run down in size, Divisions were disbanded, and military thinking stagnated. This period of peace was broken in 1853, when the disintegration of the Turkish Empire in the Balkans invited Russian domination of the Eastern Mediterranean. Acts of aggression by the forces of the Czar against Turkey early in 1854 led to declaration of war by Britain and France, who rallied immediately to the aid of the Turks by despatching troops first to Gallipoli and then to Varna in Bulgaria. In August the enemy withdrew from the Balkans, giving the politicians the chance to make peace. However anti-Russian hysteria prevailed and the Allies, not content, decided to mount an expedition to destroy the naval base of Sebastopol. Their armies re-embarked at Varna and on 14 September commenced landing at Kalamita Bay, 20 miles to the north of Sebastopol.

The British army under Lord Raglan had been formed into six divisions — 1st, 2nd, 3rd, 4th, Light and Cavalry. 3rd Division's organisation on landing was:

1st Brigade (Brig-Gen Sir John Campbell): 1st Regiment; 38th Regiment; 50th Regiment.
2nd Brigade (Maj-Gen Sir William Eyre CB): 4th Regiment; 28th Regiment; 44th Regiment.
Artillery (Lt-Col J. E. Dupuis): F and W Field Batteries RA (each 4 x 18 pdrs).

Brigades were numbered consecutively within each infantry division.

3rd Division was commanded by Lieutenant-General Sir Richard England, GCB, who unlike his colleagues had not served in the Peninsula or at Waterloo. Not that this need have mattered, but it would seem that he was by no means an energetic or thrusting commander, and perhaps he felt at a disadvantage alongside his more experienced fellows. Although most Crimean commanders had served under Wellington, his example, direction and grasp of the Principles of War, particularly of administration and logistics, had been sadly forgotten. The army in the Crimea was staffed by ignorant amateurs and supported by grossly inadequate supply and medical services. In consequence the campaign was to be marked by extreme fortitude of the soldiers in the face of appalling losses from disease, malnutrition and exposure.

The Alma, Balaclava and Inkerman

From Kalamita Bay the Allies marched south towards Sebastopol, to find a Russian army barring their way on the heights above the River Alma. On 20 September the heights were stormed and won by the gallantry of the 1st, 2nd and Light Divisions, and the skilful handling of artillery. This was the first of three major field battles in the Crimea, but 3rd Division was not closely engaged; it advanced in support behind the Guards Brigade of 1st Division, which carried its objectives without calling for assistance. 3 Div's total casualties were only 21, divided almost equally between the 4th and 44th Regiments.

After forcing the Alma, the Allied armies conducted a wide flank march to the east of Sebastopol, occupying the Chersonese uplands to the south on 27 September and investing the port on that side. The British seized the tiny

inlet of Balaclava as a base, and the Russian field armies retired to the east, to present a constant threat to the Allied flank. While Sebastopol's garrison feverishly threw up defences an immediate attack by the Allies might have taken the base, but Raglan hesitated until his heavy artillery was landed at Balaclava, and the moment passed. The siege was formally opened on 17 October with a bombardment by 180 Allied guns.

The two attempts by the Russian field army to raise the siege in 1854 led to the battles of Balaclava on 25 October and Inkerman on 5 November. As at the Alma, 3rd Division was not closely engaged at either, and it is of interest to consider why. At Balaclava the only infantry involved were the 93rd Highlanders, detached from 1st Division to cover the supply base — the other British forces engaged being the Heavy and Light Brigades and Horse Artillery of the Cavalry Division. Inkerman, the 'Soldiers Battle', was fought entirely without direction from the C-in-C, with divisions, or rather fragments of them, being thrown in on the initiative of individual commanders. 3rd Division's role, General England decided, was to remain in reserve, possibly a sensible step, but the truth becomes evident from the fact that when Colonel Bell, commanding the 1st (Royal Scots), received the order he exclaimed in disgust that he had had enough of being in reserve at the Alma, and moved his regiment up to the fighting to help repulse a Russian attack. There is no doubt that England's extreme caution as a commander contributed to the Division's lack of employment, and was a continual source of frustration to his troops.

The Siege of Sebastopol

From October 1854 until the fall of Sebastopol 11 months later, the Allied armies were continuously engaged in siege operations. 'Siege' is a somewhat flattering term, the Allies being so decimated by sickness that often they were barely able to man the trenches. Indeed it could be said that they were themselves under siege from the Russian field army hovering to the east and north; while Sebastopol itself was able to maintain communication with the outside via the Alma road, and the garrison was better fed, sheltered and armed than the forces that besieged it.

The British infantry divisions camped on the heights to the south-east of Sebastopol and with the French, constructed trench works towards the city and dockyard. The Russian defence was based on two dominating fortifications — the 'Malakoff' opposite the French sector, and the 'Redan' facing the British right wing. 3rd and 4th Divisions manned the trenches on the left wing, and therefore were not used for directly assaulting the Redan; nonetheless they were continuously employed in supporting operations on the left flank.

Many individual acts of gallantry were performed during the siege and the battles that accompanied it, and at home pressure mounted in the Press and Parliament for some method of recognising and rewarding them, irrespective of rank. After considerable discussion the Queen approved the institution of the Victoria Cross in January 1856, and recommendations in respect of individuals still living were called for. One name submitted was that of Private Grady of the 4th Regiment.

On the day following the opening of the bombardment of Sebastopol, a gun in the British trenches was put out of action by damage to its emplacement by enemy fire, and Grady volunteered to go out in front to clear debris away from the gun. He successfully completed the task under heavy fire, and became the first soldier of 3rd Division to be awarded the VC.

In November Major-General Barnard took over 1st Brigade when Sir John Campbell went to command 4th Division, and during the winter of 1854/55, 3rd Division was strengthened by five further infantry battalions; the 14th, 39th and 89th Regiments joining 1st Brigade, and the 9th and 18th going to 2nd Brigade. These were essential reinforcements as so many men of the Division were sick. Later, the 2nd Battalion, 1st Regiment joined their 1st Battalion in 1st Brigade, and the 38th was transferred to 2nd Brigade.

Among a number of officers whose letters from the Crimea have been preserved were Captain Robert Hawley of the 89th and Lieutenant Arthur Brooksbank of the 38th. Hawley arrived at Balaclava with a draft of the 89th on 5 January, and describes his impressions of the army and its condition:

'You have seen campaigning, but I doubt if your experience can give you any idea of the aspect of matters here. The vast resources that leave England are enough to occupy the quays of any large merchantile port, but to see the wretched end they come to... would astonish you. I see no activity, no moving and bustle. I believe one cart with ammunition has left the side of the creek in an hour or so. The frost has, I am glad to say, set in and the glass is now at 26°, the snow covering the ground in all directions... there is dreadful sickness amongst the men. Over 50 have died since the Regiment arrived about three weeks past... The soldiers have lost all appearance of their calling, hardly a bit of uniform to be seen. They have the look of a cross between coal-heavers and gypsies... I doubt if the Army in Spain ever reached the pitch this has...'

An example of bad planning was that many units disembarked in the Crimea still equipped with the old 'Tower Musket'. These were replaced with the muzzle-loading Minie rifle, accurate up to 1,000 yards in skilled hands, and Hawley commented:

'I landed today, went to the Ordnance Storekeeper and exchanged my 180 smooth-bores for rifles. You must do these things without asking: if you apply to Headquarters the delay would be endless. The arms are rusty but very serviceable. They are mostly those picked up after Alma and Inkerman, and bear, many of them, remnants of the strife...

'The Russian information must be very good. They know even when a regiment in the trenches is armed with rifles, and advance or withdraw their posts accordingly.'

Right: A group of officers and soldiers of the 89th Regiment in camp before Sebastopol, showing the motley dress adopted. On the left is Captain Robert Hawley and seated in the centre is the Quartermaster, Major Watson. Photograph by Roger Fenton./*National Army Museum*

4th King's Own Royal Reg.t in the Crimea · An advanced trench before Sevastopol·

It was not only equipment that was criticised. Little was thought of the C-in-C, Lord Raglan, either by the Press, who for the first time in history were able to cover a campaign at first hand, or by regimental officers. Sir William Russell, writing for *The Times*, referred to 'our men, deprived as they were of the cheering personal presence and exhortation of their Generals', and shortly after, Hawley wrote:

'.... the fault lies in a few words. Lord Raglan expected to take the place (Sebastopol) in a few days and did not, et voila le miserie (excuse the bad French). Having failed, he has shown himself QUITE inadequate to his post. He minds *The Times* though, and like a dormouse has unwound from his winter sleep and has shown himself TWICE to us...

'....The Army is not only without a general but without generals, and nothing has saved it but the down right honest hard pluck of the infantry... but now they are skeletons not only in numbers but in health.'

Hawley's opinion of the Staff is typical of all self-respecting regimental officers:

'.... Knatchball (Lieutenant Knatchball, 89th Regiment) who has very sharp eyes has just detected a staff-officer in the distance. I note it, not that the specimen is scarce but it is not of a roaming or erratic nature, confining itself to warm walls and southerly aspects, whilst we poor creatures are doubled up and shivering under a linen covering.'

On average, two-thirds of the army was incapacitated through sickness that winter. The shortage of fit men led to excessive periods of duty in the trenches. Sentries, wet through and frozen, inevitably dozed off and the Russians took the opportunity to make a number of sorties, many British soldiers being bayoneted as they slept. On 3 December 1854, the 50th Regiment lost a dozen men in this way, and their advanced trench had to be retaken by another battalion. On the night of 10 March 1855 the

Above: Winter in the trenches — the 4th (Kings Own Royal) Regiment before Sebastopol. From a contemporary coloured picture-postcard./*Kings Own Royal Border Regiment*

enemy launched what was known as the 'Great Night Sortie' against the French, with strong diversionary attacks on the 4th and Light Divisions in the British trenches. They were driven off leaving many dead and wounded abandoned in No Man's Land. A truce was arranged to recover them and Hawley wrote:

'The day but one after the Great Sortie a flag of truce was hoisted from 12 until 2... A more extraordinary scene was perhaps never before witnessed. Then the Russians crawled from their hiding-places, our fellows jumped over their trenches and, for the first time during the barbarous war, met in friendly intercourse with the Muscovites. Pipes were lighted and snuff passed between slaves (for I suppose they are) and free men. The officers chatted and took off their caps to each other. Russ is a cunning creature and asked how strong the guards of our trenches were. "15,000 always" was the grave reply, being multiplied by ten. Then they asked questions about distinctions in dress — ominous that, picking out their shots no doubt — but it won't do any harm as I think they are generally convinced a colour-sergeant, from his arm being so gaily emblazoned, was a Brigadier-General at least.'

In March 1855 a railway from Balaclava to the divisional camps was completed, greatly improving the supply position, and as spring advanced sickness decreased and the spirits of the army rose; but summer brought its own problems, as Hawley wrote on 24 May:

'....What the newspapers call Queen's weather is to be found in the Crimea as well as at home... The soldiers have now shed their red even, and come out in a brown holland shooting coat, such cool, comfortable garments, though they look exceedingly like the Russians... We

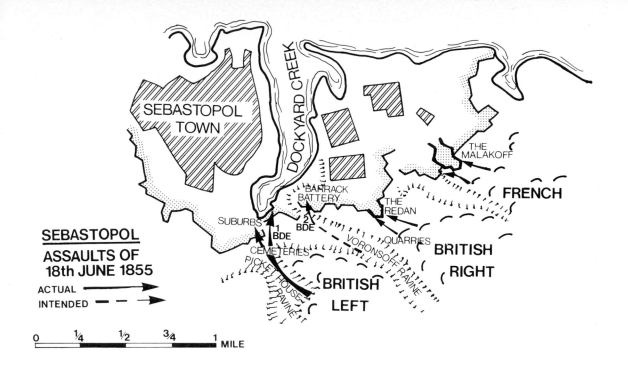

SEBASTOPOL
ASSAULTS OF
18th JUNE 1855

ACTUAL ———————▶
INTENDED — — —▶

0   ¼   ½   ¾   1   MILE

have but 29 sick in the whole Corps: of these 14 have
been struck in the trenches... We are now in the
scorching heat of May and full Summer... The sun
strikes in full force against the trenches, which stop all
draughts of air. No shelter has been provided for the men.
If they are exposed much longer it must hurt them. They
have extemporised a sort of shelter by hanging their great
coats over muskets, but this gives them small shelter...'

The Assault on The Cemeteries

On 18 June, the 2nd and Light Divisions made a major
assault on the Redan, in concert with an attack by the
French on the Malakoff, and 3rd Division was warned to
exploit success with an attack on the left wing. Eyre's 2nd
Brigade was to advance down Picket-House Ravine on
the left and attack a position known as The Cemeteries at
the head of Dockyard Creek, while Barnard's 1st Brigade
was to assault the Barrack Battery from the Voronsoff
Ravine. Both attacks were dependent on the Redan being
taken first.

The preliminary bombardment opened at 4am on the
17 June, and throughout the day the Allies rejoiced as one
by one the cannon in the Redan and Malakoff fell silent.
But it was all deception; the enemy were deliberately
withdrawing their guns to encourage attack, which now
lacked any element of surprise and when it started on the
morning of the 18th it was doomed to failure. The French
advanced too early, orders to the storming parties of the
2nd and Light Divisions were inadequate and confused
and most foolish blunder of all, the assault was made
without covering fire, and failed with terrible loss.

With the Redan still in enemy hands, 3rd Division's
attack should not have started, but in the tradition of
muddle that marks the campaign, Eyre's brigade did
advance, and Barnard's almost. Nonetheless Eyre's 2,000
men achieved a brilliant initial success. Pressing on down

the Picket-House Ravine at the double, they assaulted
and quickly took The Cemeteries at the point of the
bayonet. But then control was lost, and the brigade,
flushed with success, pushed on into the very suburbs of
Sebastopol. Here it came under fire from every side, and
individual groups of men were forced to take cover in the
houses, which they fortified for defence. Casualties
mounted and Lt Arthur Brooksbank of the 38th takes up
the story:

'At last the order came to retire; but we all agreed it was
too dangerous to attempt, and that all the wounded would
have to be left behind; so we agreed it was better to stay
where we were till dark, and then make a shift to carry
away our wounded. As soon as it was dark we collected
them together, and took off shutters and doors from the
houses, and retired upon our advanced trench. A more
dreadful day I never passed... we... lost 17 officers and
147 men killed and wounded... I believe our General
greatly exceeded his orders, for we were exposed to
batteries that ought to have been taken before we
advanced at all...'

This attack led to the award of a second VC for 3rd
Division when Colour Sergeant McWhiney of the 44th
Regiment led the brigade advance guard in the attack on
The Cemeteries. His bravery in this action confirmed the
reputation he made earlier in the siege, for while in charge
of his regiment's sharpshooters he had on separate
occasions rescued a private and a corporal who were
wounded in the open, and his exploits included the almost
unique distinction of not missing a day's duty throughout
the war.

Barnard's Brigade was fortuitously spared a similar
ordeal as Hawley describes:

'England, supposing the Redan had been taken, sent to
Barnard to advance our 1st Brigade... the last very

prudently sent to Brown (General Brown, commanding the Light Division) to know if the Redan had fallen. The reply was "No — you are already too far advanced to retire along the ravine; to advance would be but destruction", so our brigade was spared being slaughtered.'

At the close of the action the Allied troops were back where they started. 2nd Brigade had fought magnificently in its abortive advance, and it is ironic that having been committed in error, it penetrated deeper into Sebastopol than any other attack before or after.

Raglan never recovered from the disaster of the Redan; he went into decline and died of cholera 10 days later, being succeeded by the 63-year old General Simpson, who was no improvement. In August, Eyre relieved England in command of 3rd Division when the latter was invalided home. As the scorching summer dragged on

Below: The camp of the 3rd Division on the Chersonese Uplands. On the right, a battalion marches off for duty in the trenches before Sebastopol, visible in the distance. This idyllic scene, engraved in the spring of 1855, gives no indication of the dreadful camp conditions of the previous winter./*National Army Museum*

there were increasing signs that Russian morale was deteriorating, and the evacuation of Sebastopol seemed only a matter of time. But the French looked for a dramatic ending, a glorious assault, and on 8 September it took place. They captured the Malakoff, but the British again failed dismally at the Redan. There were the customary mistakes in co-ordination, but the fundamental reason for failure was Simpson's use of the worn out 2nd and Light Divisions for the assault. Alma, Inkerman and the June attacks had stripped these formations of their experienced soldiers, and they were now composed of raw recruits. Throughout the attack, Hawley wrote, 'the 3rd Division stood inactive, 5,000 strong, the finest in the Crimea.' His words sum up well the Division's potential as well as its frustration.

The day after the attack the Russians evacuated not only the Redan but the whole of Sebastopol, which was now untenable with the French holding the Malakoff.

The war dragged on officially until 30 March 1856, but without further serious fighting. The British army spent another winter at Balaclava in relatively comfortable huts and embarked for home that summer. As they departed, divisions were once again disbanded, and 3 Div was not to reform for over 40 years.

4.
The Boer War

The British Army's Shortcomings in 1899

3rd Division assembles in South Africa

Repulse at Stormberg

Advance into the Orange Free State

Disaster at Reddersberg

Formation of the Orange River Colony Garrison

Right: The Queen's South Africa Medal, 1899-1900.

'Action Front!' 77th Battery RFA
Stormberg, 10th December, 1899.

43

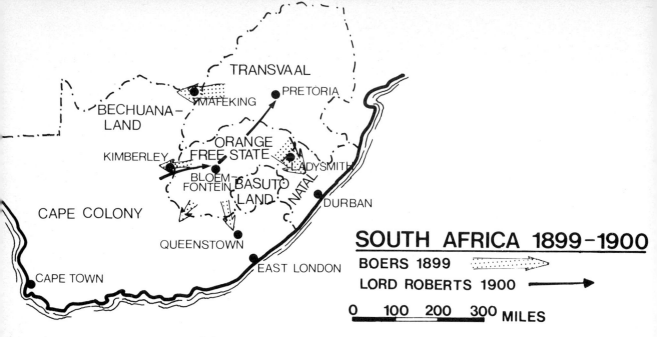

SOUTH AFRICA 1899–1900

BOERS 1899

LORD ROBERTS 1900

0   100   200   300 MILES

Above right: The enemy —
a section of Boer riflemen. Crack
shots, excellent horsemen, natural
hunters, they taught the British
Army the real meaning of fieldcraft
and mobility.
/National Army Museum

Right: The Mounted Infantry
company of the 2nd Royal Irish
Rifles crosses the Orange River,
March 1900. MI units were rapidly
expanded as the war progressed,
allowing the British infantry to meet
Boer horsemen on equal
terms./*National Army Museum*

The Boer War was to bring to an abrupt close a century of success enjoyed by the British Army, using traditional fighting methods. In 1899 the regimental qualities of courage, parade-ground precision in close order, and unthinking obedience still held sway at the expense of fieldcraft, tactics and initiative. Soldiers could fight magnificently, employing volley-fire and bayonet under the close control of their officers and NCOs, but disperse them, make casualties of their leaders and expect them to act for themselves, and they were lost. Officers regarded war as an extension of sport and few studied their profession seriously, and it is therefore not surprising that little thought had been given to the efficient use of the modern breach-loading weapons with which the army was now equipped. Conversely the Boers, though not particularly brave or well disciplined, were intelligent, self reliant, and skilled marksmen and horsemen. They were experts in the use of ground and knew how to disperse quickly, reform and fight again. The British army had much to learn from these farmers of the Veldt.

Tension between Boers and British had been increasing for some years, fostered by the Boer claim to Natal which had been annexed by Britain in 1843, and by Britain's allegations of ill treatment of her settlers in the Transvaal. The Boers were purchasing quantities of small arms and artillery from Germany, and in 1895 General Butler, the local British Commander, warned the Government that 200,000 men would be required to beat the 50,000 mounted infantry that the Boers could muster. On account of his pessimism Butler was recalled, and by October 1899, reinforcements had brought the Cape garrison to only 27,000. On 9 October Kruger, the President of the Transvaal, issued an ultimatum calling for the withdrawal of these reinforcements; two days later the ultimatum expired and a major Boer offensive into Natal was launched together with advances into Cape Colony and Bechuanaland. By early November Ladysmith, Kimberley and Mafeking were under seige.

Despite Butler's warnings no plans for despatching an expeditionary force to South Africa existed before June 1899, when a reinforcement plan was rapidly produced. Implementation was delayed until the last moment, the order to mobilise not being issued until October. An army corps of three infantry divisions and a cavalry division was formed, the 3rd Division being placed under the command of Lieutenant-General Sir William Gatacre. Initially the Division consisted of the 5th and 6th Infantry Brigades, 74th, 77th and 79th Batteries RFA and divisional cavalry, engineers and field ambulance. However on arrival at East London at the end of November only 74th and 77th Batteries, and 2nd Royal Irish Rifles from 5 Brigade remained under Gatacre's command, the remainder being diverted to Durban to reinforce the troops in Natal. In their place Gatacre took under command a variety of regular units and local forces already in the Queenstown area, and other units in the process of disembarking at East London. By 6 December the Division's composition was:

Infantry: 1st Royal Scots; 2nd Northumberland Fusiliers; 2nd Royal Berkshires (half Battalion plus mounted company and armoured train); 2nd Royal Irish Rifles; Two companies, Mounted Infantry.

Artillery: 74th Battery RFA; 77th Battery RFA.
Divisional Troops: 12th Company RE; 33rd Company Army Service Corps; 16th Field Ambulance.
Local Forces: Frontier Mounted Rifles (229 all ranks); Queenstown Rifle Volunteers (285 all ranks); Kaffrarian Rifles (285 all ranks); Detachment of Cape Mounted Police (42 all ranks).

Regular MI [Mounted Infantry] companies had been formed in 1889 in each UK District from infantry volunteers, and more recently had been formed in battalions already serving in South Africa, such as 2nd Royal Berkshires. MI were particularly suited to the open terrain and great distances of South Africa, and were to be expanded as the war progressed. The infantry personal weapon was the ten-round magazine-fed 'Long Lee-Enfield' rifle, effective at 600 yards for individual fire and at 2,000 yards for collective fire; in addition each battalion and independent MI company was equipped with one Maxim medium machine gun, the forerunner of the Vickers, with an effective range of 3,000 yards. Field Artillery Batteries were each equipped with six 15-pounder guns, with a range of 5,500 yards.

Repulse at Stormberg, 10 December 1899

3rd Division was tasked with protecting the Queenstown area from a Boer force under Olivier, which had invaded Cape Colony and occupied the important railway junction of Stormberg. By 2 December Gatacre had positioned troops as far north as Putterskraal, 30 miles from the junction, and that day he received a signal from the C-in-C, General Sir Redvers Buller, allowing him discretion either to attack the Boers, or to remain on the defensive. He chose the first alternative and decided to attack early on 10 December even though the majority of his troops and horses had only recently disembarked after a long sea voyage and were not battle-fit. However he had a numerical advantage, for the Boers were estimated at 1,700 compared with 3rd Division's regular strength of 4,500, and by using the railway a long approach march could be avoided. On 7 December Gatacre issued his orders. Leaving the Royal Scots and dismounted element of the Royal Berkshires to protect his lines of communication, the remaining regular troops were to move to Molteno pm 9 December by rail, except for the mounted infantry and Cape Mounted Police who would move by road. From Molteno the force was to march some 10 miles by night and attack the enemy before dawn on 10 December. The Boers were known to have outposts on the Kissieberg feature, two miles south of Stormberg, with their main laager in the valley between. Gatacre selected a route leading to a crossroads by Van Zyl's farm to the west of Kissieberg, so as to take the enemy outposts in the flank; with Kissicberg secured their laager would be dominated. The plan, though bold, lacked care in preparation. There were no large scale maps of the area, and no member of the divisional staff had made a route reconnaissance forward of Molteno. Surprisingly, local intelligence officers who *did* know the area were not employed and the task of guiding the force was given to a Sergeant of the Cape Mounted Police.

Through the heat of the day on 9 December the troops loaded their equipment on the train, which after some

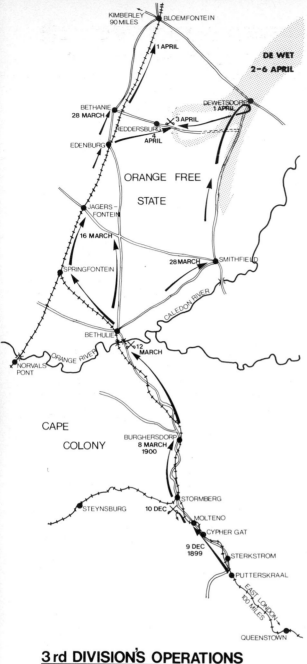

3rd DIVISION'S OPERATIONS
DECEMBER 1899 – APRIL 1900

delay left Putterskraal at 5pm. Arriving at Molteno three hours later the force quickly formed up in three groups in the following order of march:

First Group: Divisional HQ, Irish Rifles and Northumberland Fusiliers.
Second Group: Artillery escorted by mounted infantry.
Third Group: Machine-guns and field ambulance escorted by engineers.

Gatacre himself moved at the head of the first group, preceded by a scouting party from the Irish Rifles, the remainder of the column marching in fours. Guides from the mounted police accompanied each group.

At 9pm the first two groups set off from Molteno in the darkness at a good pace up the intended route, the Steynsburg road; The third group set off in error up the Stormberg road; when they realised there was no one in front they halted and enquired from the officer left in command at Molteno where the main body had gone. He was unable to help. The group returned to Molteno and stayed there, thus depriving the force of its machine guns, engineers and ambulances.

At 11pm the main body passed the track junction where it should have branched right to Van Zyl's farm. The guides led them straight on and at midnight Gatacre was puzzled when they arrived at the colliery railway and Robert's farm. On interrogation the chief guide said he knew the way and was simply taking a slightly longer but better route. Gatacre ordered an hour's halt to rest his tiring infantry, and at 2am the force pushed on again, recrossing the colliery railway and following the track to Van Zyl's from the west. The route became very bad, Gatacre questioned the guide frequently, and the atmosphere of uncertainty transmitted itself to the stumbling, weary, hungry infantry whose comments can be imagined. At 4am dawn was breaking as they reached Van Zyl's — but incredibly the guides led the force straight on up the track leading north-east; either they had lost their way, or had no idea of Gatacre's intention. As the sky lightened the column plodded on, still in fours with no skirmishers deployed, no guns unlimbered ready to fire. On their right was the northern finger of Kissieberg, and on it a small Boer picquet, much surprised to see the force winding up the valley beneath them. At 4.20am a shot rang out and a corporal in the leading company of the Irish Rifles fell dead. Rapid fire from the picquet followed and in the British column, surprised and undeployed, commanders had to act for themselves. The three leading companies of the Irish Rifles under their commanding officer, Lt-Col Eager, dashed forward and occupied a spur at the northern end of Kissieberg. The other companies and the Northumberland Fusiliers faced right and scrambled up the main ridge towards the enemy picquet, which was fast being reinforced from the laager. The field batteries swung half left at the gallop and came into action in the open 1,000 yards west of the road. On the way they were obliged to abandon a gun which, sticking in a donga (dry river bed), had its team of horses shot down and three drivers wounded, but the remaining guns brought down effective fire on the Boer positions.

The three leading companies of Irish Rifles made good progress up the northern end of the feature but the remaining infantry found the western face almost insurmountable, as they were already exhausted and a series of large boulders and vertical rock faces barred their way. The Northumberlands' CO decided that he must withdraw; five of his eight companies fell back into dead ground at the foot of the ridge, but the others failed to receive the order. They remained on the slope, as did the Irish Rifles. The gunners, assuming that the whole force was withdrawing, brought down covering fire on the

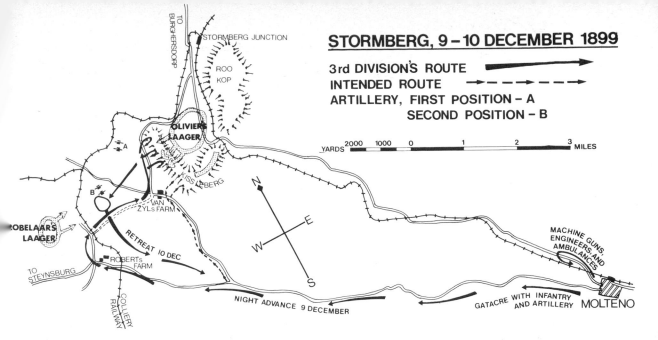

hillside, unable to see, against the rising sun, the remaining infantry clinging to the rocks. The CO of the Irish Rifles, three of his officers and three soldiers were wounded by this fire and the battalion withdrew to the foot of the hill, taking cover in a donga. The men were so exhausted that many fell asleep where they lay, as did those of the Northumberlands still on the hillside.

Gatacre now ordered a further withdrawal of the whole force to high ground 1,000 yards to the west of the donga. The artillery reached it in good order maintaining continuous covering fire by batteries, and although most of the infantry also withdrew successfully, many did not; they were either asleep or had received no instructions to retire. As Gatacre considered his next move a Boer commando under Grobelaar which, unknown to the British, had been laagered 2,000 yards further west, deployed and opened fire on the rear of Gatacre's force. 77th Field Battery turned 180 degrees and drove back Grobelaar; the two batteries were now firing trail to trail, holding back the Boers on both sides. With a further assault on Kissieberg impossible, Gatacre decided to withdraw to Molteno, unaware that many men were still missing from their units. The depleted force started back covered by the gunners and mounted infantry, with the Boers following at a respectful distance; it reached Molteno between 11am and 12.30pm, worn out, famished and thirsty. It was only when numbers were checked there that it was found that in addition to 25 killed and 110 wounded, 561 men were missing, left behind at the foot of the Kissieberg. The force entrained and returned to Cypher Gate and Sterkstrom, and so ended a most unhappy 24 hours for 3rd Division. It would not be difficult for the most junior Sandhurst officer cadet to spot the many reasons for failure, ranging from lack of reconnaissance to faulty passage of orders and complete absence of preliminary collective training.

Gatacre survived Stormberg for four months. Lord Roberts, who arrived in South Africa as C-in-C on 10 January 1900, did not wish to inflict on him the slur that dismissal would incur. Instead he decided not to employ Gatacre and his Division on offensive operations for the time being. 3 Div therefore remained in the Sterkstrom area, but the Boers showed little inclination to advance from Stormberg, and other than skirmishing between mounted patrols, no operations of importance took place on 3rd Division's front until late February 1900. By then the Division had been reinforced, its combat units now being:

Infantry: 1st Royal Scots; 2nd Royal Irish Rifles; 2nd Royal Berkshires; 2nd Northumberland Fusiliers; 1st Sherwood Foresters.
Artillery: 74th, 77th and 79th Batteries RFA.
Mounted Troops: Four companies, MI; One mounted company from each infantry battalion; Cape Mounted Rifles; De Montmorency's Scouts (a local troop raised and commanded by Captain De Montmorency VC, 21st Lancers).

Advance into the Orange Free State

In mid-February Roberts launched a counter offensive from the west, relieving Kimberley and occupying Bloemfontein on 13 March. Thus threatened in the rear the enemy opposing 3rd Division fell back from Cape Colony to the Orange Free State, and Gatacre was permitted to follow up on the axis Stormberg — Burghersdorp — Bethulie — Springfontein. On 12 March the road bridge over the Orange River at Bethulie was seized intact, through the initiative of a patrol of de Montmorency's Scouts under Lieutenant MacNiell, who kept the bridge under fire for 12 hours, thus preventing a superior force of Boers from blowing it; and by the courage of 2nd Lieutenant Popham and four private soldiers of the Foresters who crossed the bridge under fire and removed the charges.

On 16 March at Jagersfontein 3rd Division's patrols linked up with those from Roberts' army advancing south from Bloemfontein, and by 1 April the Division had assumed responsibilities for guarding the railway from

Above: The 2nd Royal Irish Rifles arrive at Springfontein station, March 1900. In South Africa, dismounted infantry relied largely on the railway system for movement./*National Army Musuem*

Springfontein to Bloemfontein, while the Royal Irish Rifles, a field battery and the Royal Scots mounted company were detached to Smithfield. Meanwhile the **Boer army** under De Wet had withdrawn to the north-east of Bloemfontein.

Disaster at Reddersberg

On 28 March Roberts asked Gatacre if he had sufficient troops to occupy Dewetsdorp. Without replying directly to the question, Gatacre despatched to Dewetsdorp three companies of the Irish Rifles from Smithfield, and reinforced them with two MI companies. The force arrived there on 1 April after a march of some 45 miles, but at midnight were ordered to withdraw again as Gatacre had received news of an advance by De Wet. Early on 2 April the force set off for Edenburg, with men and horses barely recovered from the previous three days' marching. By dawn on 3 April they had marched nearly 25 miles and were nearing Reddersburg when they were surrounded by a force of 2,000 Boers with four field guns. They held out for 27 hours, short of ammunition, lacking water, under punishing shellfire to which they had no reply, and at 9am on 4 April they were obliged to surrender. By 10.30am Gatacre with a relief force was east of Reddersburg and almost within striking distance of the enemy, but as firing had then ceased he decided not to press on; at 11am De Wet started marching his prisoners eastwards unmolested.

On 16 April Gatacre was dismissed from his command by Roberts, who held him entirely responsible for the Reddersberg disaster, in that on his own initiative he had despatched an inadequate force, largely dismounted and lacking artillery, without affording the C-in-C the opportunity to judge the desirability of his action. Gatacre was replaced by Lieutenant-General Sir Herbert Chermside GCMG, CB.

By the end of April the Division had been reinforced further, and once more the infantry were organised into two brigades, the 22nd and 23rd. As such it took part in supporting operations to recapture Dewetsdorp, and gained its two Victoria Crosses of the Boer War. These were awarded to Lieutenant W. H. S. Nickerson, RAMC, attached Mounted Infantry, and Corporal Harry Beet of the 2nd MI Company of the Foresters, both of whom attended wounded men in the open under heavy fire and stayed with them until they could be evacuated.

By June, 3rd Division has assumed responsibility for guarding the railway from Bloemfontein to Bethulie and Norval's Poort, and this static task heralded its end as a field force formation in the Boer War. Lord Roberts was about to advance on Pretoria, and to secure in his rear the **Orange River** Colony (as it had been renamed by Britain), he broke up the 3rd and 4th Divisions in early July, to provide static garrisons for principal towns and vulnerable points on the railway, and independent flying columns with which to dominate the surrounding countryside. 3rd Division went into suspended animation until March 1902 when it reformed at Bordon, Hants, subsequently moving to Bulford Camp in May 1907.

The Division's life in the Boer War had been short and not strikingly successful; blame for lack of success cannot be laid on the troops who were of as good material as ever, but on defective leadership and lack of training. However the soldiers of the Division, together with the other formations and units engaged, had learnt a great deal from the Boers concerning the value of fieldcraft, marksmanship and self reliance. These lessons were to stand them and their successors in good stead for the events that would follow in 1914.

5.
World War I

Mobilisation, August 1914

The Battle of Mons

Retreat from Mons and Advance to the Aisne

The Ypres Salient

The Somme, 1916

Arras, 1917

Eight Days in March 1918

Victory and Occupation of the Rhineland

Right: The 1914 Star with Mons Clasp.

'At your target - Rapid fire'

1st Gordon Highlanders, Mons, 23rd August, 1914.

3rd Division — Order of Battle: 1914-1918

1914-1915	1916-1917	1918
7 Brigade 3rd Worcestershire 2nd South Lancashire 1st Wiltshire 2nd Royal Irish Rifles 1st HAC (Dec 1914-Oct 1915)	Transferred to 25th Division October 1915	
8 Brigade 2nd Royal Scots 2nd Royal Irish Regt 4th Middlesex 1st Gordon Highlanders 1st HAC (Nov-Dec 1914)	2nd Royal Scots 1st Royal Scots Fusiliers 8th East Yorkshire 7th KSLI	2nd Royal Scots 1st Royal Scots Fusiliers 7th KSLI
9 Brigade 1st Northumberland Fusiliers 4th Royal Fusiliers 1st Lincolnshire 1st Royal Scots Fusiliers	1st Northumberland Fusiliers 4th Royal Fusiliers 13th Kings 12th West Yorkshire	1st Northumberland Fusiliers 4th Royal Fusiliers 13th Kings
76 Brigade Transferred from 25th Division October 1915	2nd Suffolk 1st Gordon Highlanders 8th King's Own 10th Royal Welch Fusiliers	2nd Suffolk 1st Gordon Highlanders 8th King's Own

Each Brigade had its own Trench Mortar Battery from April 1916, and its own Machine Gun Company from April 1916 to March 1918.

Mounted Troops A Squadron, 15th Hussars (Transferred to 9th Cavalry Brigade, April 1915) C Squadron, North Irish Horse (From April 1915) 3rd Cyclist Company	All mounted troops Removed from Divisional Establishment, May 1916.	
Artillery XXIII Brigade, RFA: 107, 108, 109 Batteries XL Brigade RFA: 6, 23, 49 Batteries XLII Brigade RFA: 29, 41, 45 Batteries XXX Howitzer Brigade 128, 129, 130 Howitzer Batteries 48 Heavy Battery	Transferred out, January 1917. 130 Howitzer Battery joined May 1916. 129 Howitzer Battery joined May 1916. Brigade disbanded, May 1916. Transferred out to IV Heavy Brigade, Feb 1915 X3, Y3, Z3 Medium Trench Mortar Batteries V3 Heavy Trench Mortar Battery	
Engineers 56th Field Company 57th Field Company 3rd Signal Company	56th Field Company 1st Cheshire Field Company 1st East Riding Field Company 3rd Signal Company	56th Field Company 438th Field Company 529th Field Company 3rd Signal Company
Pioneers **Machine Gun Battalion**	20th KRRC	20th KRRC 3rd Battalion MG Corps
Medical 7th, 8th, 9th Field Ambulances	⟵ 7th, 8th, 142nd Field Ambulances ⟶	
Transport	⟵ 3rd Division Train ⟶	

3rd Division — Summary of Battles: 1914-1918
(Taken from the Official History of the Great War)

1914
Mons
RETREAT FROM MONS
Solesmes (7 Brigade)
Le Cateau
The Marne
THE AISNE
Passage of the Aisne
Aisne Heights
La Bassee
Messines (7 and 9 Brigades)
Armentieres (3rd Worcesters)
YPRES
Nonne Bosschen
Wytschaete

1915
Bellewarde (1st Attack)
Hooge
Bellewarde (2nd Attack)

1916
The Bluff (76 Brigade)
St Eloi Craters
Wulverghem
THE SOMME
Bazentin Ridge
Delville Wood
The Ancre

1917
ARRAS
The Scarpe (1st, 2nd and 3rd Battles)
Arleux
Roeux
YPRES
Menin Road Ridge
Polygon Wood

1918
THE SOMME
St Quentin
Bapaume
Arras
THE LYS
Estaires
Hazebrouck
Bethune
THE ADVANCE TO VICTORY
Albert
Bapaume
Canal du Nord
Cambrai
Selle

The accounts of the Crimean and Boer Wars paint depressing pictures of inadequate preparation and low professional standards. In happy contrast the troops that went to France in 1914 were better prepared than ever before. Under the direction of Lord Haldane, War Minister from 1906 to 1909, three important measures had been initiated; the organisation of the Home Army into an expeditionary force of six infantry divisions and a cavalry division, the creation of an efficient General Staff, and the formation of the Territorial Army to supplement the Regular Army in war. The army was thus transformed from a colonial peace-keeping body into an integrated, well equipped service capable of taking its place in continental war. Within the army itself professionalism flourished, exemplified by pride in tactical skill and marksmanship, while the universal adoption of khaki uniform gave an outward sign of practical efficiency.

Major-General Hubert Hamilton CVO, CB, DSO, assumed command of 3rd Division at Bulford Camp on 1 June 1914 from Major-General Sir Henry Rawlinson. Late of the Queens Royal Regiment, Hamilton had seen active service in Burma, the Sudan and South Africa, and as he had commanded 7 Brigade at Tidworth from 1906 to 1908 he knew 3rd Division well. When he received the order to mobilise on the afternoon of 4 August, the war measures were put into operation smoothly and efficiently, and mobilisation was complete by 8 August. An infantry battalion at war strength consisted of 1,024 all ranks — four rifle companies plus machine-gun, signal and transport sections — but the average peacetime strength was 600, many of them young soldiers who would have to be sent back to Regimental Depots for further training, so a battalion might require over 500 reservists to bring it to war strength. Thus the most important task was the absorption of some thousands of

regular army reservists, men with years of experience in India and South Africa. There was no hesitation about rejoining. The Depot of the Worcestershire Regiment at Norton — their 3rd Battalion* was in 7 Brigade at Tidworth — was so crowded with reservists that they slept on the cricket pitch pending movement to battalions. Bulford Camp was the scene of particular mobilisation activity as it was the home of the three field brigades and howitzer brigade of the divisional artillery, commanded by Brigadier-General F. D. V. Wing, after whom the present artillery barracks there is named.

Between 13 and 15 August 3rd Division crossed to France with the British Expeditionary Force (BEF), up to war strength and as keen as mustard. In common with the rest of the army its soldiers had profited from the lessons of South Africa, and their standard of battlecraft and rifle shooting was excellent. The architect of British marksmanship had been Lt-Col N. R. McMahon DSO, Chief Instructor at the School of Musketry, Hythe, from 1905 to 1909. McMahon was a leading protagonist of the machine-gun, but when official parsimony prevented an increase of from two to six per battalion, he resolved to introduce rapid, accurate rifle-fire as a substitute. In 1909 he introduced a new Range Course and Musketry Training Pamphlet, and earned the nickname 'The Musketry Maniac', but his vision and energy were to save the British Army at Mons, thus influencing the course of the war. In 1914 this remarkable officer, whose achievements have been largely unrecognised, was commanding the 4th Royal Fusiliers in 9 Brigade.

By 20 August the BEF was concentrated near the Belgian frontier at Mauberge, on the left wing of the Allied armies. The British were to co-operate with the French 5th Army, sweeping forward into Belgium to meet the Germans. Further south other French armies intended to regain Alsace and Lorraine, lost after the Franco-

---

* Normally Regiments of the Line each consisted of two regular battalions; certain regiments however were permitted to maintain four battalions owing to their excellent recruiting, and of these the Royal Fusiliers, Worcestershires and Middlesex, were all represented in 3rd Division.

Below: Bulford Camp, 1912, looking west from Beacon Hill over Salisbury Plain. Here 3rd Division trained for the War in which it was to earn the nickname 'Iron Division'./*HQ Bulford Garrison*

SALISBURY PLAIN, BULFORD CAMP.

Prussian War of 1870-71. This French offensive took little account of the strength and direction of the enemy's movements under the German 'Schlieffen Plan', which involved a great wheeling advance through Belgium aimed at outflanking the Allied line. In fact neither opponent took much account of the other's movements, despite accurate reports from pilots of their newly formed flying corps. A fumbling head on clash of arms in Belgium was to be the inevitable result.

THE WESTERN FRONT

THE WESTERN FRONT

BATTLE ZONE,
OCTOBER 1914
TO FEBRUARY 1918

HINDENBURG LINE ▲▲▲▲▲▲▲

LIMIT OF GERMAN
ADVANCE, MARCH 1918

5   0   5   10   15   20
MILES

The Battle of Mons

3rd Division entered Belgium on 21 August and the following day reached the Mons-Condé canal either side of Mons. They had been marching for a week and though weary were eager for action. They had not long to wait, for news arrived that on the BEF's right enemy had thrown the French back nine miles, exposing a dangerous gap, while on the left, cavalry and aeroplane patrols reported German columns moving round the British flank. It was decided that the BEF would remain on the Mons-Condé canal for 24 hours and then withdraw if necessary. Meanwhile six infantry divisions of the German 1st Army were marching headlong for the 3rd and 5th Divisions forming 2nd Corps on the left of the BEF.

As a defensive position the canal line had many drawbacks, the countryside being studded with mining villages and slag heaps, which restricted deployment and fields of fire. The canal itself was crossed by a number of bridges, and as a further advance had not been entirely ruled out their demolition was postponed. The most serious problem, affecting 3rd Division alone, was the canal loop north of Mons. The battalions holding it occupied a most uncomfortable salient which could be shot at from three sides.

As Sunday 23 August dawned, the outpost platoons of 8 and 9 Brigades forward of the canal peered through the early morning mist and soon saw groups of German cavalry trotting towards them. The fire orders rang out, and the first shots of the war sent the enemy troopers clattering back, leaving behind two wounded officers as prisoners of the Middlesex. German infantry appeared shortly after, and the forward sections could scarcely believe their eyes, for the enemy were massed shoulder to shoulder: 'At your target in front — At seven hundred — Rapid Fire!' — and 15 aimed shots a minute from every rifle tore into the German companies, reducing them to grey heaps of dead and dying. Those that followed took cover behind the bodies of their fallen comrades and tried to form a firing line, but the British, using a trick learnt from the Boers, ceased rapid fire and told off crack shots to engage suitable targets independently.

However, enemy pressure against the salient was relentless, particularly around the Nimy Bridges, and it was here that the 4th Royal Fusiliers and 3rd Division won the first two Victoria Crosses of the war. They were awarded to Lieutenant Maurice Dease, commanding the machine-gun section and to Private Godley, a member of his section. Another machine-gunner, Private Barnard, remembers the battle well:
'We had a gun posted on either side of the railway running over the bridge. I was on the left hand gun, as Number 3 — the ammunition number. We had mounted

Left: Mons, the morning of 22 August 1914 — the scene in the Grand Place. 4th Royal Fusiliers are resting before moving up into the Canal Salient. Within 24 hours this battalion was to win the first two Victoria Crosses of the war./*Mr H. C. Barnard*

THE BATTLE OF MONS, 23rd AUGUST 1914

UNIT BOUNDARIES, 23rd AUGUST ——||——
8 & 9 BRIGADE LOCATIONS, am 24th AUGUST — — ×— —

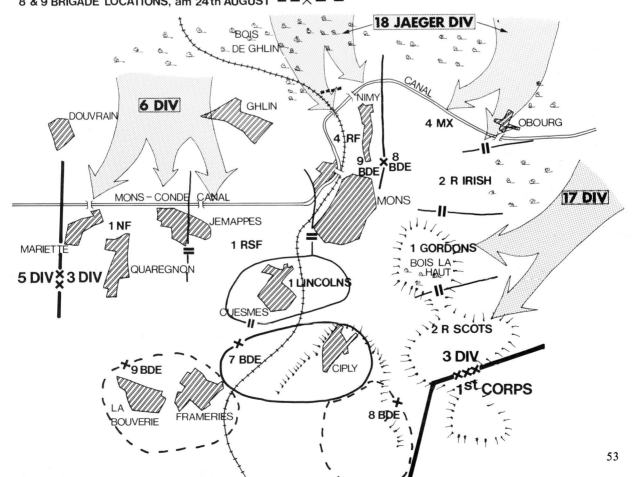

the guns the night before and protected them with sacks from a nearby flour mill, filled with shingle.

'The first I saw of the Germans was one of their aeroplanes flying low over us at about 7am, the pilot looking down at us. I remember the plane had wings shaped like a bird's. Shortly after, enemy infantry advanced down the railway line, and we and the rifle platoon near us shot them to pieces. Next we were heavily shelled, many of our men being hit, and by 8am I had taken over as Number 1 on the gun. The Germans occupied a row of houses about 400 yards away and started firing at us. I ignored the normal drill of "tapping" the gun left and right — I just loosened the clamp and sprayed the windows backwards and forwards — and there was no more firing from those houses.

'The section continued to suffer casualties. I saw both Lieutenant Dease and Sergeant Haylock fall — they had been controlling the guns from the middle of the bridge. I was the only man left on my gun, and all the crew of the other had been knocked out, so Corporal Parminter, the section corporal, took it over. I had just seen two enemy machine-gun teams move to a hayrick half right, so I shouted to Parminter — "You take the right, I'll take the left". We pumped them, and they never opened fire.

'We kept on engaging other targets, but at some stage I was wounded in the foot, and I seemed to be black and blue all over from splinters. The gun was also hit twice, and jammed, but I managed to clear the stoppages. Finally sometime about midday the gun was hit again and stopped completely. I gave the rest of my ammo to some riflemen nearby, and crawled to the bottom of the railway embankment. I couldn't move back when the rest of the battalion withdrew later. The Germans came up the railway, and my foot was bandaged by two young Danish medical orderlies.* Then a German NCO arrived and I thought he was going to strike me, but a German officer on the embankment ordered him not to, and I shouted up "Thank You". He shouted back "All's fair in Love and War".'

After Barnard's gun had been knocked out Lt Steele, commanding the rifle platoon by the bridge, took command of the other gun and under his control Private Godley fired it for two hours after being severely wounded and then, when the Fusiliers withdrew, Godley continued to fire the gun on his own to cover them. He was carried to Mons hospital by Belgian civilians, and later taken prisoner. Meanwhile Dease had died of the wounds received while controlling his guns, and in recommending the award of the VC, Lt-Col McMahon wrote:

'Lt Dease was wounded and man after man of his detachment was hit. He appears to have received a second wound after neglecting a first wound in his leg. Taking a little time to recover, he managed to return to the gun and kept it in action. He was then incapacitated by a third wound. Thus his conduct was heroic indeed,

* Denmark was neutral but a number of Danes volunteered for the German Army as non-combatants.

and of the greatest service in delaying the crossing of the enemy.'

Maurice Dease was in fact wounded five times before he finally succumbed.

While the Royal Fusiliers were gallantly defending the Nimy bridges, the German assault fell on the remainder of 9 Brigade. This brigade was justly proud of being largely a 'Fusilier Brigade', and Mons was to be the start of an outstanding fighting record during World War I. The 1st Royal Scots Fusiliers and 1st Northumberland Fusiliers (the 5th Fusiliers who had served in 3 Div in the Peninsula and South Africa) were soon in action against the enemy 6th Division. The Northumberlands were astounded to see infantry advancing in close order towards the bridge at Mariette. Their rapid fire shredded the German ranks, the survivors being forced to retreat before advancing again more cautiously. The Northumberland's outposts ambushed them once more at a road block before withdrawing to the canal, where the battalion had little difficulty in holding the enemy.

At midday the attack enveloped the right flank of 8 Brigade, with the German 17th Division assaulting the strong positions on the Bois la Haut held by the Gordons and Royal Scots. The enemy were beaten off, but meanwhile the Middlesex and Royal Irish in the salient came under heavy pressure, the machine-gunners of the Royal Irish repulsing a cavalry attack only to be destroyed themselves by German shellfire. By mid-afternoon a withdrawal from the salient was ordered and the battalions fought their way back, section by section, in full view of the enemy. The Gordons covered the Middlesex and Royal Irish, the Lincolns doing likewise for the Royal Fusiliers. It was a confused and desperate battle, but by late afternoon battalions had reassembled in new positions around Ciply.

While the infantry battled the destruction of the canal bridges was authorised, and the divisional engineers won 3rd Division's third and fourth VCs of the war. On the Jemappes bridge, Lance Corporal Jarvis of 57 Field Company worked for 12 hours under heavy fire to place the demolition charges and successfully blow the bridge. At Mariette, Captain Theodore Wright although wounded in the head and under continuous fire made two attempts to connect the firing circuit. He was mortally wounded three weeks later on the Aisne when assisting 5th Cavalry Brigade across a pontoon bridge. Both sappers were gazetted for their awards on 16 November 1914.

Towards evening the Germans again attacked 8 Brigade, just as their supporting artillery were withdrawing from the Bois la Haut. It was a running fight; 23rd Battery RFA were ambushed on the way back by enemy filtering through Mons, and the leading gun teams suffered heavily. The Gordons counter-attacked and cleared the way for the gunners, and together with the Royal Scots and Royal Irish broke up all further attacks and the Germans retreated, badly mauled. Shortly afterwards the weary Scots and Irish heard enemy bugles sounding 'Cease Fire', and 8 Brigade with its gunners withdrew unmolested during darkness, being complete in the new position by 3am.

The first day's fighting of World War I had involved 3rd Division more heavily than any other formation. The deadly fire of the British regulars had cut to pieces the massed conscripts of the German Army, but in return the enemy artillery fire had been heavy and accurate, and had accounted for most of the 3 Div's casualties, the Middlesex suffering 400 and the Royal Irish over 300.

The Division now occupied a strong, compact position on rising ground to the South of Mons; however the situation on the flanks of the BEF compelled a general withdrawal on 24 August. The final action in 3rd Division's sector was fought by the 2nd South Lancashires of 7 Brigade and the 1st Lincolns around Ciply and Frameries, as the remainder broke contact and marched rearward. Supported by 109th Battery RFA, they brought the German 6th Division to a bloody halt, a German officer recording that as his men moved forward to support the leading companies, they found only dead and wounded. 'Tommy seems to have waited for the moment of the assault — suddenly, when we were well in the open, he turned his machine-guns on (the rapid rifle-fire of the Lincolns). Up to all the tricks of the trade from their experience of small wars, the English veterans brilliantly understood how to slip off at the last moment.'

The Retreat from Mons

The German advance through Belgium swung southwards like a giant scythe, threatening the Allied rear, and the BEF's withdrawal was a race to escape the scythe. The 13 days of gruelling marches under a blazing sun, punctuated by short rearguard actions including the battle of Le Cateau, is acknowledged as an outstanding example of the discipline, standard of training, and dogged good humour of the British regular soldier.

On the 24 and 25 August, 30 miles were covered at the end of which the weary troops of 2nd Corps went into billets on the line Caudry-Le Cateau, but meanwhile 1st Corps had made a detour to the east of the Forest of Mormal thus opening a gap between the two Corps. German cavalry were pressing hard on the heels of 2nd Corps and at 2am on the morning of the 26 August General Smith-Dorrien, the Corps Commander, asked Hamilton if the 3rd Division could resume the retreat at once. Hamilton replied that he could not possibly start before 9am and Smith-Dorrien therefore decided to stand and fight that morning at Le Cateau.

The Germans did not attack frontally with massed infantry, having learnt their lesson at Mons. Instead they subjected 2nd Corps to heavy shelling, behind which their infantry carefully filtered forward. 4th and 5th Divisions holding the flanks on either side of 3rd Division came under heavy pressure and shortly after midday they started a difficult withdrawal, endeavouring to prevent the enemy from enveloping them. 3rd Division's retirement was assisted by a very gallant action fought by the Gordons and a detachment of the Royal Scots. These units were in the centre of the line and in the confusion the order to retire never reached them. When the Division withdrew in the early evening, the Gordons and Royal Scots remained to beat off repeated enemy attacks, and by nightfall although outflanked the Jocks were still holding their ground. At midnight they started to slip away and were almost clear, but at 3am they ran into strong enemy

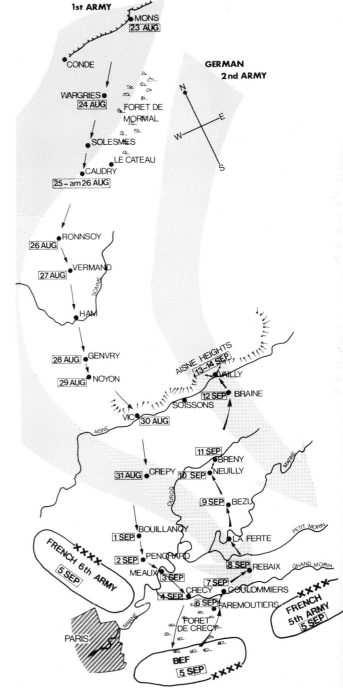

THE RETREAT FROM MONS
AND
ADVANCE TO THE AISNE
23rd AUGUST – 14th SEPTEMBER 1914

ROUTE OF 3rd DIVISION
RETREAT →
ADVANCE ⟶

forces and after a fierce battle, and surrounded by the main body of the German Army, they were forced to surrender.

The retreat continued by day and night with soldiers losing track of time and place; between 28 and 30 August 3rd Division recorded a march of 68 miles in 50 hours. While the infantry slogged along the dusty roads, the mounted troops — A Squadron, 15th Hussars and 3rd Cyclist Company — were watching the enemy vanguard, guiding stragglers, and maintaining contact with flanking formations. The Hussars were to add a further honour to 3rd Division's already impressive list. During the time that A Squadron was covering the right flank it found itself hemmed in by barbed wire, but Corporal Charles Garforth under heavy fire and without thought for his own safety managed to cut the wire, enabling the Squadron to withdraw. He then rescued a wounded comrade and carried him back. Later, when his Troop Sergeant's horse was hit by machine-gun fire, Garforth pulled the Sergeant from under the horse, and covered his withdrawal with rapid rifle fire. For his repeated coolness and gallantry during the retreat, Garforth was awarded the Victoria Cross.

The Advance to the Aisne

By 1 September the BEF was winning the race, marching an average of 15 miles a day against the German's 10, and on 5 September was concentrated in the Foret de Crecy. Meanwhile Joffre, the French C-in-C, had formed a new army, the 6th, to the north of Paris to threaten the enemy flank. By 3 September the German advance had lost cohesion and Joffre prepared his counter-stroke. The following day he made his decision; the 5th and 6th Armies were to counter-attack on 6 September, and at an emotional meeting the day before he invited Field Marshal French to co-operate by advancing into the gap that had opened between the German 1st and 2nd Armies. The British C-in-C agreed to do so willingly, the order to advance was received with cheers by British troops in the early hours of 6 September, and late that

Above: Corporal Charles Garforth, 15th Hussars, opens fire to cover the withdrawal of his Troop Sergeant. This was the third act of gallantry during the retreat that earned Garforth the Victoria Cross. From a painting by G. D. Rowlandson./*15th/19th Kings Royal Hussars*

day the 1st Wiltshires leading the BEF's advance forced the crossing of the Grand Morin. Everywhere the Germans were found in disorderly retreat, and on 9 September north of the Marne the 1st Lincolns by skilful infiltration surrounded and captured a battery of guns. The pursuit quickened and by 14th September the Division was crossing the Aisne. The Allied intention was to secure the high ground north of the river, but since 11 September there had been two developments; the weather turned very wet, and the Germans contrived to bring up two corps from other sectors, and with these they formed a front on the Aisne heights. Between 15 and 23 September in a series of attacks and counter-attacks, the war of movement slowed to a standstill on the muddy downland, and both sides dug in, laying the foundations of four years of trench warfare. Yet there was still hope of maintaining mobility and allowing tactical skill to flourish, for the area of northern France and Flanders provided room for manoeuvre, and like two opposing rugby teams, each side now attempted to find 'one man over' before being forced into touch in the North Sea.

Northward to Ypres

3 Div was relieved on the Aisne by French troops by 2 October and with the rest of the BEF hurried 80 miles north. Between 13 and 27 October the Division was fighting fiercely around Aubers Ridge and Neuve Chappelle, the last sentence of the Divisional War Diary for 14 October reading simply: 'General Hamilton was killed'. The GOC had been struck down by shellfire when visiting his forward troops. 1st Wiltshire's War Diary records on 30 October that the battalion's casualties in the first 10 weeks fighting had been 20 officers and over

1,000 men. This was typical of battalions in the Division and indicates how quickly the strength of the regular army was draining away.

Major-General Mackenzie took command of the Division but within 10 days was invalided home. The CRA, Brigadier-General Wing, assumed command temporarily, and under him 3rd Division moved 20 miles north to the Ypres salient for the final battles before trench warfare paralysed the Western Front. On 6 November the Division repulsed heavy attacks at Poelcappelle, and two days later moved south to the Menin Road, along which the German Guard Corps was making its final effort to break through. 9 Brigade was heavily engaged in the bloody and confused fighting that followed, with the Royal Scots Fusiliers and Northumberland Fusiliers successfully counter attacking at Nonne Bosschen. At one point the Germans captured a farm in the British lines but an 18-pounder field gun was manhandled up, six shells were pumped into the farm, and CSM Gibbon of the Northumberlands led a counter-attack which ejected the enemy after hand-to-hand fighting. His posthumous DCM was one of many gallantry awards won during the First Battle of Ypres. 3rd Division's casualties during the November fighting alone were 130 officers and 3,126 soldiers, and by the end of the year the prewar regular army had virtually ceased to exist, units having been reinforced with young men who had responded to Kitchener's call for 100,000 volunteers.

On 21 November Major-General J. A. L. Haldane assumed command of the Division. A cousin of the famous War Secretary, Aylmer Haldane had been commissioned into the Gordon Highlanders in 1882, and more recently had commanded 10 Brigade (4th Division) in the Retreat from Mons and the subsequent fighting. He was a tireless, resolute commander whose interest in the administration and well-being of his soldiers matched his tactical drive. His attention to detail bordered perhaps on fussiness, but while the men of the Division experienced the hardships of trench life during the cold, wet winter of 1914-15 his care for them was constant, and he insisted on comfortable rest areas for battalions out of the line, the pattern of duty during this period being four days in the trenches alternating with four days in billets. During Haldane's period in command the 3rd Division achieved a particular reputation for reliability, and throughout 1915 was repeatedly used to reinforce, take over vulnerable sectors, and recover lost ground. Haldane recounts that more than once the Germans shouted from their lines 'When the 3rd Division leave we will retake the trenches'. By 1916 the Divison was known throughout the army as the 'Iron Division'.

On the day that Haldane assumed command, the Division was reinforced by the 1st Battalion, Honourable Artillery Company. It is indicative of the gravity of the situation during 'First Ypres' that 1st HAC, a Territorial unit manned by potential officer material from the City of London, should have been rushed into the line. Initially the HAC reinforced regular battalions with individual companies, and won its first honours (a MC and DCM) on the first night of duty with the 2nd Royal Scots. On 9 December it went into line as a battalion with 7 Brigade, and within three days suffered casualties amounting to 12 officers and 250 soldiers. Fortunately by January the HAC's officer potential was realised and early in the month 23 privates were ordered to report to battalions in 3rd Division as platoon commanders, several of them being killed before their commissions were gazetted. 1st HAC continued to fight gallantly with the Division until October 1915, when the battalion was placed under GHQ command as an officer producing unit.

During the winter of 1914-15 3rd Division quickly adapted to the requirements of trench warfare. On 21 January 1915 the War Diary recorded that experiments with trench mortars and grenade launchers had succeeded; that members of the divisional cyclist company had been trained as specialist bombing teams; that a visual signalling method by which the infantry could direct the fire of the artillery on to enemy trenches had been perfected; and that sappers were to be attached

Below: 'If you can find a better hole!' — Jocks of the 1st Royal Scots Fusiliers (9 Brigade) in the Ypres Salient, 1915./*Imperial War Museum*

to each infantry strong point to make good the ravages of enemy shelling.

The divisional engineers featured in some of the hardest fighting. On 12 March 1915, Lieutenant (now Brigadier) Cyril Martin of 56 Field Company commanded a raiding party of 16 sappers, and although wounded early in the action he led the party into the enemy's trenches and held back their reinforcements for nearly 2½ hours. For conspicuous bravery he was awarded the Victoria Cross, and six of his party received the Distinguished Conduct Medal. Lieutenant Martin had earlier won the DSO during the Retreat from Mons.

In October 1915, in addition to losing 1st HAC, 3rd Division said farewell to 7 Brigade. As part of a leavening of 'New Army' divisions, this experienced brigade joined 25th Division, and in its place came 76 Brigade with four New Army battalions — 7th KSLI, 13th Kings, 8th Kings Own and 10th Royal Welsh Fusiliers. Haldane then ordered a series of exchanges within the Division, aimed at balancing experience between brigades.

3rd Division remained locked in trench warfare in the Ypres sector throughout the first half of 1916, and on 27 March launched an operation which was to result in the winning of the first VC by a Chaplain in the war. The 1st Northumberland Fusiliers, supported by the 4th Royal Fusiliers, assaulted and took the first and second line of enemy trenches at St Eloi, south of Ypres. The Fusiliers' brilliant success was followed by days of heavy German counter-attacks and shelling, and it was during this period that Padre Edward Mellish, attached to the Royal Fusiliers, distinguished himself. His citation read:
'During heavy fighting on three consecutive days he repeatedly went backwards and forwards under continuous and heavy shell and machine-gun fire, between our original trenches and those captured from the enemy, in order to tend and rescue wounded men. He brought in 10 badly-wounded men on the first day from ground swept by machine-gun fire. The battalion to which

he was attached was relieved on the second day, but he went back and brought in twelve more wounded men. On the night of the third day he took charge of a party of volunteers, and once more returned to the trenches to rescue the remaining wounded. This splendid work was quite voluntary and outside the scope of his ordinary duties'.

Space does not permit a detailed account of all 3rd Division's remaining actions in World War I. Attention will therefore be focussed on three major battles in which the Division played a significant part — the Somme, 1916; Arras, 1917; and the Great German Offensive of March 1918.

The Somme Offensive, 1916

The battles of the Somme in 1916 have been recognised as the bloodiest and most costly ever fought by the British Army. Originally planned as a joint Franco-British offensive, the French were prevented from taking a major part by the massive German onslaught on Verdun, 100 miles to the south-west, which started in February. Thus by the summer, the main aim of the Somme offensive had become the relief of pressure on the French, holding out tenaciously in the forts and trenches around Verdun.

The first attack on the Somme was launched on 1 July by eighteen British divisions, supported on the right by five French divisions. 3rd Division was required to enter the battle during the follow up phase and on the 1 July was training for the operation. Despite appalling losses the initial Allied assault drove a salient into the German lines some two miles deep on the 13th Corps front as far as Montauban, and on 4 July 3rd Division was warned to reinforce 13th Corps and prepared to join the offensive. Haldane was ordered to attack the trenches north of Montauban, on the front Longueval Village exclusive to **Bazentin-le-Grand** Wood exclusive, and on 7 and 8 July the Division moved forward and relieved 18th

Left: 1st Northumberland Fusiliers display their trophies after capturing the St Eloi position, 27 March 1916. The reputation of this battalion stood high — Brigadier Page, late 3 Div Artillery, told the author that if any CO in the Division had been asked to name the best battalion he would have replied that, after his own, the 'Fighting Fifth' was without doubt the finest./*Imperial War Museum*

Right: St Eloi, March 1916 — German prisoners taken during the assault guarded by a young signaller of the 8th Kings Own. /*Imperial War Museum*

Division in the trenches north of Montauban, overlooking Caterpillar Wood. The GOC-in-C 4th Army, General Rawlinson ordered the new offensive to start on 14 July and on 10 July the British artillery opened a slow but steady preparation aimed at destroying the enemy's wire.

The Official History does not say who originally recommended that assaulting divisions should form up by night in No Mans Land before delivering a dawn attack at 3.25am on 14 July, but in his book *A Soldier's Saga* Haldane himself claims the credit:

'I was anxious that the attack should be a surprise . . . and I urged that not only my division but the others on my flanks (7th and 9th) should, under cover of darkness, cross the intervening space and, lying close to the enemy's trenches, attack at dawn without preliminary bombardment. After some demur my proposal was approved . . . neither Congreve (GOC-in-C 13th Corps) nor Rawlinson did more than acquaint themselves with my plans, and I was determined that their confidence should not be misplaced . . .'

The C-in-C, Sir Douglas Haig subsequently raised objections to the proposal, but after a personal approach by Rawlinson he finally agreed to the plan on 12 July. The concept of forming up under cover of darkness 250 yards from the enemy's trenches was bold, exciting and, judged by contemporary tactics, revolutionary. It was also risky, for secrecy would be difficult to maintain and the troops were entirely without experience of set-piece night attacks. To minimise these risks painstaking and imaginative staff work was essential, and fortunately this was forthcoming.

During the five nights before the assault, dumps of combat supplies were built up in Caterpillar Wood in No Man's Land, remaining unprotected and undiscovered due to Allied air superiority. At last light on 13 July picquets of Lewis gunners crept forward and established a protective screen only 200 yards from the enemy

trenches. Behind them brigade staff officers and sappers silently laid out in white tape the 'Forming Up Point' for no fewer than six assault brigades, 22,000 men in all. In 3rd Division's sector the foremost tape — the Start Line — was only 250 yards from the enemy. Still the Germans remained in ignorance of the preparations — three of them who blundered into an 8 Brigade picquet were silently captured and turned out to be deserters from the Guard Fusiliers and they confirmed that their comrades were not expecting an attack.

At 12.25am, the assault battalions quietly filed up from Caterpillar Wood and edged their way along the tapes. The formation was : on the left, 9 Brigade with 12th West Yorkshires and 13th Kings in the assault line, 1st Northumberland Fusiliers in support and 4th Royal Fusiliers in reserve; and on the right 8 Brigade with 7th KSLI and 8th East Yorkshires in the assault line, 1st Royal Scots Fusiliers in support and 2nd Royal Scots in reserve. Haldane retained 76 Brigade in divisional reserve, intending to use it to exploit the success he confidently expected. By 1.45 all were in position and there was no sign that they were detected, reflecting great credit on the discipline and patience of these soldiers, many of whom had been in the army only a few months, and who made up a total of 24 battalions. Meanwhile the artillery kept up a steady bombardment, but not so heavy as to alert the enemy.

At 2am the men of the assault battalions started to creep slowly forward — 20 yards every 15 minutes until only 120 yards from the enemy. 10 minutes to zero — the sky was lightening but a ground mist still concealed them; the old hands could scarcely believe it — out in No Mans Land without a shot being fired at them. Then at 3.20am, the enemy trenches were struck by a five-minute hurricane of shells and machine-gun fire on fixed lines, another novel feature of the attack. The enemy would expect a lengthy bombardment to precede an assault, and after five minutes they would be sheltering in their dug

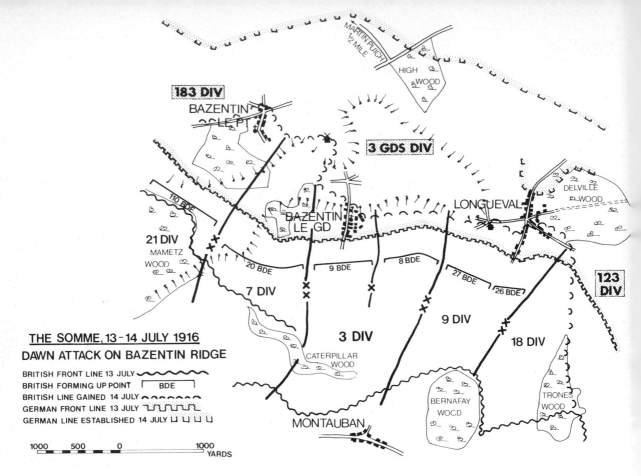

THE SOMME, 13-14 JULY 1916
DAWN ATTACK ON BAZENTIN RIDGE

BRITISH FRONT LINE 13 JULY
BRITISH FORMING UP POINT ⌐ BDE ⌐
BRITISH LINE GAINED 14 JULY
GERMAN FRONT LINE 13 JULY
GERMAN LINE ESTABLISHED 14 JULY

1000   500   0   1000
                      YARDS

outs, resigned to a long wait, and unaware that their opponents were almost upon them. At 3.25 the barrage stopped abruptly. The men of the assault battalions rose and rushed the enemy trenches in the half light. A few Germans scrambled up to their fire positions, but 9 Brigade took and cleared the whole of the first line with ease after a short sharp fight. The assault battalions pushed on, seizing Bazentin-Le-Grand village and consolidating on its northern edge by 6.30am. Within three hours from zero 9 Brigade had cleared a salient 700 yards deep, and there seemed to be no sign of enemy in front of them.

On the right, 8 Brigade was not so fortunate. Although surprise was complete, the KSLI and East Yorkshires found that by some mischance the enemy's wire was still largely intact. Their initial rush was held up, and the enemy recovered himself. Only the CO of the KSLI, Lt-Col Negus and a handful of his men, and two platoons of the Yorkshires got through and into the enemy's trenches. The remainder of the assault battalions established a firing line in shell holes along the wire, and there was an imminent danger of the attack in this sector bogging down like so many others in the previous two years. At this crucial stage Captain Kelly, Brigade Major of 8 Brigade took decisive action. After artillery fire had been directed on the enemy lines, he organised the move forward of bombing parties from the Royal Scots and Royal Scots Fusiliers. Entering the enemy trenches from 9 Brigade's sector, and in the places where the isolated parties of KSLI and East Yorkshires were doggedly

retaining a foot-hold, the Jocks bombed their way inwards and outwards. For 1½ hours a grim battle was fought below ground level, the bloody sequence of grenade blast, bullet and bayonet being repeated again and again. Steadily the Scots clawed their way along the trenches, and by 1pm 8 Brigade's objective was secure to a depth of 200 yards. 3rd Division's task was now in theory complete, and the way seemed to be open for a breakthough; the CRE (Lt-Col Elliott) and Commander 9 Brigade (Brigadier-General Potter) were able to walk forward some distance towards High Wood without seeing enemy or attracting fire. Haldane sought permission to launch 76 Brigade, fresh and ready, towards the wood, but his request was turned down; 76 Brigade was to be held back to deal with counter-attacks, and anyway, he was told, the 2nd Indian Cavalry Division was moving up to exploit. However the cavalry were still far away, having 12 miles to cover from their assembly area over rough slippery ground, and the leading brigade, the Secunderabad Brigade, did not pass through 3 Div until 7pm. At 9.30pm, when it was too dark to continue, the cavalry consolidated between Longueval and High Wood. On their left, 91 Brigade of 7 Division had advanced up to the edge of the wood during the evening, but could get no further. That night the Germans established a defence line running from High Wood to the northern edge of Longueval and Delville Wood, and by the following day it was clear that a further costly break-in battle would be necessary.

Above: Bazentin Ridge, 14 July 1916. German prisoners-of-war being escorted back after 9 Brigade's brilliantly successful dawn assault. On the skyline is the village of Bazentin Le Grand. */Imperial War Museum*

Left: The Deccan Horse of the Secunderabad Brigade, 2nd Indian Cavalry Division, forming up to exploit 3rd Division's dawn assault of 14 July 1916. They had been held too far back, and by nightfall the brigade had penetrated only 2,000 yards beyond 3 Div's gains. */Imperial War Museum*

On 3rd Division's right, 9th Division had been unable to complete the capture of Longueval and Delville Wood on 14 July, and it was decided that before any further assault could be made in the centre, the enemy salient in the northern half of Longueval-Delville Wood should be destroyed. On 17 July Haldane was ordered to clear the salient 'at all costs' by attacking from the west at dawn on 18 July, and 76 Brigade were detailed for the task. Concurrently the Germans were also planning a massive counter-attack to retake the south end of the feature. The agony of Longueval-Delville Wood was about to begin, lasting for 3rd Division until 25 July, the ebb and flow of battle taking place in what was now no more than a heap of rubble and blackened tree stumps.

At dawn on 18 July 76 Brigade, with the Gordons leading and the Kings Own in support, successfully assaulted the northern half of the Village and the north west corner of the Wood. But at 9am an enemy bombardment 'of unparalleled intensity' fell on both village and wood. 76 Brigade's battalions, lying in the open, were withdrawn to save them from total destruction. Most of the South African Brigade of 9th Division, holding the north east part of the wood were killed or wounded. The enemy counter-attack that followed suffered heavy casualties, but regained a lodgement in the village and wood. On 20 July 3 Div side stepped and took over the whole of the southern edge of the village and wood from 9 Div, and 76 Brigade put in a further attack with 2nd Suffolks and 10th Royal Welch Fusiliers. Both battalions were virtually annihilated — two companies of the Suffolks, disappearing into a maelstrom in the northern end of the village, were never seen again.

On 22 July subsidiary attacks at night were made by 2nd Royal Scots and 7th KSLI to assist a major attack from the west by another division, which failed. Then on 23 July, at dawn, 3 Div was ordered to attack at short notice to finally clear the village and wood, and 9 Brigade assaulted from the west after inadequate preparation, reconnaissance or coordination. The attack nearly succeeded, for despite very heavy losses parties of the Northumberlands and West Yorkshires fought their way through to the northern edge of the wood, but being too few to consolidate were ordered to withdraw again. Finally during the night 25/26 July the Division was relieved in the line by 2 Div.

During the period 14-27 July the Division had suffered total casualties of 6,102; killed 1,100, wounded 4,092, missing 910. Most had occurred during the seven days in Longueval and Delville Wood, after the failure to exploit early success on Bazentin Ridge. For 3rd Division, the trauma of the Somme continued until November. In August it took part in four major attacks at Guillemont which came to a halt despite initial success, and on 13 November came the final agony, the attack on Serre. In thick fog and a morass of mud, the assault by 8 and 76 Brigades went in at dawn and the Official History comments:

'The story may be told in a few words. Starting in good order, the leading battalions were soon struggling through mud which in places was waist-deep . . . groups of men forced their way into the German trenches in the face of an alert enemy, to carry on the fight the best they could.'

These gallant groups were too few, and during the day those that survived were ordered to withdraw. On 17 November all offensive operations on the Somme were discontinued.

'The Somme' has often been criticised for its apparent lack of success, yet its benefits should be acknowledged. On 10 July the Germans were obliged to close down their assault on Verdun; and more significantly, they were so shaken by their Somme casualties (which exceeded those of the Allies: 650,000 against 613,000) that for the remainder of the war they never fought again with the same determination and self-confidence.

Haldane had left the Division on 6 August, being appointed to command 6th Corps. Under him the Iron Division had become greatly respected in both the British and German armies, and it is interesting to note that he contrived to keep his old Division in 6th Corps for the battle of Arras in 1917, and throughout most of 1918. He was succeeded in command in his own words by 'the man whom before all others I would have chosen' — Major-General C. J. Deverell, late of the Prince of Wales Own West Yorkshire Regiment, who shortly before had commanded 20 Brigade (7th Division) during the attacks on High Wood. He was an energetic commander, noted for his policy of 'offensive defence' — domination of the battlefield by raids during static periods.

Arras, Spring 1917

'SOLDIERS OF THE 3rd DIVISION. On the eve of the battle in which we are about to engage I wish to express my pride and admiration of the splendid spirit pervading All Ranks. The importance of carrying out our task cannot be over estimated. No difficulties must stop us and the whole-hearted effort of every one of us is required. I am confident that the great traditions of the Division will be enhanced and that the work of the Division in battle will be both famous in our own country, and a terror to our foes. Forward the 3rd Division, as thorough in its conduct of the fight as it has been in the preparations for it.'

The tone of this Special Order of the Day, issued by Deverell on 7 April, indicates the scale and importance of the Allied Spring Offensive of 1917. Earlier the Germans had withdrawn voluntarily to the newly prepared and formidable Hindenburg Line, stretching from the high ground immediately east of Arras to Vailly on the Aisne. The Allied plan was to attack concentrically on two fronts; the British opposite Arras to break the northern hinge, the French northwards across the Aisne to outflank the German line. If successful, the two thrusts would meet at Cambrai. 6th Corps (3rd, 12th and 15th Divisions) had moved up in February from the Somme to Arras, and their task was to assault on 9 April, on the axis of the Arras — Cambrai road, with 3rd Division on the south of the road. Objectives were laid down as a series of lines — Black, Blue and Brown.

Preparations for the offensive were made in great detail, helped considerably by the presence of extensive underground cellars and caves in Arras. These were used for the assembly of assault divisions, who by way of existing sewers and newly dug tunnels could move underground direct to their attack positions, arriving relatively fresh and in good order. The infantry soldier in the assault carried, in addition to rifle, bayonet, and steel helmet: entrenching tool, full waterbottle, groundsheet, two days' rations, three sandbags, 170 rounds of rifle ammunition, two Mills bombs, and a ground flare; the latter for indicating the position of forward troops to reconnaissance aircraft. In addition specialists carried Stokes mortars, shells, extra bombs, wire and pickets. Small men humped almost half their own weight in weapons and equipment, so the ability to move up without the exhausting frustrations of mud, shelling and darkness was a welcome novelty. The unseasonable weather — sleet and snow — was disappointing and opinions differed as to whether or not greatcoats should be carried in the assault; in 3rd Division they were to be brought up quickly on reorganisation. Other preparations included the use of tanks — 3 Div had No 9 Company in support for the first two phases — and a narrow gauge railway to ensure a constant supply of shells for the massive artillery preparation. The careful planning calls into question the tone of Siegfried Sassoon's poem 'The General', 1917:

' "Good morning, Good morning!" the General said,
When we met him last week on our way to the line.
Now the soldiers he smiled at are most of 'em dead,
And we're cursing his staff for incompetent swine.
"He's a cheery old card" grunted Harry to Jack
As they slogged up to Arras with rifle and pack . . .
But he did for them both by his plan of attack.'

3rd Division's attack plan was simple and straightforward; each brigade would in turn take one of the objective lines — Black by 76, Blue by 9 and Brown by 8 in that order. At zero hour, 5.30am, 1st Gordons and 10th Royal Welch Fusiliers advanced behind an artillery barrage described in the War Diary as 'truly magnificent', to which was added a hurricane bombardment of Stokes mortars and overhead Vickers machine-gun fire. Both battalions quickly took their objectives, and with scarcely a pause 9 Brigade passed through at 7am, the infantry advancing with sections in file — for speed of movement and ease of control — but ready to extend into line for the final assault. 2nd Suffolks had reinforced 9 Brigade, for the objective was a formidable one, including Tilloy village on the left and the 'Harp' trench systems on the right. Behind a creeping barrage the five battalions advanced with great determination, fighting through their objectives — outflanking and bombing, company passing through company. The thorough training of February and March proved its worth and by late morning Blue line was taken. 9 Brigade had fought a magnificent infantry battle for their expected tank support had been disrupted by boggy ground and only one tank was able to accompany the assault.

At midday 8 Brigade passed through; pockets of enemy isolated in Tilloy village surrendered at the sight of fresh waves of infantry, and the brigade pushed on across the 3,000 yards of open ground towards the Brown line and Chapel Hill. It was a long advance, and artillery support could not be as precise or as heavy as in the earlier stages. As the KSLI and Royal Scots started up Chapel Hill they were enfiladed by numerous machine guns in strong points around Feuchy Chapel, and the brigade was pinned down. Deverell quickly arranged an artillery bombardment followed by an attack by two fresh battalions from 76 Brigade, the Gordons and Kings Own. But the planning was hurried, and the Kings Own received their orders too late. The Gordons advanced gallantly, unsupported, but were forced back, and all battalions dug in for the night 800 yards short of the objective.

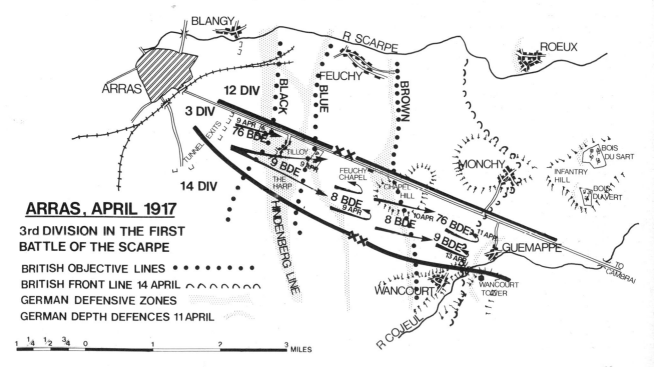

ARRAS, APRIL 1917
3rd DIVISION IN THE FIRST BATTLE OF THE SCARPE

BRITISH OBJECTIVE LINES ● ● ● ● ● ● ●
BRITISH FRONT LINE 14 APRIL ∩∩∩∩∩∩
GERMAN DEFENSIVE ZONES
GERMAN DEPTH DEFENCES 11 APRIL

The following morning a properly planned attack by all four battalions of 8 Brigade was launched, preceded by a barrage involving six field batteries, four 4.5 howitzer batteries, and all divisional machine-guns. It was entirely successful, contrasting strongly with the previous evening's failure. The problem of launching quick attacks when deep inside enemy territory was one of communication, for fire support could be requested or controlled only by telephone (which took time to lay) or runner, and it lacked the flexibility that radio was later to provide.

3 Div and the remainder of 6th Corps had now taken all initial objectives. Success had been due to thorough preparation, excellent fire support, and determined infantry set-piece fighting. But such success took time, time in which the enemy was able to establish fresh defences on the line Roeux-Monchy-le-Preux-Guemappe-Wancourt Tower, and the Arras fighting now repeated the pattern of many previous offensives. On 11 April 76 Brigade assaulted Guemappe, but was halted 500 yards from the objective by enfilade fire from Wancourt. Orders then arrived saying that 3 Div was to be relieved by 29 Div on the night 13/14 April, but before this could take place the Division became involved on its right flank in a 7th Corps operation, with regrettable results. 50th Division (7th Corps) was due to advance on 14 April up the Cojeul valley and Wilkinson, commanding 50 Div, asked Deverell to assist by clearing Guemappe first. Although 3rd Division had been through a gruelling period and was about to be relieved Deverell agreed, understanding that Wilkinson would seize the Wancourt Tower feature simultaneously. Misunderstanding led to confusion, orders were issued only 25 minutes before

Fire Support at Arras: Above: A Stokes Mortar of the 12th West Yorkshires (9 Brigade). This weapon was the direct ancestor of the 3-inch Mortar of 1939-45 and today's 81mm Mortar.
/Imperial War Museum

Left: A 9.45-inch Trench Mortar manned by the Divisional Artillery's Heavy Trench Mortar Battery.
/Imperial War Museum

Right: A 9.2-inch Howitzer of the Third Army Artillery in action, 9 April 1917.
/Imperial War Museum

zero, and when the Northumberlands, Royal Fusiliers and West Yorkshires of 9 Brigade advanced on Guemappe, they were exposed to devastating flanking fire from Wancourt Tower where Germans were seen standing in the open to fire across the valley. The attack was broken off after 9 Brigade had lost 313 men. That night 3 Div was relieved, having suffered 2,767 casualties since 9 April.

While the Division was out of the line a second offensive was launched on the Arras front. In 6th Corps sector this resulted in advances of up to 2,000 yards on the axis of the Cambrai Road. On the 24 April 3 Div came up again and relieved 29 Div, this time around Monchy-le-Preux. 'Monchy' — as it was known to all who served there — is situated on a dominating spur and had already been the scene of bitter fighting when captured by 37th Division on 11 April. To support the French who were still heavily engaged on the Aisne, it was decided to continue the offensive with a fresh attack starting on 3 May. This would require 3rd Division to assault eastwards from Monchy, the objective being the horseshoe of high ground Bois du Sart — Infantry Hill — Bois du Vert.

The plan for the assault on 3 May contained a serious flaw. Instead of fixing zero hour for dawn — 4.5am — when troops could see sufficiently well to fight (as on 14 July 1916) — the time was advanced to 3.45am. The 20 minutes of darkness could lead to disorganisation and confusion during the assault and worse, at 3.30am the full moon would be setting directly behind the assembling troops, silhouetting them and drawing heavy fire. The comment of the Official History is conclusive:

'That British troops, with their tradition of skill in estimating the effect of the lights of the heavens and turning it to their own advantage, should have been suffered to fall into this trap is one of the most melancholy features of a melancholy episode; a striking contrast to the attack of the 14 July 1916 where, on favourable ground and after the most careful preparations, success was achieved. A surprise assault in darkness may have good prospects of success; an assault in darkness which is expected by the enemy cannot.'

Perhaps Siegfried Sassoon was right after all.

When 3 Div's four leading battalions, 13th Kings and 4th Royal Fusiliers (9 Brigade) and 1st Royal Scots Fusiliers and 2nd Royal Scots (8 Brigade) advanced, they were met by a hail of fire as they stumbled forward groping for their objectives. 2nd Lieutenant Rashleigh Williams was a 19-year old platoon commander in Z company, 4th Royal Fusiliers:

'We advanced in the darkness behind a deafening barrage, but the Germans hidden in the Bois du Sart seemed to know we were coming. They opened up at us with machine-guns from many directions, and I was soon hit badly in the arm and side, and collapsed. When I came to it was daylight, and shells and bullets were falling all around. My arm was limp and useless, so I strapped my lanyard round it and started to crawl back. I was blown by a shell burst into a crater, and discovered there were some other badly wounded men there. Together we started to crawl back again along a gully, and found it piled high with dead. The men who were following me didn't like the idea of crawling over them but I said it was the only way to get back alive. We made it eventually, to another battalion. While their stretcher bearers were

carrying us back we were shelled with gas, but somehow they got us through. I heard afterwards that when reinforcements reached the battalion that afternoon they found only 120 men under the command of a Corporal.'

In a few places 3 Div gained a foothold in the new German defence line, and at great cost battalions hung on to these all day but after dark were withdrawn to their original positions. This situation was repeated in every division of Third Army, with the exception of 12th Division which held a gain of 500 yards made by 7th Royal Sussex at Roeux, three miles north of Monchy.

Rashleigh Williams underwent four years' of treatment for his wounds. His memories of 4½ months with the Division before his evacuation remain vivid, and emphasise its unfailing morale:

'I was a 19-year old boy in charge of a platoon of men of all ages. I still wonder how the older men, 40-year olds, kept going. Sometimes in the trenches my platoon sergeant and I had to break the ice from their trousers and help them up at stand-to. By the time the buckets of stew reached us from the transport lines they were covered in mud and frozen solid and we thawed it out in tins held over candles. The discomforts were worse than the fighting but despite them everyone was always cheerful and ready to do anything, and we were all very proud to be in 3 Div.'

The Division's total casualties amounted to 5,388 by the time the Arras offensive staggered to a close on 24 May. Although there was no breakthrough, it nonetheless achieved significant and far reaching results. The dominating ground between Tilloy and Monchy on which the northern hinge of the Hindenburg line rested had been seized, placing the Germans at a grave disadvantage for the remainder of the war. Their efforts to regain it in March 1918 were to involve 3 Div in further violent fighting.

Eight Days in March 1918

The Treaty of Brest — Litovsk between Germany and Bolshevik Russia in March 1917 allowed the enemy to move massive forces from the East in an endeavour to win victory in France before American troops arrived in strength. An offensive was planned for March 1918 aimed at breaking through on a broad front between the Oise and the Scarpe, followed by a thrust northwards to the channel. The assault was to fall mainly on the British Third Army (Byng) and Fifth Army (Gough). By 21 March 71 German divisions supported by 2,500 heavy guns faced 26 British divisions and 976 heavy guns.

After taking part in the Third Battle of Ypres — remembered as 'Passchendaele' — during Autumn 1917, 3rd Division returned to the Arras sector and by March 1918, as part of 6th Corps, Third Army, it was holding the sector from Guemappe to Croisilles. In February, due to Britain's manpower shortage, Brigades had each been reduced in strength to three battalions.

The Allies had copied the defensive system of the Hindenburg Line, and the new layout consisted of a Forward Zone of lightly held trenches, with behind it a Battle Zone up to five miles deep, studded with redoubts and machine-gun nests. A Rear Zone known as the 'Green Line', was also planned but in some places, due to labour shortages, it was marked out but not dug.

The first phase of the German assault, codenamed 'Michael', started at 4.40am 21 March with a shattering bombardment followed by massed infantry attacks. 'Michael' struck the 34th Division sector to the south of 3rd Division which, as the enemy punched deeper and deeper, was to find itself being steadily outflanked, and 9 Brigade on the right swung back to the Sensee River Valley to cover penetration into 34 Div's Sector by elements from six German divisions. Then as a fresh German attack on 22 March drove 34 Div back to, and from the Green Line, 9 Brigade formed a defensive flank facing south, with 13th Kings and 20th KRRC (Pioneers). Their Gunner OP officers had the

mortification of seeing massed German infantry to the south, but out of range. Meanwhile on 3 Div's right the Guards Division moved up in reserve behind 34 Div.

During the day Haldane ordered 3 Div and 15 Div to withdraw to the rear of the Battle Zone, to conform with loss of ground on the right and that night the withdrawal was executed successfully. On 23 March from 5 to 8am, a heavy German bombardment fell on positions previously evacuated by 3 Div. At 10am the Germans realised their error and closed up, but stopped short of the new position and there was no more than an exchange of rifle fire, some of the young reinforcements newly arrived from England standing up 'to get a shot at Fritz'.

At dawn the following day the Guards Div moved into the line on 3 Div's right. That morning the Germans

THE GERMAN OFFENSIVE
MARCH 1918

FORWARD DEFENSIVE ZONE
REAR DEFENSIVE ZONE
(GREEN LINE)
BRITISH POSITION LINES

Below left: The remains of the Hindenburg Line — 13th Kings (9 Brigade) in Tilloy, with captured German weapons. Left centre is an enemy mobile pillbox, mounted on wheels./*Imperial War Museum*

Below: A 60-pounder battery of the Corps Artillery moves back during the German offensive of March 1918, in the course of which the Allies were forced to withdraw a distance of 25 miles between the Somme and the Aisne.
/*Imperial War Museum*

attacked strongly north-west on the axis Henin-Neuvelle, aimed at seizing high ground vital to the Arras position. The brunt of the attack fell on 8 Brigade, which inflicted great loss on the enemy. Attacks continued all day but no ground was lost. The War Diary records that at 5.45pm 'a large party of enemy approached with a white flag; they were immediately fired on and dispersed'.

On 25 March in the south the German thrust on the Somme reached Albert, and 6th Corps was instructed to withdraw to conform. Pivoting on the right of 3 Div, which was to stand fast in the Battle Zone, the Guards Div was to wheel back with its right lying on Boisleux. The move was completed at dawn, 26 March. The enemy then filtered forward to the new line opposite the Guards Div, while the German advance in the south continued. By 27 March, 3 and 15 Divs were still holding the rear portion of the Battle Zone, having evacuated the forward portion during the night of 25/26 March to conform with the withdrawal in the south. Apart from shelling, it was a quiet day in 3 Div's sector, but there were indications that a major attack on Arras was imminent.

The second phase of the German offensive, nicknamed 'Mars', was about to start. It was aimed at smashing the British pivot on the high ground east of Arras, and driving on to the final objective, Boulogne. To quote Cyril Falls in his book *The First World War:* 'unluckily for the gambler Ludendorff, his nine divisions assaulting on 28 March struck four British as good as Britain could then show, Regular (3rd and 4th), New Army (15th Scottish) and Territorial (56th London)'.

At 3am on 28 March a violent bombardment fell on 3 Div, including heavy gas shelling of gun areas. At 5.30am 8 and 9 Brigades on the right and centre were assaulted by the 6th Bavarian and 26th Reserve Divisions and an hour later 76 Brigade on the left was attacked by 236th Division. 3 Div met the Germans with every description of fire, and although communications were cut the divisional artillery identified the changes in range as the Germans advanced and initially no penetrations were made on 3 Div's front. But from 7am onwards the three enemy divisions continued their assaults, each preceded by a heavy bombardment and throughout the day 3 Div, with the 15 and 4 Divs on the left, conducted one of the hardest fought defensive battles on record. 7th KSLI's action, as reported by the Commanding Officer was typical of those fought by the division that day:
'A barrage of great intensity was again put on the front line and at 7.15am the enemy again attacked and forced an entry into the trench at the junction of the two front companies and commenced to bomb his way outwards. The right-hand company held him for some time until the bombs gave out, and then attempted to hold him by rifle fire but were forced back as far as the junction of the reserve line. The left-hand company who had suffered heavily from the bombardment formed a block in the trench, but the enemy worked his way in considerable strength round their flank and they withdrew — again the enemy got behind them and the survivors — about 15 — together with the right-hand company of 13th Kings fought their way back to the reserve line.'

Here the enemy was held, and the CO's report concludes:

'The conduct of the last draft, boys of 19, was particularly praiseworthy and in spite of shelling they did considerable execution with their rifles on the enemy as he attempted to advance on the reserve line. Great difficulty was experienced in keeping Lewis guns in action owing to their constantly being clogged with dust from exploding shells. It was necessary to clean them frequently. Stretcher Bearers displayed marked gallantry in carrying out their duties — Machine-guns and field artillery afforded invaluable assistance, a direct hit from the latter knocked out a gun being brought into action near Henin. The battalion's casualties were 16 officers and 378 other ranks.'

By 4pm the whole division had carried out a methodical fighting withdrawal to the Green Line. At each successive stage it had subjected the enemy to punishing small arms and artillery fire, sapping his momentum. By 5pm the assault had been brought to a standstill, and 'Mars' had failed. The concluding German report ran: 'As the sun set behind rain clouds, there also vanished the hopes which OHL (German High Command) had placed in the attack' and Cyril Falls writes: 'The British achievement should be inscribed in gold letters on Britain's roll of honour. The defence of 28 March not only killed Ludendorff's plan to expand the battle but virtually ended the battle itself'.

3rd Division's casualties during the period were 3,527 all ranks killed, wounded and missing. When on 29 March it was relieved in the line by 2nd Canadian Division, and moved to First Army in the Bethune area, General Byng (Third Army) issued this order of the day:
'I cannot allow the 3rd Division to leave my Army without endeavouring to express my admiration of their conduct during the past fortnight. By their conduct they have established a standard of endurance and determination that will be a model for all time.'

3rd Division continued in the forefront of the fighting in 1918, halting the German offensive at La Bassee in April, and taking part in the ultimate advance to victory. In the last six weeks of war the Division sustained over 4,000 casualties, showing that the final days were as hard fought as any. On 15 November the 3rd Division entered Germany.

The Division's performance in World War I speaks for itself. Although by 1918 there was probably not a man in it who had opened rapid fire on the Mons-Condé canal on that first misty morning of 23 August 1914, the tradition of fearless discipline and steadiness set by the prewar regular army had been maintained throughout.

3rd Division remained with the British Army of the Rhine until 1920. The units that had fought so gallantly in the war were quickly sent home for demobilisation, and were replaced by Young Soldiers' battalions of the Northumberland Fusiliers, the Kings Liverpool, the York and Lancasters and the Durham Light Infantry. In 1920 the Divisional Headquarters reassembled at Bulford, once again taking under its wing 7, 8, and 9 Brigades of the regular army, and settled down to peacetime soldiering, secure in the knowledge that they had helped to win the 'War to end Wars'.

6.
The Road to Dunkirk

Right: The 1939-1945 Star.

Bray Dunes – Dawn, 18ᵗ June 1940.
1ˢᵗ Bn. Coldstream Guards.

Above: A rifle section of the King's Company, 1st Grenadier Guards, in the Gort Line, November 1939. The British public expected a repeat of 1914-18, and in this posed photograph the Section Commander checks his watch, ready to give the whistle signal which will send his section 'over the top'./*Imperial War Museum*

In the Summer of 1937 3rd Division was located as it had been in 1920 — Divisional headquarters at Bulford Camp, with 7 Brigade at Tidworth, 8 Brigade at Plymouth and 9 Brigade at Portsmouth. The tempo of life had changed little in the intervening years. Although a new weapon, the Bren light machine-gun, had made its appearance to replace the Lewis gun of 1914-18, tactics had changed little since World War I, and despite the lessons of the Spanish Civil War noted by younger officers, static warfare undisturbed by air power or armour provided the scenario for exercises.

However in August the routine of life for 9 Brigade changed abruptly following the appointment of Brigadier Bernard Montgomery as its commander. Montgomery had already gained a reputation for himself while commanding his battalion, the 1st Royal Warwicks, in Egypt, and also during his tour as chief instructor of the Staff College at Quetta in India. He held radical views, was very outspoken and had made a number of enemies; however his immediate superiors appreciated his worth and had given him their support. Having experienced the shambles of 1914-18 he was convinced that battles could and should be won without crippling loss. Careful planning and thorough training were his prescription, and 3rd Division was to feel the benefit of his influence in the coming years.

Despite the tragic loss of his wife two months after taking over, Montgomery soon impressed his personality and methods on 9 Brigade. He trained them hard for the war which he knew was to come, and by 1938 the reputation of his brigade was second to none. In July he organised an amphibious exercise, landing his troops from HMS *Southampton* on the South Devon coast. The antiquity of the equipment was laughable — most of the troops landing from rowing boats — but the fact that the exercise took place at all was due to the energy and imagination of Montgomery. Later in 1938 his brigade was selected to carry out secret gas trials on Salisbury Plain and General Wavell, then GOC-in-C Southern Command, paid it particular tribute. In October Montgomery was promoted to major-general and left for Palestine — but was to be back as GOC 3rd Division within a year.

During Montgomery's absence the growing threat of Hitler and Nazi Germany did promote a re-equipment programme for the British Army. In late 1938 the infantry received the tracked Bren-gun carrier, which provided the battalion commander with a mobile reserve of fire power. The carrier could carry out a variety of tasks, and it was one of the infantry's 'best buys', remaining in service until the 1950s. They also received the .55inch Boys anti-tank rifle, of limited penetrating power, and a small number of 3-inch mortars. The divisional artillery was re-equipped with the 25 pounder — an excellent close support weapon, and the divisional anti-tank regiment received the new 2 pounder. This was an accurate gun and could penetrate the side armour of the Panzer Mark I and II at 800 yards. However, misconceived anti-armour tactical thought led to a design with all-round traverse. Thus the silhouette was excessively high, the gun difficult to conceal, and the crew exposed and vulnerable. Moreover there was little opportunity for infantry to train with tanks and

appreciate their characteristics, and an isolated demonstration of infantry tank co-operation laid on at great effort by 2nd Lincolns (9 Brigade) with a tank company at Bovington in early 1939, was viewed with surprise and some incredulity by spectators. The lack of readiness for war compared with 1914 will be noted and Montgomery commented in his memoirs that in 1939 'the British Army was totally unfit to fight a first class war on the continent of Europe...' It was fortunate that this army was not precipitated into battle as it had been in August 1914.

Mobilisation — September 1939

On arriving home from Palestine in August 1939 Montgomery had first to defeat the War Office ruling that all appointments were suspended on mobilisation, which was then imminent. He quickly persuaded the Military Secretary's branch otherwise, and assumed command of the Division from Major-General Bernard on 28 August. On 1 September Germany invaded Poland and 3rd Division mobilised on the following order of battle:

7 Guards Brigade: 1st Grenadier Guards; 2nd Grenadier Guards; 1st Coldstream Guards.
8 Infantry Brigade: 1st Suffolk; 2nd East Yorkshire; 2nd Gloucestershire.
9 Infantry Brigade: 2nd Lincolnshire; 1st Kings Own Scottish Borderers; 2nd Royal Ulster Rifles.
Artillery: 7th, 23rd and 33rd Field Regiments; 20th Anti-tank Regiment.
Engineers: 17th, 246th and 253rd Field Companies; 15th Field Park Company.
Divisional Troops: 15th/19th Kings Royal Hussars (Armoured Reconnaissance); 2nd Middlesex (Machine gun battalion); 3 Div Signal Regiment; 3 Div Column RASC; 7, 8 and 9 Field Ambulances, RAMC; 3 Div Ordnance Field Park; 3 Div Provost Company.

As in 1914 and in former wars, the Division's order of battle was founded on the backbone of the army — the regular battalions of the infantry of the line. However 7 Guards Brigade had replaced 7 Infantry Brigade in 1938, and brought to 3rd Division that happy blend of unswerving loyalty and relaxed independence characteristic of Household Troops, and the traditional excellence of a Brigade of Foot Guards blended well with 3rd Division's special qualities to form an exceptionally efficient and reliable fighting formation.

The soldiers who made up the Division were disciplined, cheerful and a blend of youth and maturity — young regulars waiting to join their overseas battalions and rejoined reservists who had completed seven years colour service. In 7 Guards Brigade there was less of an age gap, as guardsmen served for only three years with the colours before joining the reserve. In the infantry the ratio of reservists to serving regulars was about 50:50, but in gunner regiments it was much higher, due to a very rapid expansion of the Royal Regiment on mobilisation. In mid-September 3 Div moved to a concentration area in Dorset and Somerset where units shook themselves out and waited to be called forward for embarkation. Meanwhile Montgomery was visiting the soldiers of his new Division. Major Jim Gibson, East Yorkshires, still remembers the GOC's brief remarks to the battalion: 'We are regular soldiers, you and I' said Monty, 'and we are going to war with the 3rd Division. I knew it in the last war — it was known as the "Iron Division" then, and it is going to be known as the "Iron Division" in this war. Good Luck'. The nickname has been retained ever since.

3rd Division, as part of 2nd Corps (Lt-Gen A. F. Brooke) moved to France in early October with personnel crossing from Southampton to Cherbourg, and vehicles travelling from the Bristol Channel to Brest. After an uncomfortable 24-hour train journey north, personnel were reunited with their vehicles on the Franco-Belgian frontier between Armentieres and Maulde. Here the British Expeditionary Force, under General Gort, together with the French 7th and 1st Armies on its left and right, dug fixed defences on the frontier, thus extending the Maginot line from the border with Luxembourg northwards to the channel. There was no immediate threat of a German attack for Hitler had hoped that the mere speed of his Polish conquest would persuade the Allies to negotiate. When overtures were not forthcoming, his army required time for preparation before launching an offensive in the West.

3rd Division's sector of the 'Gort Line' lay to the east of Lille, and throughout the autumn soldiers marched forward daily from their billets with pick and shovel to work on their positions. In November it started to rain, and digging went on in a daily misery of mud, which hardly dried from their newly issued battledress overnight before work started again the following morning. However this filthy weather had one beneficial result, for the morass in the Low Countries forced Hitler to postpone an offensive planned for November until the January freeze.

Montgomery prepares for Battle

During November, the French High Command appreciated that the Germans would attack through Belgium as well as the Saar, and in this situation the Allies would be obliged to advance to Belgium's aid. The apparent advantages of such an advance were that the Allied line would be shorter and that the Germans would be stopped short of French territory. Furthermore, the Belgian army contribution in theory was considerable. However the Allies could only gain full benefit from these advantages provided they had sufficient time to make the advance in good order. The Belgians claimed that they were strong enough to hold the enemy while the Allies advanced, and the plan therefore appeared acceptable. General Brooke considered that the idea of abandoning the Gort Line and dashing forward to meet the enemy was most unsound, but nonetheless orders were issued for this operation, and Montgomery and his Division prepared for the consequences. The new plan would mean a 75-mile move under threat of air attack to the River Dyle covering Brussels. That winter and spring the Division and its brigades repeatedly practised such a move followed by occupation of a defensive position. This type of operation is successful only if rehearsed to perfection and carefully controlled at all levels from

Below: Billets behind the Gort line — one of the less comfortable. A platoon of 1st Suffolks in a barn./*Imperial War Museum*

Below right: Battalion Command Post of 2nd Lincolns in a 15-cwt truck, on a Divisional movement exercise, Winter 1939/40. Lt-Col Newbery is in the centre, with left to right: RSM Martin, 2-Lt Fennel (Intelligence Officer), Major Lowe (2IC) and 2-Lt Noble (Signals Officer)./*Imperial War Museum*

section to divisional HQ. The dozens of vehicles involved, including two platoons of RASC troop-carriers loaned to the Division, would move throughout the night using only convoy lights; these had been thought up and developed by 7th Field Regiment RA, and consisted of a hidden light illuminating the white-painted rear differential of each lorry. On arrival at the new location every element in the Division was required to disperse quickly and quietly to its battle positions, dig in, site weapons, be fed and be ready to meet the enemy at first light. But Montgomery's thoughts ranged far ahead of the plan to advance into Belgium, for he also insisted that his Division trained for withdrawal, by day or night, in contact with the enemy. The complexities of such an operation were manifold, for the withdrawal would be dogged by enemy aircraft, as well as mobile ground forces; transport may not be available, roads may be blocked, and the infantry may have to march, dig, fight, and march again. Montgomery's foresight was to be fully justified by later events.

Meanwhile he made himself known to every man in 3rd Division, and impressed on them that he was their leader. He made a point of knowing everything about his command and it became a joke among visitors to try to find a question he could not answer. Many officers in the Division who by tradition played down the cult of personality found Montgomery's self-assertive manner difficult to swallow, but nonetheless they respected him as a highly efficient commander. They also knew that inefficiency in themselves was likely to result in a one-way ticket home. Montgomery also had firm ideas on domination of the battlefield, believing that since 1918 patrolling and sniping had become lost arts. He instructed every battalion to form a specialist fighting patrol consisting of an officer and 12 men, and a sniper section. Members of fighting patrols were to be specially selected

and would form separate and permanent sub-units, and together with carrier platoons would be regarded as 'corps d'elite'. This unusual concept compares with today's very proper policy of regarding patrolling as a basic skill of every infantryman.

8 Brigade in the Maginot Line

Hitler postponed his January offensive until the early summer, and invaded Denmark and Norway instead. Meanwhile brigades of the BEF were sent in rotation to occupy forward positions of the Maginot Line opposite the German frontier south-east of Luxembourg, the aim being to give troops experience of contact with the enemy. 8 Brigade went there in January, and Lt (later Lt-Col) Robin Turner, who was signal officer with the 2nd East Yorkshires, recalls their tour in the Maginot Line:

'The main dispositions down to and including platoon outposts remained static throughout the brigade's tour of duty. Each battalion did its "stint" (approx one week) in the *Ligne de Contact* whilst the rest of the brigade deployed in depth in the *Ligne de Receuil*, just forward of the main Maginot defences.

'The battalion in *Ligne de Contact* required special support from the rest of the brigade. Virtually no wheeled transport was possible forward of Battalion HQ in the deep snow and ice in the exposed positions of platoon outposts, hence two companies of "porters" were required to keep the outposts fully maintained in the mere seven hours of daylight each 24 hours. Also two regimental signal platoons were required to run the complicated line circuits (speech) and a morse fuller-phone circuit went right down through company HQ to each platoon.

'The Fighting Patrol elements of each battalion were brigaded and remained forward in the Contact Line throughout; the Fighting Patrols were highly trained

specialists — they even had special camouflaged snow clothing — and were bravely led by two senior subalterns of the Gloucestershires and East Yorkshires — McKenzie and Dobbie — and a 2-Lt of the Suffolks. Their greatest success came one night out in the vast, moonlit snow fields of No Man's Land when a combined patrol led by McKenzie watched, stalked and finally ambushed an enemy fighting patrol. The ensuing action was short and sharp — for our part consisting of concentrated fire at close range from Thompson sub-machine-guns (the famous Tommy Gun of gangster days).

'For identification purposes one of the dead Germans was manhandled three or four miles back to base through deep snow fields — and finally to the RAP at Battalion HQ. There this young German soldier was laid out for examination by the Intelligence Officer and the MO.

'I remember entering the RAP to see my first dead enemy soldier — a curious feeling — for some unaccountable reason imagining in my youth that a dead German would be something different from anyone else dead! This feeling soon disappeard when in amazement we found that although the unfortunate man had been hit by a positive fist-full of .45 Tommy Gun bullets, only one had killed him — all the others were lodged in his heavy clothing and the various straps and webbing of his equipment. This was a shock and momentarily impaired our faith in the beautiful new sub-machine-guns which had only so recently come our way'.

In January 1940 the newly mobilised Territorial Army divisions arrived in France to reinforce the BEF. As their standard of training did not match that of the regular divisions, Gort ordered an exchange of units between divisions, and after returning from the Maginot Line 8

Brigade received the 4th Royal Berkshires in place of the Gloucestershires, and in the Divisional Artillery 76th (Highland) Field Regiment replaced 23rd Field Regiment.

Blitzkrieg

The German plan for their early summer offensive was a 'Blitzkrieg' main assault by armoured and motorised forces closely supported by the Luftwaffe, through the Ardennes region of south Belgium and Luxembourg. The French expected an attack least of all here as the country was wooded and mountainous, and they had built no Maginot defences in the area. To the north of this main thrust Reichenau's Sixth Army of 16 infantry divisions was to invade northern Belgium, quickly reduce the strong fortifications on the Albert Canal, and pin down the Allied forces there. This was an important element of the German plan, for if the Allies were allowed to consolidate in Belgium, they could release divisions to counter the main German assault in the south.

Early summer brought beautiful weather, and Thursday 9 May found the soldiers of 3rd Division, like the rest of the BEF, enjoying the sunshine and looking forward to the weekend. The Germans were also looking forward with tense excitement to something very different. They were assembled in the wooded countryside west of the Rhine under orders to invade Belgium early the following morning, and after a Special Order of the Day from the Führer was read out they seized a few hours sleep before H-hour.

That night the soldiers of the BEF in their billets behind the Gort Line were woken by the noise of German aircraft attacking airfields in their rear, and 'Alerts 1, 2 and 3' were issued by the French GHQ at 5.45am, followed an hour later by the order to move into Belgium. 3rd Division led 2nd Corps forward, starting late in the

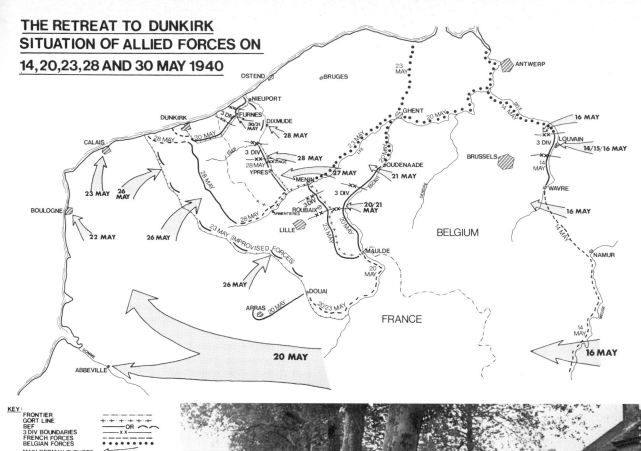

THE RETREAT TO DUNKIRK
SITUATION OF ALLIED FORCES ON
14, 20, 23, 28 AND 30 MAY 1940

KEY:
FRONTIER
GORT LINE
BEF
3 DIV BOUNDARIES
FRENCH FORCES
BELGIAN FORCES
MAIN GERMAN THRUSTS

Above left: The GOC visits
7 Guards Brigade in November
1939. Left to right: Brigadier
Whitaker, Major-General
Montgomery, Lt-Col Cornish (CO
2nd Grenadiers), Major Colvin
(Senior Major 2nd Grenadiers) and
Captain Des Voeux (Adjutant
2nd Grenadiers). Montgomery was
the first Senior Officer to wear
battledress./*Imperial War Museum*

Right: The end of the Phoney War.
A 15-cwt truck of 3rd Division
moves up to Louvain past Belgian
Chasseurs, 11 May 1940./*Imperial
War Museum*

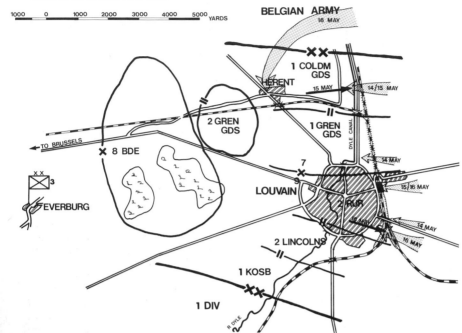

THE DEFENCE OF THE DYLE
14–16 MAY 1940

GERMAN ATTACKS ▷

BRITISH COUNTER ATTACKS ⟶

1000 0 1000 2000 3000 4000 5000 YARDS

BELGIAN ARMY
16 MAY

XX
1 COLDM
GDS

HERENT

15 MAY   14/15 MAY

2 GREN
GDS

1 GREN
GDS

TO BRUSSELS
× 8 BDE

DYLE CANAL

14 MAY

XX
3

EVERBURG

7
9
×

LOUVAIN

15/16 MAY

R DYLE

14 MAY

16 MAY

2 LINCOLNS

1 KOSB

XX

1 DIV

Below: Carriers and Light Tanks of
the 15th/19th Kings Royal Hussars
withdraw through Louvain as the
Dyle bridges are blown, 14 May
1940./*Imperial War Museum*

afternoon. The 15-cwt truck leading one of the columns found the frontier barrier closed, with the faithful but ill-informed official demanding the normal 'permit to enter Belgium'. The truck charged the barrier and the move continued smoothly. The BEF was left free from air attack deliberately, as the Germans wanted it forward in Belgium, where it could not influence the Ardennes breakthrough. When the divisional advance parties reached Louvain at about midnight they were surprised to find the Belgian 6me Chasseurs — newly mobilised cycle troops — in position on the eastern edge of the town, and nothing would budge them. Though it had been agreed previously that Louvain should be the BEF's responsibility, the Belgians stated that they themselves would defend the historic city. The Chasseurs were already jumpy as a result of bombing and reports of parachutists, and when the 2nd Middlesex reached the outskirts they were fired on by the Belgians and lost a man wounded.

Montgomery told his units to wait behind Louvain while he went to see the Belgian commander. Meanwhile his Corps commander took the matter up personally with the King of the Belgians, but Montgomery had already reached an agreement whereby 3rd Division would be 'in support' of the Belgians, and his units interspersed themselves among the Chasseurs. Brooke remarked, 'poor Belgian commander, how little he knows the viper he is harbouring'. It was crowded and unsatisfactory in the forward positions, and those chosen by the Belgians were poorly sited. However Montgomery knew how it would end, and later, when the first German shells fell and patrols appeared, the Chasseurs doubled to the rear to whistle signals and pedalled away, leaving 3 Div with a free hand to meet the enemy.

The Defence of the Dyle

The 15th/19th Kings Royal Hussars, watching the approaches to Louvain with their light tanks and carriers, were obliged to fall back during 14 May to conform with hard-pressed units on their flanks, and in the afternoon they withdrew across the Dyle bridges which were blown at 4pm. In section post and gun line 3rd Division's soldiers — very few of whom wore World War I ribbons — waited for the enemy and privately wondered how they would react under fire. Captain (later Lt-Col) Billy Faure Walker was with HQ 7 Guards Brigade and recalls that when the mortaring and shelling of brigade headquarters started:

'This was my first experience of shelling, and I think it was a great fault in our training that none of us had been prepared for receiving shellfire. Nobody had told us or warned us what it was like and what was dangerous and what could be ignored. So every time a shell went off or we heard a shell whistling towards us, we thought it was coming directly at us and we dived into the nearest ditch or lay down on the ground, a very undignified and unnecessary procedure. Many of these shells were so far away as to be completely harmless. We found that provided a shell landed more than 25 yards away you were very unlucky if it did you any harm. However, I think that this lack of psychological training was remedied soon after, because a lot of people felt the same as I did.'

Meanwhile at HQ 9 Brigade enemy shelling which was directed by Henschel spotting aircraft was remarkably accurate. The staff soon discovered why, for a civilian was found cutting marks in the grass pointing to the headquarters. He was arrested and summarily shot on the orders of the brigade commander.

The shelling was followed by enemy motorcycle reconnaissance units and lorried infantry, who patrolled and probed 7 and 9 Brigades' positions throughout the night, giving Bren gunners and OP officers their first experience of live targets. Some minor infiltration of 7 Brigade's sector was reported to Divisional headquarters, and in the enthusiasm of inexperience a staff officer woke Montgomery to tell him the news. His reply was short and typical: 'Go away and don't bother me — tell the Brigadier there to turn them out'. No one ever disturbed Montgomery's sleep again. At dawn 1st Coldstream destroyed an enemy patrol which had established itself on the west bank of the Dyle canal.

Having located the Division's forward positions the Germans attacked vigorously on 15 May. The first to feel the effect of the enemy artillery were the Ulster Rifles, who endured two hours of shelling which reduced the railway line on the forward edge of their defences to a shambles of smashed wagons and twisted rails. Determined infantry attacks followed, the fighting centering round the goods sidings and the main railway station. Here the fire fight ranged from platform to platform, but Lt Garstin and his platoon, using the subway system to deploy their Bren groups, held the enemy on the far side of the rails. Immediately north of the station 2-Lt (later Brigadier) 'Digger' Tighe-Woods' 9 platoon was positioned astride the line, and he takes up the story in mid-morning:

'After a very busy night the company commander, Major "Slappy" Reid, thought I could do with a bit of sleep and sent Lt "Bala" Bredin, who was held as a spare officer in the company, forward to take over my platoon whilst I had a little shuteye at company HQ. This was fortunate for me, because after a few hours' slumber, the Germans arrived and after a bit of prodding attacked the position in some force. I went forward with all the spare details from company HQ and occupied a trench about 30 yards behind, and below, the platoon on the embankment. The only way to reach this position was up a ladder with 27 rungs. Rolling off the top into the trench was hazardous and better performed by night than day. This meant the position was virtually isolated during daylight.

'The enemy were now occupying a railway administrative building, three storeys high, on their side of the embankment, which made the forward section position, immediately below, untenable. This section withdrew, on Bala's order, under covering fire from the main position and joined the rest of the platoon. One rifleman was hit in the dash across the rails, falling midway between opposing sides. A section commander, Cpl Gibbens, left the trench and ran to the fallen man, being greeted by a hail of fire and falling beside him. When the fire had ceased he leaped to his feet and sprinted with the casualty back into the safety of the trench. The fact that the soldier was dead in no way lessened the bravery of the deed, which was to be surpassed, with the loss of his own life, later in the day. The Germans now opened a heavy

fire on the trench, and were able to rake it from the top floor of the railway building. The rifles and Brens of No 9 platoon blazed back. Casualties were now occurring and as these were all in the head were mostly fatal; one luckier rifleman had his ear shot off by a bullet.

'The enemy now got a spandau across the line between the Rifles and the 1st Grenadiers on the left. This opened up on the platoon from the rear, the bullets striking the wall at the top of the ladder and the parados of the trench. About the same time they worked a heavy 20mm machine-gun forward and this opened up on the position from about 100yd range, the heavy armour-piercing bullets knocking the parapet back into the trench and filling the air with the cinders and earth of which it was composed. The shouts of German NCOs, accompanied by the blowing of whistles, could now be heard above the din as they formed-up to rush the position. A line of railway trucks on their side of the embankment gave them some shelter. Cpl Gibbens had now taken over a Bren, and to get a better aim at them through the wheels of the trucks he laid across the parapet firing until he was hit and knocked back into the trench. He heaved himself and his Bren back into the open again and kept his gun hammering away until he was killed.

'Opposite the supporting trench, now occupied by the company HQ details, was a tunnel under the main embankment. A German in a shiny helmet, which had obviously known applications of black boot polish, stuck his head round to see if the way was clear. It wasn't, and that was the last corner he looked round.

'The firing from No 9 Platoon had now ceased; although the Grenadiers had dealt with the infiltrating spandau from the left rear, the enemy fire from the front was as heavy as before, and the shouts and whistles of the Germans forming up continued. I thought it was all up

Above: The enemy — A Wehrmacht infantry squad advances confidently through Belgium, May 1940./*Imperial War Museum*

Above right: A Vickers detachment of 2nd Middlesex in action in support of 2nd Royal Ulster Rifles, Louvain, 14 May 1940. /*Imperial War Museum*

and the rush would come any minute. Suddenly above the din I heard Bala's voice shout "Fix swords" and above the top of the trench a line of bayonets appeared as they were clamped on to the rifles. It was a wonderful moment and I knew if the enemy came they were going to be met halfway in the open.

'But another and decisive Arm now took a hand, with a shriek and a roar a concentration of our own artillery descended on the area. 7 Field Regiment had done their ranging* and an enormous weight of fire (I believe Monty put a divisional concentration down — the first ever fired in anger?) engulfed the position. The opposing sides were only 30 or 40 yards apart and some shells fell around our positions. As we were well dug-in, and the enemy were not, the result was complete. When the crash of shells suddenly ceased there was an extraordinary silence, it seemed uncanny after the noise that had gone before. The only sound to break the silence was when a wall or a chimney pot collapsed, and tiles and slates came slithering off the roofs. After a considerable pause some German shouts and whistles were heard again. But very different this time, they were sorting themselves out and were pulling back. Their firing had ceased altogether, and

* In fact they had not! Colonel Bernard Mallinson, who was Adjutant of 7th Field at the time, tells me that only one gun per troop had been calibrated! — Author

when they tried to get the heavy MG back it blew up on mines that No 7 Platoon, occupying the railway station itself, had placed in some long grass.

'We buried Cpl Gibbens and the other casualties in a grave below the embankment, Bala reading the service from the back of the FSPB. I went back up the ladder, pulling up boxes of ammunition and grenades, and Bala returned to his rightful place at company HQ, and I have no doubt to a bottle of champagne, of which there seemed no shortage there. I thought my platoon might make me feel that I had not been around when the need was greatest. But they could not have been nicer and seemed really glad to see me; perhaps they felt that having Bala around was almost as lethal as the Germans.'

Lt (later Major-General) 'Bala' Bredin's comments on the effectiveness of 7th Field Regiment's concentration are very definite: 'We realised the Germans were forming up to rush us, and we were throwing hand grenades and preparing for hand-to-hand encounter. The business was settled by what became known as an "Uncle Target" being centred on 9 Platoon. It was terrifying and breathtaking but preferable to being overrun, and was highly successful. Don't let anyone underrate the ability of the Royal Regiment to save the Infantry's bacon'.

Meanwhile opposite 7 Brigade the enemy crossed the Dyle canal and again made a lodgement in 1st Coldstream's sector, and consequently a counter-attack, supported by medium and field artillery and two troops of the 5th Royal Inniskilling Dragoon Guards, was mounted by a reserve company of the Coldstream. The 'Skins' — normally 4th Division's armoured reconnaissance regiment — were temporarily supporting 3rd Division and their Adjutant was Lt (later General) 'Monkey' Blacker who was to command the Division 25

years later. He remembers that the counter-attack had little difficulty in restoring the situation, the enemy having pulled back under the weight of artillery fire.

The Vickers machine-guns of 2nd Middlesex had been closely supporting forward battalions throughout the fighting. Lt-Col (later Lt-Gen) Brian Horrocks, who had taken command of the battalion two days before, made a point of visiting each of his detached platoons daily and explaining the overall situation to them from a map brought up to date every few hours. As time progressed, 3rd Division's sector on the map began to resemble a rock, past which a torrent of red arrows was flowing. These arrows represented German penetrations of the Belgian Army immediately to the north of the Division, and to the south of the BEF where French formations had given way. The expanding torrent could have only one result and on 16 May orders were issued for the BEF to start withdrawing that night to the line of the Escaut, pausing on the River Dendre on the 18 May. The Escaut position was to be occupied by midnight 19 May.

Throughout 3rd Division soldiers received the order with incredulity, for they had seen off a number of determined and well supported attacks. Their successful defence had been noted by the enemy whose 19th Infantry Division, which had been attacking Louvain, expressed alarm at the British ability to counter-attack. A report from the enemy, commenting on the Ulster Rifles' and Coldstream's actions stated that the British had broken in; and extra formations, including a panzer division, were alerted to intervene if necessary. The reluctance of the men of the Iron Division to withdraw was understandable, but they accepted the order when the position on the flanks was explained. At last light on 16 May thinning out started, with the Ulster Rifles and 1st Grenadiers withdrawing from Louvain without trouble. However on the extreme left the Germans had broken through the Belgian sector and outflanked the Coldstream. A very determined defence by the guardsmen prevented the Germans from penetrating further, and at last light the forward companies withdrew with their wounded through the village of Herent. There was some enemy infiltration, but the route was held open by the determined efforts of Headquarters Company and a reserve rifle company. The battalion broke clear, and the last elements were lifted away by the light tanks of the 5th Inniskillings.

Thus started a withdrawal which was to end only when the troops of 3rd Division arrived at Dover from Dunkirk 16 days later. It was to involve the occupation of five intermediate positions and continuous movement on foot and in vehicles, and the thorough training of the winter and early spring paid dividends. Captain (later Brigadier) Douglas Wilson, who was attached to HQ 9 Brigade from the Lincolns, recalls:

'Although there was hard fighting during the retreat and everyone was extremely tired, the Division as a whole was never off balance. Whenever a complicated withdrawal was ordered, we managed it somehow whatever the problems. We simply did what we had practised and despite our weariness we automatically knew what to do. The Division always had something in reserve and some answer for the unexpected, and units were able to break contact at the right moment, thanks to the good judgement of commanders and the steadiness of the soldiers. We were certain that we were the best trained and led division in the BEF.'

The Withdrawal to the Escaut

8 Brigade covered the withdrawal of the forward brigades, and then handed over to an armoured reconnaissance screen of 15th/19th Hussars and 5th Inniskillings. The infantry marched some 25 miles to their embussing points west of Brussels, and by last light 17 May were digging in on the line of the River Dendre. The following morning German reconnaissance elements approached the river, and among unusual targets engaged by the 2nd Grenadiers were two officers in a blue saloon car and a group of cyclists who, it is related, impressed the guardsmen by pedalling in step. As the day wore on the enemy made no determined effort to force the obstacle in strength, but contented himself with shelling and mortaring. Infiltrators started to cause considerable annoyance, and reserve companies were engaged in dealing with snipers in the rear.

Having delayed the enemy on the Dendre for 24 hours, the Division started its withdrawal to the Escaut early on 19 May, threading back in brilliant weather along roads choked with refugees. The infantry of 9 Brigade were carried in a motley selection of impressed Belgian vehicles ranging from some hundreds of bicycles to an enormous bright red 20-ton transporter, driven by a subaltern in the Royal Ulster Rifles; his platoon was thankful that the Belgian roads were very straight. In the rear and covering the withdrawal with their machine-guns were the Middlesex. One of their sergeants, acting as a platoon commander, described in his report to the Adjutant, Captain (later Major-General) John Willoughby, an incident which typified the conditions of the move:

'I was leading the platoon and on coming to a railway bridge we found a large RASC truck about 50 yards in front of it with the occupants apparently dead. I halted the platoon to see if any aid could be given to them, but all the truck personnel were found to be dead. They had evidently been machine-gunned from the air. This was our first sight of death and it wasn't at all nice. It proved however to be our salvation. Instead of getting on my truck and moving on, something or other prompted me to walk the remaining 50 yards to the bridge and see what lay beyond around the corner, and there I received a most severe jolt; proceeding toward me were six German tanks roughly 800 yards away. For a moment or two I was stupified, and then realised we must have gone round in a complete circle and were almost back at our starting point. Fear lent me wings and all Olympic records were shattered in my sprint back to the trucks. It was hopeless for us with our exceedingly low stock of ammunition to try and engage six tanks, with the prospect of even more behind them. It was more than I dare do to tell our own truck drivers that these enemy tanks were just around the corner — I could well imagine the confusion and mechanical breakdowns that would ensue. Our immediate concern however was to get away as far as we could and rejoin the Company. So I just gave a hint to the drivers that we had almost completed a circle and that the enemy were not far off. The words were hardly out of my mouth when the trucks were whisked round and we were going hell for leather back the way we had come. We were fortunate enough to meet the Bn 2nd IC and he put us on the right road where we very thankfully rejoined our own Company.'

General 'Bala' Bredin recalls another incident which illustrates the Divisional commander's influence:

'We were covering a crossroads prior to making a complete break with the enemy, and Montgomery arrived in his car saying "Well, what are you doing here?" I gave him a brief account of the situation as we saw it locally finishing up with "And I don't think you ought to hang around here, Sir" as shells began to fall. He drove off but apparently in no particular hurry and his visit had a very steadying, business as usual, effect on us. He made it all seem like some rather special exercise.'

On the evening of 19 May 3 Div assembled in rear of its sector of the Escaut, hoping for a night's sleep in billets before occupying battle positions; however they were disappointed, for that afternoon Montgomery told his brigade commanders that there were now no troops between the Division and the advancing Germans, and occupation was to start at once. Battalions moved forward immediately and dug in, their discipline and training overcoming the effects of exhaustion caused by nine days constant fighting and movement.

Defence of The Escaut

The River Escaut was a fair obstacle, despite a drop in level due to inundations down river. However the countryside was flat and featureless save for lines of poplars and hedgerows, and the home bank of the river lacked dominating ground to provide observation and blocking positions for our troops. 3rd Division was

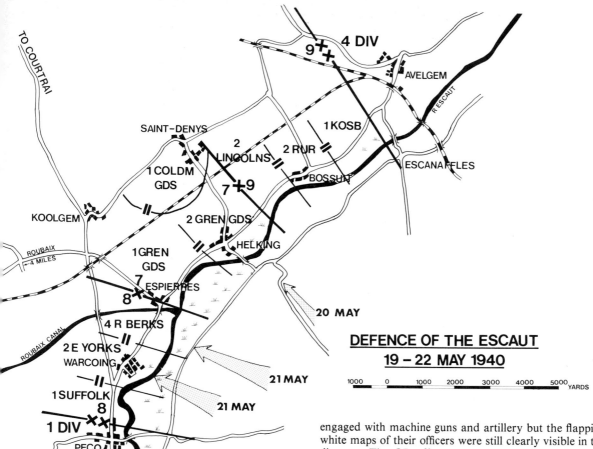

**DEFENCE OF THE ESCAUT
19 – 22 MAY 1940**

1000	0	1000	2000	3000	4000	5000

YARDS

responsible for a stretch 12,000 yards long between Avelgem and Pecq, and in order to cover the river with maximum fire power and prevent any crossing, all three brigades were deployed forward.

While the Division dug in on the river line, the situation to the south of the BEF was deteriorating. On 20 May the leading enemy panzer divisions reached the coast near Abbeville, thus cutting off the British together with the French Army Group No 1 and the Belgian Army. Gort therefore started assembling reserve TA divisions and improvised forces along the waterways from St Omer to Douai to cover his rear. It was clear to him that evacuation by sea would be necessary, but six days were to pass before the reality of the situation was appreciated by the War Cabinet and Gort permitted to give orders for evacuation.

Back on the Escaut, 3rd Division waited for the enemy. 20 May passed relatively peacefully, except in the 2nd Grenadiers sector, where a German patrol which had sneaked over the river was spotted by an officer visiting his outposts. The Grenadiers stood-to in time to witness a considerable number of Germans moving forward with bridging equipment. The enemy withdrew after being

engaged with machine guns and artillery but the flapping white maps of their officers were still clearly visible in the distance. The OP officers with the Grenadiers had the mortification of being unable to take full advantage of these tantalising targets owing to a shortage of shells, as the BEF was now cut off from its main L of C and combat supplies were becoming increasingly scarce. The 2nd Grenadiers also dealt with an outbreak of fifth column activity in their rear. They rounded up 17 snipers in Helkin and summarily executed them, while in 8 Brigade an enemy sniper claimed the life of Lt-Col Fraser, CO of the Suffolks.

At 6.30am on 21 May the enemy commenced heavy shelling of 8 Brigade's sector, and during the morning attacks developed against the Royal Berkshires on the left and the East Yorkshires holding Warcoing in the centre. With artillery and MMG support, both battalions engaged and broke up these attacks before they could cross the river. Meanwhile the enemy gained a temporary lodgement in 1st Division's sector on the right, but others who tried to cross opposite the Suffolks in rubber boats were killed before they could land. During the day a personal message from Gort was relayed to the troops of the BEF that they were now to stand and fight. This is just what everyone wanted to hear, for they were confident in their ability to do so.

22 May passed without incident in 3rd Division's sector, but despite Gort's reassuring message of the previous day the news from elsewhere was not promising. To the north the Germans had penetrated the Escaut in 44th Division's sector, and 70 miles to the south-west Gort's improvised forces were hard pressed in front of

Arras. The prepared defences of the Gort line were only a few miles in rear and the C-in-C therefore obtained the **agreement** of his allies to withdraw to it, with the Belgians in the north conforming by pulling back to the River Lys. This river was a good obstacle, but the plan resulted in the Belgian line lying at right angles to the British, inviting a German attack at the vulnerable hinge, and furthermore the Belgians would be holding a longer front than previously.

Return to the Gort Line

Orders for the withdrawal went out on the afternoon of 22 May, together with the information that the BEF was to be placed on half rations. From that moment 3rd Division never fed better, their cooks' trucks being crammed with local beef, pork, chickens and eggs. Hidden depths of butchery talent appeared everywhere and an entry in the War Diary for 24 May reads 'CRASC collected 60 cows to form Divisional Dairy Farm'. Units thinned out at 11.30 that night and marched 10 miles to the Gort Line. The carrier platoons were brigaded to cover the withdrawal and the new position was reached by first light 23 May.

The troops occupied the prepared defences of the Gort Line covering Roubaix and Tourcoing with some bemusement, wondering whether the dash forward into Belgium had really been necessary. Now they were back where they started in far less favourable circumstances, weakened by casualties and the stress of withdrawal. No battalion occupied the same position it had prepared, as the Divisional sector was six miles to the north of the one they had dug so carefully the previous autumn covering Lille. Furthermore the defences had been allowed to deteriorate during 14 days' neglect.

During the five days 3rd Division spent in the Gort Line the Germans limited their activity to shelling, as their offensive efforts were directed against the Belgians in the north and against the south-western flank of the Allied pocket, their intention being to cut the BEF off from the coast. However Montgomery was not content to let his Division sit in its defences and wait, so he ordered the mounting of an operation which has been remembered ever since with distaste by those who took part in it.

The Wattrelos Counter-Attack

The Divisional commander evidently decided that it was time to raise the morale of his troops by giving them a taste of the offensive, the chance to go forward rather than back. On 24 May he instructed 8 Brigade, which so far had been least heavily engaged, to advance some 3,000 yards from their sector at Wattrelos, seize prisoners, and withdraw. The operation was to take place in daylight that evening with H-Hour at 7pm. It has since been described variously as a 'counter-attack', 'reconnaissance in force', or 'raid', but its sole aim was to raise morale; prisoners and information could have been obtained more easily by patrol action.

The brigade plan was for elements of each battalion to advance to the railway line which crossed their front and seize prisoners from the German positions thought to be in the villages of Herseaux, La Boutellerie and Estampius. Two companies only from each battalion would be used as the brigade still had to hold its sector of the Gort Line,

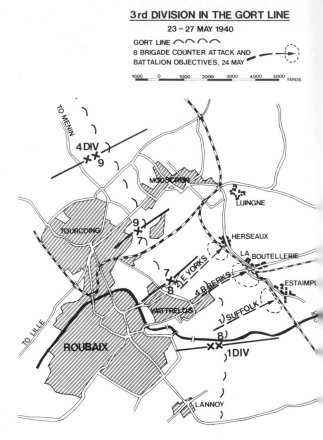

3rd DIVISION IN THE GORT LINE
23 – 27 MAY 1940

GORT LINE ∩∩∩∩
8 BRIGADE COUNTER ATTACK AND
BATTALION OBJECTIVES, 24 MAY

hence the attacking battalions were to have nothing in reserve. The attack was to be 'silent', ie no artillery support unless called for during the attack, despite the face that a reconnaissance patrol of the Suffolks had located enemy machine-gun positions on the axis and flank of their advance. Lt-Col Milnes, who had taken command of the Suffolks when Fraser was killed, requested covering fire but was informed that the plan would not be altered. Battalions were ordered to lead with their carriers, as if they were tanks; evidently the success of these vehicles in counter-penetration and withdrawal **operations** had resulted in an exaggerated idea of their capabilities. Detailed orders for the attack were not given out until midday 24 May, leaving little time for reconnaissance and preparation. Also as exits through defensive minefields had to be opened up in full daylight, the enemy were thoroughly alerted. The carrier platoon of **the Royal Berkshires** was commanded by 2-Lt (later Brigadier) Bob Flood, and he remembers that:

'At the O Group we were very surprised to hear that my carriers were to lead, but this was the brigade plan and there was no option but to accept it.

'At H hour I took the carriers through the minefields following a sketch map given me by the CO at the O Group. Once we were clear of the gap I deployed my **three sections** up as we had a large frontage to cover, and when we had advanced a short distance we came under **machine-gun** and rifle fire. I ordered my sections (by coloured flag signals!) into mounted action behind hedges

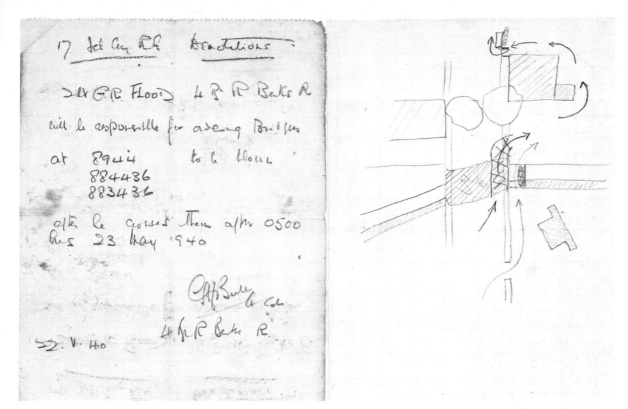

and banks, and in some cases it was possible to come into dismounted action from farm buildings.

'It soon became evident that the Germans were using armour-piercing small arms ammunition, as two of my carriers suffered casualties from bullets which penetrated their ¼-inch side armour. While I was trying to locate the enemy a bullet shattered my binoculars, wounding me in the head and temporarily blinding me. My driver drove my carrier to the platoon sergeant who took over from me and I was evacuated. I learned afterwards that five of my carriers were knocked out, although two were subsequently recovered. After getting the platoon back from the Dyle unscathed it was galling to have the carriers thrown away like this. They were excellent for providing mobile fire support and covering a withdrawal, and the Germans had considerable respect for them, but to use them for a head-on assault was nonsense, and illustrates how much ignorance there was at the time concerning the characteristics of carriers, and their misuse as tanks.'

In spite of the carrier platoon's losses, C and D companies of the Royal Berkshires fought their way forward, took prisoners, and returned. However they suffered more casualties than they inflicted.

The Suffolks' attack on the right is described by Captain (later Colonel) William Heal, who was adjutant of the battalion.

'It was clear to us at battalion HQ that the operation would be a very sticky one and Lt-Col Milnes wanted to go with the two companies himself. I managed to persuade him that this would do no good but that he would do better to establish a forward HQ with one of the

Above: Pages from a carrier platoon commander's field pocket book.
Left: His authority to order the blowing of bridges by 17 Field Company RE during the withdrawal from the Escaut. Today, the 'AFW 4012C' delegating authority to the Demolition Guard Commander consists of four sheets of foolscap.
Right: His route through the Gort Line minefield when leading the Wattrelos counter-attack, 24 May 1940. Sketched by the CO, 4th Royal Berkshires at the Battalion O Group./*Brigadier G. R. Flood*

remaining companies. This we did and were in close touch with the whole ill conceived affair.

'The advance started at 7pm as planned. A Company on the left did not get more than 500 yards and D Company on the right about 300 yards. There was very heavy enemy small arms, mortar and artillery fire and the two companies, unsupported by anything but a machine-gun platoon of the Middlesex (which was knocked out by a direct hit from a shell early on) were quite unable to advance'.

At this stage the Suffolks called for artillery support, but there was a failure in communication to the guns and the support was not forthcoming. Heals account continues:
'There were some very gallant local actions by sections and individuals but these were mainly when they were trying to extricate themselves. The battalion stretcher-bearers were outstanding in their bravery in bringing in casualties. By 2200hrs it was all over and the rest of the night was spent sorting things out.

'Casualties in 1st Suffolks were three officers killed, three wounded, two warrant officer platoon commanders killed and 67 soldiers killed and wounded. Four carriers were lost. There was a very strong feeling, which lasts to this day, about the entirely unnecessary nature of the affair.'

Only the East Yorkshires were able to show a credit balance, for they encountered little opposition and brought back a German officer prisoner.

The casualties suffered by the other battalions — particularly among officers and NCOs, were to be sorely felt during the remainder of the campaign. The question must be asked — who was responsible? Responsibility, as ever, rests at the top. Both the concept and detailed plan were questionable, and although the latter was a brigade responsibility, the Divisional commander must have been aware of it. How Montgomery, invariably so thorough and sound in his planning and preparation, could have countenanced let alone approved this operation, is difficult, with hindsight, to understand.

During the 24 May the German efforts to cut off the BEF developed with their infantry divisions attacking the Belgian Army holding the Lys. By the end of the day they were across the river in a number of places, the most serious penetration being north of Menin. Belgian morale deteriorated badly and there were indications that their army was about to withdraw north-east to Bruges for a final stand on Belgian territory, rather than north-west in conformity with the BEF. Such a move would leave a yawning gap between the two armies.

The seriousness of the situation was confirmed decisively by information gained that day as a result of the gallant action of Sergeant Burford, 1/7th Middlesex, whose machine-guns had been temporarily in support of 3rd Division until 24 May. While patrolling northwards across the Lys, Burford had ambushed a German staff car, killing its occupants and capturing a briefcase, which he brought back to HQ 3rd Division. Whilst the Divisional staff were examining the documents it contained the Corps commander arrived and immediately ordered them to be sent to GHQ. They included a complete order of battle of the German army, and the plan for the German offensive through the Belgian sector. This showed that a total of three German corps were to be used, thrusting at Ypres and beyond to cut off the BEF's escape route. To meet this threat Gort moved the 5th and 50th Divisions on 25 May north to the Ypres-Comines canal. On the following day he was authorised to evacuate the BEF from Dunkirk.

While these momentous decisions were being taken life for the Division remained relatively quiet, the soldiers being intrigued to hear on the radio from Lord Haw Haw* that not only was 3rd Division notorious for its looting, but also that it had been entirely destroyed.

During this pause Montgomery took the opportunity to present the ribbons of decorations to those honoured in the first list of awards. Among these were Lieutenant-Colonel Cazenove of 1st Coldstream and Lieutenant-Colonel Knox of 2nd Royal Ulster Rifles, who received

the DSO for their battalions' defence of Louvain. Other awards were a MC, DCM and MM for 1st Coldstream, a MC and MM for 2nd Middlesex, and a MC and four MMs for 2nd Ulster Rifles.

By 27 May the Belgian army north of the Lys was disintegrating under relentless German pressure, and the BEF started a series of side steps northwards to cover its vulnerable eastern flank during the withdrawal to the sea. The collapse of Belgian resistance resulted in the disappearance of all troops opposing the Germans north of 50th Division at Boezinge on the Yser canal. General Brooke, whose 2nd Corps was responsible for the eastern flank, was gravely concerned for he knew from the documents captured by Sergeant Burford that the Germans were heading for this gap. He therefore ordered 3rd Division to disengage from the Gort Line and move back to fill the void on the Yser canal by first light 28 May. This was a daunting instruction, for it required the Division to execute a difficult and complex manoeuvre — a night flank march across the front of attack. The move was to follow a maze of minor roads in an area congested with refugees, requisitioned and military vehicles, French cavalry and horsed transport, soldiers on foot and on bicycles, formed units and stragglers, some following firm instructions, others using their own initiative. The distance to be covered was 50 miles and there was insufficient troop carrying transport for the whole division. The route ran only a few thousand yards in rear of 5th Division, at that time under very heavy pressure, and which could conceivably give way at any moment. The machine-guns of the 2nd Middlesex and armoured cars of 12th Lancers — under command for this operation — went ahead on the afternoon of 27 May, to establish a screen on the canal until the main body completed its move. They formed a fragile front but something had to be done quickly for at any moment the Germans might approach the canal. Meanwhile to provide sufficient transport to make up the deficiency in troop carriers, all non-essential stores were unloaded from unit vehicles and hidden under bales of cotton in the factory warehouses of Roubaix or dumped in the canal. By last light the military police and sappers who were to mark and keep open the route were in position, and the move started. The night was dark and wet, and enemy shells were arching overhead and falling to the west of the column with rounds falling short and added to the confusion on the already chaotic roads. 'Bala' Bredin recalls:

'We appeared to be driving just behind the front line for mile after mile encountering crossroads after crossroads that was covered by shell fire. I have never admired the Divisional RMPs so much as that night as they stood in the centre of each crossroads with the light of shell bursts glinting on their red hats, trying to gauge the gap between shells to let the traffic through, and there was always another to fill the gap when the policeman on duty became a casualty.'

In the early hours of 28 May the leading companies were met by guides from their advance parties, shown their positions and by first light 8 and 9 Brigades were dug in behind the canal and ready for the enemy. 'It was with a feeling of intense relief that I found Monty in position'

---

* William Joyce, who broadcasted for the enemy and was executed for treason after the war.

wrote Brooke afterwards; 'I found he had, as usual, accomplished almost the impossible'. By 10am 7 Guards Brigade were in reserve around Oostvleteren, covering the Yser bridge at Elsendamme on one of the main withdrawal routes. That morning the Division heard the news that King Leopold of the Belgians had surrendered with his army.

The Defence of the Yser Canal

3rd Division was now covering the vital sector of the eastern flank of the BEF's withdrawal route to Dunkirk, a sector which was to face the next phase of the German attempt to cut off the BEF. On their right 50th Division was firm, but the left flank, from Noordschote to Nieuport, was uncovered due to the Belgian surrender. Montgomery appreciated that the enemy had only to shift his effort a few miles further north, and not only 3rd Division but the whole BEF would be outflanked. He still had the 12th Lancers under command and he sent them off to watch his left flank on the line of the Loo canal, between the Yser and Furnes. Lt-Col Lumsden commanding the Lancers felt more anxious even than Montgomery, for he had a hunch that as a result of the Belgian capitulation, the bridges to his front over the Yser at Dixmude and Nieuport would not only be undefended, but intact. Lumsden therefore sent off a troop to Dixmude and a squadron to Nieuport, together with sappers of the Royal Monmouthshire RE to blow the bridges. It was a wise and fortunate move, for both bridges were found intact and the sappers blew them in time, that at Dixmude only minutes before the arrival of German reconnaissance troops. For the next six hours a troop of the Lancers commanded by 2-Lt Mann

prevented elements of two enemy divisions from crossing, enabling Brooke to move up further units to hold the Yser. Mann was awarded the DSO for his tenacious and spirited defence.

Meanwhile, on 3rd Division's right flank, pressure on the 50th Division was increasing. The task of these two divisions was to hold the line of the canal while the BEF pulled back northwards behind them. A partial withdrawal was planned for the evening of the 28 May when 50th Division would wheel back to the Poperhinge canal, and 9 Brigade would conform by swinging back to the line Luzerne-Woestern. It was vital to the overall plan that units should maintain their positions during each phase of the withdrawal, and then break cleanly, and it was clear to everyone that this was to be an extremely tricky operation. Brigadier Robb, commanding 9 Brigade, recalled that by this stage he was in the habit of prefixing his orders by saying: '9 Brigade has already extricated itself from several fantastic situations, and there is no reason why we shouldn't get out of this one, provided we keep our heads.' He also remembered that there was a gallant but fastidious staff officer at Divisional Headquarters, whose particular fear of being captured was based on the probable inability, while a POW, of obtaining a change of clothes. When things became dicey, this officer wore two sets of underwear, but on 28 May he appeared bulky enough to be wearing at least three.

Enemy pressure against 3rd Division on 28 May fell initially on the battle hardened Ulster Rifles holding Boezinge at the junction with 50th Division. Artillery and mortar fire was followed by probing attacks which were beaten off with the ever effective support of a Vickers section of 2nd Middlesex. That evening the Ulster Rifles

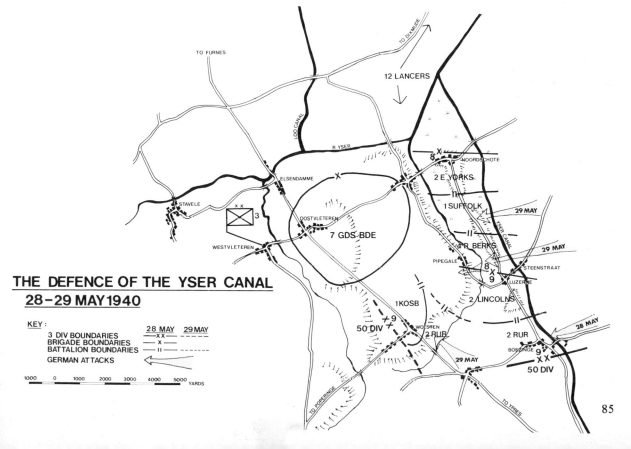

THE DEFENCE OF THE YSER CANAL
28-29 MAY 1940

KEY:

	28 MAY	29 MAY
3 DIV BOUNDARIES	— xx —	- - - - -
BRIGADE BOUNDARIES	— x —	
BATTALION BOUNDARIES	— ii —	- - - - -
GERMAN ATTACKS	←	

1000 0 1000 2000 3000 4000 5000 YARDS

were able to withdraw as arranged in good order to the intermediate position at Woesten. Behind them the rearward movement of British and French troops gathered momentum, so far as the congested routes would allow. One casualty of this confusion was Colonel 'Marino' Brown, Royal Marines, 3rd Division's GSO 1. While on his way to Corps Headquarters, he had to leave his car to walk through a block of French vehicles and was shot dead.

29 May was a vital day for the withdrawal of the BEF. While the 2nd, 4th and 44th Divisions threaded their way back to Dunkirk, 3rd and 50th Divisions held the line Noordschote to Poperhinge via the 'hinge' at Luzerne. This village was also the junction of 8 and 9 Brigades, against whom the enemy's 19th and 30th Divisions launched furious attacks aimed at closing the BEF's escape route. The first assault, with heavy artillery support, fell on the 4th Royal Berkshires at Steenstrat. Enemy infantry were soon working round the flanks of the forward companies holding the apex of the hinge, and with one company commander killed and two wounded, their men withdrew some 700 yards to shorten the line. This operation was touch and go, but sterling work by the depleted carrier platoon which covered the withdrawal enabled them to be established on higher ground around Pipegale by 3pm. Meanwhile on their left the 1st Suffolks were also attacked, and two forward platoons were overrun before the enemy were stopped by companies in depth.

The history of the Royal Ulster Rifles records that the day spent at Woesten was one of the most unpleasant experienced by the 2nd Battalion. They were shelled continuously, suffering numerous casualties including six in battalion headquarters which received a direct hit. As the battalion started to thin out at 9pm in preparation for withdrawal to the Dunkirk perimeter, the Germans struck. The withdrawal became a series of confused running battles, sometimes hand to hand, in the fading light, but every section and platoon held its position until the time laid down for 'final abandonment'. One isolated forward platoon was saved by a splendid action by a carrier section of 2nd Lincolns, which came forward and having destroyed two enemy machine-guns, lifted the riflemen back. The Ulster Rifles' carriers then took over the rearguard, blazing away with their Brens while the battalions finally broke contact. The Lincolns' carriers under Captain Rowell MC, had had a busy time for earlier they had rescued a company of 8th Durham Light Infantry of 50th Division, which had been cut off, and they completed the day's work by ambushing a party of enemy motorcyclists who were following up. Before the Lincolns themselves finally withdrew they put in a counter-attack on their left where the Germans had driven a wedge between them and the Royal Berkshires, and were threatening the route back. Their commanding officer and adjutant were wounded during the withdrawal, and Capt Cartland who remained behind with the rearguard firing a Bren to the last was the fourth officer of his company to be killed that day.

Meanwhile 8 Brigade was also withdrawing under pressure, and as the Royal Berkshires drew back their battalion second-in-command, Major Roper, covered the final move with a Bren. He survived to take over

Camarades!

Telle est la situation!
En tout cas, la guerre est finie pour vous!
    Vos chefs vont s'enfuir par avion.
A bas les armes!

British Soldiers!

Look at this map: it gives your true situation!
Your troops are entirely surrounded —
    stop fighting!
Put down your arms!

Above: Leaflet dropped by German aircraft at Woesten, 28 May 1940. These leaflets heartened 3 Div's soldiers — they understood the position to be far worse./*Major H. W. Bruce*

command of the battalion later that evening when his CO, Lt-Col Bull, was mortally wounded by shell fire. The battalion suffered seven further officer casualties that evening.

Thus 8 and 9 Brigades held the ring while the BEF withdrew, but the cost had been heavy. The effective strength of each battalion was now nearer the equivalent of two companies, with few officers left. It was fortunate that 7 Guards Brigade was still relatively strong, and had moved back early that afternoon to Furnes on the Dunkirk perimeter, to provide a foundation for the Division's final defence. The withdrawal of 7 Brigade to Furnes as described by Faure Walker brought its hazards and tragedies:

'Furnes was the corner of the outer perimeter through which all the means of communication, road, rail and canal passed, and it was of vital importance to prevent the Germans getting it because otherwise they would have been able to roll up the whole of the embarkation on beaches around Dunkirk. It had been ordered that no vehicles whatsoever other than ambulances and a few staff cars could be brought into the perimeter. So Brigadier Jack Whitaker decided that our vehicles should be immobilised, we did this by emptying the oil out of the engines, and running the engines until they seized up, and we set off by march-route down the main road to Furnes. Without a doubt it was one of the most unpleasant marches that I have ever taken part in. We were within easy range of the German artillery and we were shelled constantly along the whole length of the road. As we set out, we were passed by innumerable vehicles full of troops who were driving down towards the perimeter and presumably, we hoped, would immobilise their vehicles before we got there. It was a great relief that ambulances frequently patrolled up and down the road to pick up the casualties from shellfire. The shelling was particularly unpleasant because the shells used to burst on hitting the tops of the trees which lined the road. Some people wisely avoided the road and marched along the farmland within a few hundred yards of the road, and as I gazed out of my ditch as the shells were burst all round, I very much wished that we had the sense to do the same. However, eventually we fetched up at Furnes, a small town which had not been touched in the First World War and had two or three main roads passing through it over bridges across a deep and wide canal. As we arrived on the outskirts of the town, the Adjutant of the 2nd Grenadiers rushed up to me almost in tears and said that his Commanding Officer and two other officers had just been killed. I immediately said "Is Jack, Brigadier Jack, alright?" "Yes, he fortunately turned off the street a few yards before this firing started and he is alright." What happened was that German motorcyclists had infiltrated through the Belgian lines, I think they were probably dressed in civvy clothes, and had taken up sniping positions in the town. They were in fact winkled out and dealt with later on but we had lost the very lovable Commanding Officer in Jackie Lloyd who would undoubtedly have risen to very great heights in the army. It was a very great loss to the Brigade.'

As the headquarters of 7 Guards Brigade marched on into Furnes, Faure Walker saw a dejected figure, who he recognised as Montgomery, standing in the market place. 'My Guardsmen were themselves feeling shaken at the news of Colonel Lloyd's death, but I told them to march at attention and "put it on" for the Divisional commander. As we swung past we gave him a terrific "eyes left", and Monty suddenly straightened up and gave us a great salute in return. Afterwards he told me that he

had been saddened by the death of his driver shortly before we arrived, and I like to think that our "eyes left" did the trick and helped him revert to his normal self.'

During the night 29/30 May the weary battalions of 8 and 9 Brigades withdrew, but found the bridge at Elsendamme destroyed by bombing. The sapper field companies built a pontoon, but this also was hit and set on fire. Undismayed the column motored down minor roads to the next village, Stavele, found a bridge intact and continued their grind north to the Furnes-Bergues canal near Wulveringhem where they abandoned and set fire to their vehicles and continued the move on foot. By first light 30 May these exhausted brigades had occupied their sectors on either side of the Guards.

The Dunkirk Perimeter

By the time 3rd Division arrived at Furnes nearly 100,000 troops, British and French, had already left. The plan was for evacuation to continue behind the defended perimeter until the night of 31 May/1 June when 2nd Corps, holding the eastern sector, would be withdrawn from the beaches of La Panne.

From 30 May 3rd Division was continually engaged in preventing the Wehrmacht's 56th and 216th Divisions from overrunning the Dunkirk perimeter from the east. Although the country was flat and intersected with ditches and inundations which hindered the attacker, the defenders were limited to digging their defences along the edges of roads and banks, where they could be easily located. The Nieuport-Furnes-Bergues canal, on which the defence was based, was only 30 yards wide, and its embankments gave the enemy a covered approach. Their full force fell initially on 4th Royal Berkshires immediately to the north of Furnes, at dawn on 30 May.

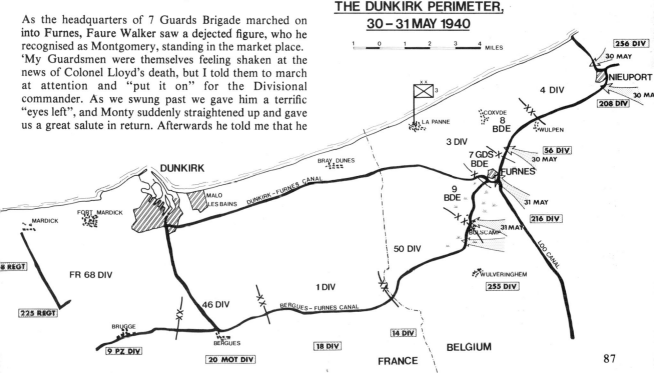

THE DUNKIRK PERIMETER, 30 – 31 MAY 1940

87

The battalion was by now reduced to a fighting strength of 50, with only two officers in addition to the commanding officer and adjutant. They were reinforced by sappers from the 17th and 152nd Field Companies and gunners from 20th Anti-Tank Regiment, all fighting as infantry, and throughout the day they were exposed to relentless enemy pressure. In some places the Germans crossed the canal, and during the confused fighting that followed both the 1st Coldstream and carriers of 2nd Grenadiers mounted counter-attacks to restore the situation. The fierceness of this fighting can be judged by the fact that the Coldstream lost two Company Commanders killed, and Lt-Col Arnold Cazenove sent his Adjutant, Captain (later Major-General Sir George) Burns, to take command of the remaining troops. With his imperturbable manner, Burns soon had the situation in hand. Under his direction the near side of the canal was cleared of enemy, and at dawn the Divisional front was intact.

Meanwhile Gort had ordered a thinning out of senior officers from the beachhead in order to ensure that a minimum with sufficient experience and knowledge would be available to provide a nucleus on which to rebuild the army in the future. As part of this plan Brooke returned to UK, and before he left he appointed Montgomery, his most junior divisional commander, as his relief. Brigadier Anderson, commanding 14 Brigade of 4th Division, was appointed GOC 3rd Division while Horrocks of 2nd Middlesex was sent off down the beaches to find 14 Brigade, tell Anderson the news and take over his brigade. That evening Anderson was in command. The evacuation of leaders had also been applied at more junior levels and units had each sent home two experienced officers, warrant officers and NCOs.

During 31 May the Germans continued in their attempt to smash through 3rd Division's sector of the perimeter defence. The first attack fell on 1st KOSB, 9 Brigade's right hand battalion, but this was seen off by the Borderers and by two battalions of Durham Light Infantry on their right. The enemy then returned to the assault of Furnes, which had been the scene of continual gun battles and shelling since the Grenadiers had thrown out infiltrators two days earlier. This time the Germans made a determined effort to seize the town. Every street and house became a battlefield, but the guardsmen, supported by the excellent defensive fire of the divisional artillery, which had sufficient ammunition for just one day's intensive firing, prevented the enemy from making any further inroads.

During the day orders for the Division's evacuation were issued, the O Group of 7 Guards Brigade being held in a trench dug in a manure heap which provided particularly effective protection from shell splinters. Thinning out started at dusk, and rearguard companies withdrew at 2.30am. The Gunners' methods of providing covering fire during the last few hours were perhaps unique, and are recorded in 7th Field Regiment's War Diary:
'Six guns were left in action, two in support of each battalion in 8 Brigade. The remaining 13 guns were left in position, but with their sights and breech blocks removed so that, should a section be shelled out of one position, it could move to and fire from any other position by transferring personnel, ammunition, dial sights and

breech blocks. Sufficient men were left with each section to provide reliefs, so that three or even four guns could be fired in each troop.

'Each troop had a certain number of targets recorded; these were fired in turn and other targets engaged from the map — the pundits of the School of Artillery would have been horrified by some of the methods of shooting adopted — map shooting from a 1/250,000 map with considerable success — E troop under Lieut J. de G. Dill fired several barrages from two guns — the infantry asked for them and considered them successful! About 3,000 rounds were available for six guns, and practically the whole of this was fired. This needed prodigious efforts on the part of gun detachments, who did their best to return shot for shot with the far more numerous German artillery.'

What better illustration could there have been of the Corps Commander's reminder to them, made during a visit in March, that 'its shells that count — not guns'.

The assembly of the Division on the beaches at La Panne is recalled by 'Bala' Bredin:
'We withdrew stealthily from our positions near Furnes and approached La Panne which appeared to be the target for every German gun for miles. There seemed to be no way round it so through the middle we went, in groups from wall to wall trying to anticipate where the next shell would fall. There were an awful lot of casualties lying around for whom one could do little, many of them from 7 Guards Brigade who appeared to have passed through a short time before. One unfortunate guardsman, appearing to recognise me as an officer, motioned to me in the light of the flames from burning buildings. I leant down to see if there was anything I could do. All he said was "Leave to fall out, sir, please", having said which he appeared to feel quite justified in dying. He had done his duty and maintained the sort of standard to which we all aspire.'

During the evening of 31 May enemy air attacks and shelling had completely disrupted the embarkation arrangements and when units arrived at the beach they found the piers smashed and the ships lying off shore. They were told they would have to move along to Dunkirk, 10 miles away. A few groups managed to launch or recover small craft stranded on the beach, and get out to the ships, but the majority started the long trudge through the dunes to Dunkirk. As dawn broke the Stukas and Messerschmitts arrived, adding to the agony of the toiling columns, but fortunately the soft sand absorbed much of the lethality of bomb and bullet. At Bray dunes some parties joined the queue at the still intact vehicle pier, but the rest plodded on to Dunkirk, where the embarkation system was operating efficiently, and were taken off from the East Mole by a variety of craft.

So the short but memorable Dunkirk campaign ended. 3rd Division had displayed a very high professional standard throughout, and its performance is summed up well in the Royal Ulster Rifle's history:
'There was no spirit of defeat when the battalion disembarked at Dover. Every officer and rifleman was convinced that the battalion had fought the enemy to a standstill when it was allowed to do so. No section had

Left: 'There was no spirit of defeat'. Members of the 2nd Royal Ulster Rifles on the vehicle pier at Braye Dunes. Lt-Col Knox DSO is in the centre, bareheaded; behind him, 2-Lt Carberry. Left and right centre, 2-Lt Sturgeon and Lt St Maur Shiel, left and right foreground Captain Garratt and L Cpl Delaney (CO's Driver)./*Imperial War Museum*

lost an inch of ground, nor withdrawn a second before the appointed time.'

and by Lt-Col Wedderburn-Maxwell, commanding 7th Field Regiment:
'It was a great experience to see officers and men turn into veterans of the highest calibre in under three weeks, and to serve in a Division that never lost cohesion nor its high state of discipline.'

Reorganisation in the United Kingdom

After being cleared from Dover and Ramsgate to the length and breadth of the UK, all 3 Div personnel were instructed to report to Frome, and by 10 June the Division had reassembled in Wiltshire, Dorset and Somerset. Reinforcements arrived and, surprisingly, a complete replacement of weapons and equipment was issued. There was only sufficient in UK for one division — and 3rd Division received the lot, for it was under orders to return to north-west France to continue the fight. Brooke, who had been appointed C-in-C of this new expedition, had chosen 3rd Division to go — a considerable compliment — and Montgomery was back as GOC after acting as GOC 2nd Corps during the evacuation. Then, on 17 June, France capitulated and the expedition was cancelled.

During the period of reorganisation the 4th Royal Berkshires left the Division, for the battalion had returned from Dunkirk only 47 strong, and needed time to reform. Its place in 8 Brigade was taken by the 1st Battalion, South Lancashire Regiment, which was later to enrich the reputation of 3rd Division by being one of the first units to land on D-Day. Horrocks also returned to command 9 Brigade, Brigadier Robb having suffered a heart attack

Below: His Majesty King George VI inspecting the 2nd East Yorkshires at Frome on 8 June, within days of reassembling after evacuation. Montgomery accompanies the King; immediately behind the GOC is Lt-Col T. F. Given, the CO, who was decorated by the King with the DSO in recognition of the battalion's defence of the Yser canal./*Lt-Col M. R. R. Turner*

during the evacuation. 3rd Division, now fully equipped and up to strength, moved down to the Sussex coast and took over a sector from Brighton to Littlehampton. The Division was to prepare the area for defence against the expected invasion, and in Montgomery's words it descended 'like an avalanche' on the resorts of Sussex by the Sea. To the chagrin of local councils and residents, weapon slits were dug in the gardens, machine-guns sited on the promenades, and piers taken over as observation posts. Montgomery was ruthless in ramming home the truth of the emergency to the residents, for whom the 1940 holiday season was clearly to be an unusual one.

However a static coast defence task rankled with Montgomery for his was the only fully equipped division in the country. In France and Belgium 3rd Division had demonstrated its skill in manoeuvre and rapid deployment, and when Churchill visited him on 2 July, Montgomery requested that 3 Div be made fully mobile with buses and formed into a counter attack force. The next day the following minute was issued from 10 Downing Street:

'Action this Day

3.VII.40

Prime Minister to Secretary of State for War

I was disturbed to find the 3rd Division spread along thirty miles of coast; instead of being, as I had imagined, held back concentrated in reserve, ready to move against any serious head of invasion. But much more astonishing was the fact that the infantry of this division, which is otherwise fully mobile, are not provided with the buses necessary to move them to the point of action. This provision of buses, waiting always ready and close at hand, is essential to all mobile units, and to none more than the 3rd Division while spread about the coast.

I heard the same complaint from Portsmouth that the troops had not got their transport ready and close at hand. Considering the great masses of transport, both buses and lorries, which there are in this country, and the large numbers of drivers brought back from the BEF, it should be possible to remedy these deficiencies at once. I hope, at any rate, that the GOC 3rd Division will be told today to take up, as he would like to do, the large number of buses which are even now plying for pleasure traffic up and down the sea front at Brighton.'

It is therefore no surprise that by the end of July 3rd Division was in Gloucestershire training for the mobile reserve role, having handed over its coastal task to a TA division. Montgomery's views on the striking power of his

Iron Division had also set many other minds a-thinking, for he was told to prepare simultaneously for operations in the Azores, Cape Verde Islands, and Eire!

In July Montgomery was promoted to command 5th Corps and handed over 3rd Division to Major-General S. A. H. Gammell CB, DSO, MC. In the autumn the Division returned to the south-west as mobile reserve where it remained until early summer 1941, when it moved to Buckinghamshire. That year it was decided to form a Guards Armoured Division, and the units of 7 Guards Brigade were selected to form part of it. The loss of this fine brigade which had proved a pillar of strength during the retreat to Dunkirk was regrettable, but the 3rd Division's loss was the Guards Armoured's gain. In its place the Division received 33 Tank Brigade, consisting of 43 RTR and 144 and 148 Regiments, RAC. It trained as a 'mixed division' until 1943, when it reverted to its traditional role as an infantry division. 33 Tank Brigade was replaced by 185 Infantry Brigade — the 2nd Royal Warwicks, 1st Royal Norfolks, and 2nd Kings Shropshire Light Infantry. This brigade was to prove a worthy successor to 7 Guards Brigade as the third point of the divisional triangle, in the memorable days that lay ahead.

Right: 3rd Reconnaissance Regiment training with Standard 'Beaverettes' in 1942. These vehicles were armour-plated civilian cars with no cross-country performance, and were soon replaced by carriers and purpose-built armoured cars. Formed from 8th Royal Northumberland Fusiliers (Motor Cycle Battalion) in 1941, 3rd Recce Regt replaced 15th/19th King's Royal Hussars as 3rd Division's reconnaissance unit./*Imperial War Museum*

7.
Assault Division, 1944

3 Div Prepares to Invade Europe
D-Day
The Battle for Caen
Lebisey, Cambes and La Londe
CANLOAN
Operation Goodwood
Breakout from Normandy

Right: The France and Germany Star.

La Londe, 27th June, 1944.

1st Battalion, The South Lancashire Regiment.

Above: In Scotland the Divisional Engineers prepare to breach the Atlantic Wall: Cpl Wood (left) and two sappers of 246 Field Company RE build replicas of the German defences, and then train to destroy them./*Lt-Col R. M. S. Maude*

Centre right: A sapper, carrying an 80lb 'Beehive' charge follows an escorting infantryman of 8 Brigade. Beehives were used for destroying pillboxes./*Lt-Col R. M. S. Maude*

Bottom right: The CRE, Lt-Col 'Tiger' Urquart, watches a trial of a rocket grapnel, designed to carry detonating cable across minefields. In the left foreground is Cpl Thompson 246 Fd Coy. The weapon was never used in action as its flight was extremely unpredictable.
/*Lt-Col R. M. S. Maude*

By 1943, 3rd Division had spent 2½ years in the United Kingdom, training hard but firing not a shot in anger. Meanwhile other divisions were achieving fame in North Africa, while raids on the mainland of Europe were giving commandos and parachute troops a glamour all of their own. The officers and men of 3rd Division could have been excused an eagerness to transfer to other formations and get back to the fight, but few did so. They were confident that 3rd Division's day would come, and they were determined not to miss it.

Their long wait was broken early in the year when 3 Div was ordered to start training in the Scottish lowlands for the invasion of Sicily. Then came frustrating news, 1st Canadian Division was to replace 3 Div in the Sicily landings. The decision was disappointing but understandable, for Canadian forces had been training in UK for three years and so far had seen no action. But the Division's setback was soon followed by the excellent news that it was to take part in the assault on North West Europe, and its commander, Major-General Ramsden, secured an undertaking from General Alanbrooke, the CIGS, that 3 Div would be the first British infantry division ashore. This undertaking was honoured, although subsequently, when Montgomery increased the size of the assault wave, the assignment was shared with 50th Division.

Henceforward the training in the damp, misty hills of Dumfriesshire assumed new meaning, for the men of 3 Div had been entrusted with the task that every allied soldier had waited for — the assault on Hitler's 'Atlantic Wall' and the thrust into Germany that would lead to final victory in Europe. The programme of preparation was the most vigorous and realistic ever experienced in the British army. The Divisional Battle School at Moffat, commanded by Lt-Col Carse, East Lancashire Regiment, became well known to every company in the Division; there they learnt to assault a wide variety of fixed defences while the divisional engineers experimented with

new devices for the destruction of concrete strongpoints. The realism of all arms training was extreme; for example, young officers on their battle course found that DF from supporting gunners was falling only 18 yards in front of their slit trenches.

As the autumn progressed, units commenced combined operations training with the Royal Navy. This was centred on Inverary in Argyll, and exercises ranged up and down the west coast of Scotland between Rhum and Bute. Soldiers experiencing the agonies of seasickness were not reassured by the issue of both tablets and vomit bags at the same time, but splashing ashore to terra firma, even in the cold autumn sea, therefore had its compensations. Gunners practised loading and disembarking their new equipment, consisting of Priest SP guns in the field regiments and American M10 SP guns in 20th Anti-tank Regiment, and perfected the art of firing from the decks of landing craft during the approach, since this was to be an integral part of the assault fire plan.

In December the Division moved north to Inverness on the Moray Firth. Here it met Force S, the naval task force under Rear-Admiral A. G. Talbot which was to lift it to the beaches. It also married up with the large number of specialist units placed under command for the landing. These were 27 Armoured Brigade, including 13th/18th Hussars with Duplex-Drive (Amphibious) tanks; 101 Beach Area, a Port Operating Group, two anti-aircraft regiments, 53 Medium Regiment RA, No 1 Special Service (Commando) Brigade, 5 Assault Regiment RE, two specialist field engineer companies, and a host of minor service units. The size of the Division was thereby doubled and it is remarkable that the Divisional HQ Staff, with few increments, was able to administer and command them, and at the same time plan for D-Day

Below: Major-General Tom Rennie with Montgomery, who as C-in-C 21st Army Group was to command all Allied land forces on D-Day./*Mrs H. E. Richardson*

Left: The D-Day team at Abelour, Speyside, March 1944. Left to right: Colonel Montgomery (Comd Beach Sub-Area), Brigadier Cass (Comd, 8 Brigade), Colonel Cameron (ADMS), Brigadier Mears (CRA), Lt-Col Rea (AA & QMG), Brigadier Smith (Comd, 185 Brigade), Lt-Col Hussey (CO, 33 Fd Regt RA), Major-General Rennie, Commander Duckworth RN (SO(Ops), Force S), Lt-Col Browne (GSOl), Lt-Col Foster (CO, 76 Fd Regt RA), Brigadier Cunningham (Comd, 9 Brigade), RN Liaison Officer, Force S. */Brigadier J. C. Cunningham*

Below right: Extract from a secret Wehrmacht publication *Das Britische Kriegsheer*, giving Orders of Battle of British Divisions in February 1944. The enemy had failed to identify 185 Brigade which had replaced 7 Guards Brigade after Dunkirk, or the 1st South Lancashires, which had replaced the 4th Royal Berkshires; and furthermore thought that 3 Div was in North Africa. The enemy's failure to identify 3 Div in Normandy was the official British excuse for the lack of publicity given to the Division for the first three weeks of the Normandy campaign./*Intelligence Corps Museum*

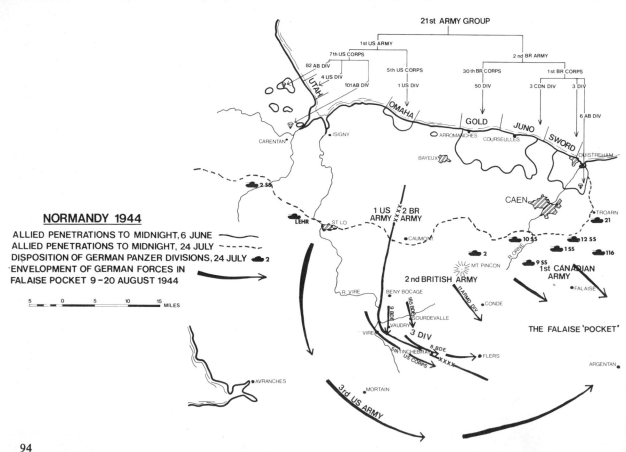

NORMANDY 1944

ALLIED PENETRATIONS TO MIDNIGHT, 6 JUNE
ALLIED PENETRATIONS TO MIDNIGHT, 24 JULY
DISPOSITION OF GERMAN PANZER DIVISIONS, 24 JULY
ENVELOPMENT OF GERMAN FORCES IN
FALAISE POCKET 9–20 AUGUST 1944

5   0   5   10   15 MILES

itself. The Divisional planning team was at the time working in London with the Overlord planning staff.

In December, General Sir Bernard Montgomery was appointed to command 21st Army Group, and Major-General T. G. Rennie DSO, MBE, came to 3rd Division to take over from Ramsden. Tom Rennie, late of the Black Watch, had served since 1939 with that great fighting formation, 51st (Highland) Division. He had been taken prisoner at St Valery in June 1940, but within 10 days he had made a remarkable escape, and later won his DSO commanding the Black Watch at El Alamein.

Under Rennie and Talbot, 3rd Division and Force S perfected their landing techniques for this highly complex operation. Between December and March seven full scale exercises were held in the Moray Firth, practising every aspect from marshalling in the mounting area to reinforcement of the beach head. The weather was often vile. The tale is told of an officer of 20th Anti-tank regiment who asked the coxwain of his craft what course they were supposed to be steering. 'I don't know, Sir', was the reply; 'I'm following the craft ahead'. 'Where is the craft ahead?' 'I don't know, I haven't seen it for about an hour'. When the fourth exercise, 'Grab', was mounted, the wind was blowing force 6, and it was bitterly cold. Talbot and Rennie decided nevertheless to go ahead with the landing, and the fact that it was successfully accomplished gave immense confidence to everyone when later D-Day itself turned out to be grey and rough. Lt-Col (later General Sir Richard) Goodwin, who was commanding the Suffolks, recalls: 'I have never in my life

seen troops so tough and fit. Despite the extreme cold and wet, their enthusiasm on these exercises was quite outstanding.'

While this intense training was in progress, plans for the invasion were being finalised. 3rd Division was to be the extreme left-hand assault division of 21st Army Group, landing opposite Caen. The Division would land on a one-brigade front on the 'Queen' sector of 'Sword' beach, with 8 Brigade leading and 185 Brigade following up and passing through. 9 Brigade, in reserve, would land last. The Division's immediate task was to secure the high ground north of Caen and if possible Caen itself. It was also to relieve 6th Airborne Division of responsibility for the bridges over the Caen Canal and River Orne, which were to be seized by glider-borne troops during the preceding night.

It is important throughout to understand how Montgomery, who was in overall command of Allied ground forces, intended to conduct the Normandy battle after the initial landing. His concept was to build up for a breakthrough by the 1st US Army on the right, while the enemy squandered his panzer reserves against 2nd British Army on the left. Relentless pressure by the British, rather than remarkable progress, would be required in order to absorb the German reserves.

In April the Division moved south through an England made bright and green by a warm and gentle spring. Units occupied camps in the woods of south Hampshire and apart from one rehearsal exercise on the Sussex coast they had little to do but wait expectantly and keep fit. On

Englische Infan-   terie-Divisionen

Nr. bzw. Name	englische Inf. Brig.Nr.	Inf. Bataillone	Unter-Artillerie	stellte sonstige Truppen	war eingesetzt	Abzeichen an Kfz.	Bemerkungen
1.	2	I./Loyals II./N.Staffs. VI./Gordons	engl.Feld-Artl.Rgt. 2 Stab, 35.,42., 53./87.Abt.	? (M.G.Btl.) engl.Aufkl.Abt. 1	Nordfrankreich 1939	Weißes, gleich-seitiges Dreieck auf schwarz. Quadrat	In Nord-Afrika
	3	I./D.W.R. II./Foresters I./K.S.L.I.	engl.Feld-Artl.Rgt. 19 Stab, 29.,96., 39./97.Abt.	engl.Pz.Jäger-Abt. 81 Stab, BB.,294.,297.Kp. engl.le.Flak-Abt. 90 Stab, 311.,312.,313.le.Battr.	Flandern 1940 Großbritannien 1940/42		
	24 Garde	V./Gren.Gds. I./S.G. I./I.G.	engl.Feld-Artl.Rgt. 67 Stab, 265.,266.,446.Abt.	23.,238.,248.engl.Pi.Kp. 6.engl.Pi.Park-Kp. engl.Inf.Div.Nachr.Abt. 1	Tunesien 1943		
2.	4	I./R.S. II./Norfolk w. 1/VIII./L.F.	w. engl.Feld-Artl.Rgt. 10 Stab, 30./46., 51.,54.Abt.	? (M.G.Btl.) w.engl.Aufkl.Abt. 2	Nordfrankreich 1939	Gekreuztes weißes Schlüssel-paar auf schwarzem Quadrat	In Indien
	5	II./Dorset I./Camerons VII./Worc.R.	engl.Feld-Artl.Rgt. 16 Stab, 27.,34., 72./86.Abt.	engl.Pz.Jäger-Abt. ? Stab, engl.le.Flak-Abt. ? Stab,	Flandern 1940 Großbritannien 1940/41		
	6	I./R.W.F. I./R.Berks. II./D.L.I.	engl.Feld-Artl.Rgt. 99 Stab, 393.,394.,472.Abt.	5.,506.engl.Pi.Kp. 21.engl.Pi.Park-Kp. engl.Inf.Div.Nachr.Abt. 2	Indien 1942		
3.	8	I./Suffolk II./E.Yorks.	w. engl.Feld-Artl.Rgt. 7 Stab, 9./17., 16.,43.Abt.	w. II./Mx. (M.G.Btl.) w. engl.Aufkl.Abt. 3 w. engl.Pz.Jäger-Abt. ? Stab,	Nordfrankreich 1939	3 aneinand. stoßende schwarze Dreiecke in roter, kreis-förmiger Fläche	(mot.) In Nord-Afrika
	9	II./Lincolns. I./K.O.S.B. II./R.U.R.	w. engl.Feld-Artl.Rgt. 33 Stab, 101.,109., 113./114.Abt. engl.Feld-Artl.Rgt. 76 Stab, 302.,303.,454.Abt.	engl.le.Flak-Abt. ? Stab, 17.,253.engl.Pi.Kp. 15.engl.Pi.Park-Kp. engl.Inf.Div.Nachr.Abt. 3	Flandern 1940 Großbritannien 1940/43		
4.	10	II./Bedfs.Herts. II./D.C.L.I. 1/VI./Surreys	engl.Feld-Artl.Rgt. 22 Stab, 32.,33.,36.Abt.	w. IV./N.F. (M.G.Btl.) engl.Aufkl.Abt. 4 engl.Pz.Jäger-Abt. 14 Stab, 38.,61.,88. Kp.	Nordfrankreich 1939	3/4 einer roten Kreisfläche, 1/4 links oben etwas heraus-ragend	(mot.) In Nord-Afrika
	12	II./R.F. VI./B.W. I./R.W.K.	engl.Feld-Artl.Rgt. 30 Stab, 104.,111.,112.Abt. engl.Feld-Artl.Rgt. 77 Stab, 305.,306.,307.Abt.	engl.le.Flak-Abt. 91 Stab, 314.,315.,316.le.Battr. 7.,59.,225.engl.Pi.Kp. 18.engl.Pi.Park-Kp. engl.Inf.Div.Nachr.Abt. 4	Flandern 1940 Großbritannien 1940/42 Tunesien 1943		

Friday 26 May came the final preparations. French francs and phrasebooks were issued, camps were sealed and detailed briefing of all ranks started. This briefing was most comprehensive, but the numerous maps, models and aids still bore codenames. Real names and locations would not be known until specially overprinted battle maps were issued after embarkation.

On Tuesday 30 May, men were basking in the warm sun when the quiet order was given for them to get their kits on and fall in. The embarkation machinery went into motion, and by Saturday 3 June all were aboard, but meanwhile the weather had turned squally and grey. They remained at anchor in Portsmouth harbour and waited. D-Day, intended for 5 June, was postponed, but a favourable forecast enabled Eisenhower to order the landing for 6 June. The fleet sailed on 5 June into a grey and heaving channel. As the men of the Division sailed with Force S out of Spithead they saw their joint commanders, Talbot and Rennie, standing together on the Headquarters ship, HMS *Largs,* with the Signal 'Good Luck — Drive On' flying from her yard-arm.

The fleet steamed to the assembly area south-east of the Isle of Wight where it formed into columns and laid course for Normandy. Throughout the afternoon and night of 5 June the force rolled and pitched southwards and as dawn was breaking reached the 'Lowering Position' seven miles offshore. Ahead, the minesweeper force was clearing a channel to the beaches, and the

Right: Letter from Eisenhower to General Rennie, written after the Supreme Commander's visit to 3 Div in its concentration area on 13 May 1944./*Mrs H. E. Richardson*

Below: Major Alastair Rennie and men of D Company, 1st Kings Own Scottish Borderers, watch an infantry flame-thrower demonstration, while waiting in the Overlord concentration area. /*Imperial War Museum*

Supreme Headquarters
ALLIED EXPEDITIONARY FORCE
Office of the Supreme Commander

15 May, 1944

Dear Rennie:

I must write to tell you what a great pleasure it was for me to visit your Division on Saturday. I had heard so much about you all from General Montgomery; he certainly did not exaggerate anything he told me. It was good to see your Division looking so fit and in such good spirits.

Will you please thank all ranks who were concerned in making my visit to you such a pleasant one.

Good luck to you all and I shall look forward very much to our next meeting.

sincerely
Dwight D Eisenhower

Major General T.G.Rennie, D.S.O., O.B.E.,
Headquarters,
3rd Division,
c/o A.P.O.,
England.

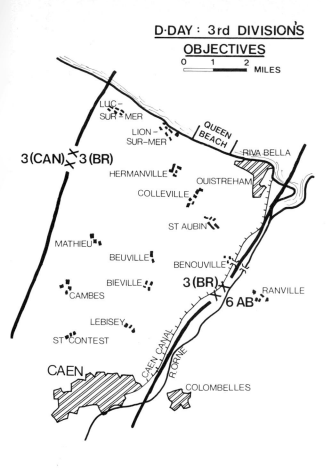

D·DAY : 3rd DIVISION'S OBJECTIVES

0   1   2 MILES

3(CAN) X 3(BR)

LUC-SUR-MER
LION-SUR-MER
QUEEN BEACH
RIVA BELLA
HERMANVILLE
OUISTREHAM
COLLEVILLE
ST AUBIN
MATHIEU
BEUVILLE
BENOUVILLE
CAMBES
BIEVILLE
3 (BR)
RANVILLE
6 AB
LEBISEY
ST CONTEST
CAEN
CAEN CANAL
R. ORNE
COLOMBELLES

Below: Section of specially overprinted map showing German obstacles and defences on 'Queen' Beach. The defended complex to the west of La Breche is Strongpoint 'Cod'./*Brigadier G. G. Mears*

waiting infantrymen could see to the east the flash of heavy guns as the warships of the Royal Navy commenced their bombardment of the coast defences.

The Assault Plan

Before following the fortunes of the Division during the landing it is as well to know the assault procedure from the 'Lowering Position', and the detailed plan once ashore.

At the 'Lowering Position' the assault battalions aboard the Land Ships Infantry (LSI) were to file into the Landing Craft Assault (LCA) carried at the LSI's davits. The LCAs, each carrying a platoon, would be lowered, circle the LSI, form up and head for the beach, close behind the assault engineers, whose Assault Vehicles RE (AVRE) were carried in Landing Craft Tank (LCT). The SP guns of the divisional artillery would follow some 2½ miles behind in further LCTs. But ahead of all these units would be men with the most hazardous task of all — the tank crews of the 13th/18th Hussars driving their DD (Duplex-Drive) amphibious Sherman tanks. They were to provide the immediate close armoured support so vital for the sappers and infantry fighting on the beaches. It was to take skill and courage to manoeuvre their inherently unseaworthy vehicles towards the hostile beach.

Once ashore the tactical plan was as follows. The leading assault battalions of 8 Brigade, the South Lancashires and the East Yorkshires, were to destroy the beach defences including a strongpoint nicknamed 'Cod'. The South Lancashires were then to clear an exit from the beach road to Hermanville while on the left the East Yorkshires destroyed strongpoints 'Sole' and 'Daimler' behind Riva Bella, and struck south to St Aubin. Finally the Suffolks, in brigade reserve, would move up the centre to secure the high ground south of Colleville. 1st Special Service Brigade, landing after the East Yorkshires on Queen Red, were to secure Ouistreham and the bridge at Benouville, seized earlier by glider troops of 6th Airborne

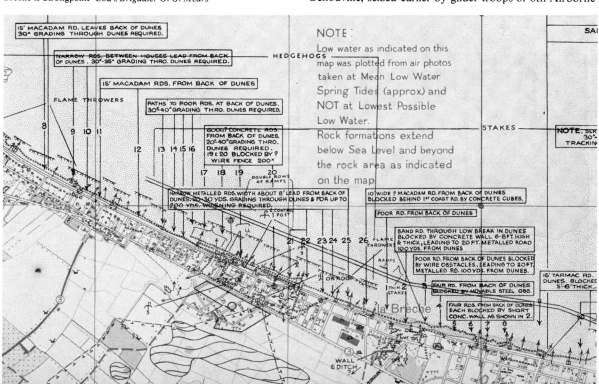

15' MACADAM RD. LEAVES BACK OF DUNES 30" GRADING THROUGH DUNES REQUIRED.

NARROW RDS. BETWEEN HOUSES LEAD FROM BACK OF DUNES. 30"-35" GRADING THRO. DUNES REQUIRED.

HEDGEHOGS

NOTE: Low water as indicated on this map was plotted from air photos taken at Mean Low Water Spring Tides (approx) and NOT at Lowest Possible Low Water. Rock formations extend below Sea Level and beyond the rock area as indicated on the map.

SAI

15' MACADAM RDS. FROM BACK OF DUNES

FLAME THROWERS

PATHS TO POOR RDS. AT BACK OF DUNES. 30"-40" GRADING THRO. DUNES REQUIRED.

8   9 10 11

GOOD? CONCRETE RDS. FROM BACK OF DUNES. 20"-40" GRADING THRO. DUNES REQUIRED. 19 & 20 BLOCKED BY ? WIRE FENCE 200"

STAKES

NOTE. SER 30"- TRACKIN

12   13 14 15 16

17 18 19   20 DOUBLE ROWS OF RAMPS

NARROW METALLED RDS. WIDTH ABOUT 8' LEAD FROM BACK OF DUNES. 20-30 YDS. GRADING THROUGH DUNES & FOR UP TO 200 YDS. WIDENING REQUIRED.

10' WIDE ? MACADAM RD. FROM BACK OF DUNES BLOCKED BEHIND 1st COAST RD. BY CONCRETE CUBES.

POOR RD. FROM BACK OF DUNES

21 22 23 24 25 26 FLAME THROWER

SAND RD. THROUGH LOW BREAK IN DUNES BLOCKED BY CONCRETE WALL 6-8 FT. HIGH & THICK, LEADING TO 20 FT. METALLED ROAD 100 YDS. FROM DUNES.

POOR RD. FROM BACK OF DUNES BLOCKED BY WIRE OBSTACLES, LEADING TO 20 FT. METALLED RD. 100 YDS. FROM DUNES.

FAIR RD. FROM BACK OF DUNES BLOCKED BY MOVABLE STEEL OBS.

16' TARMAC RD. DUNES. BLOCKED 5'-6' THICK.

FAIR RDS. FROM BACK OF DUNES EACH BLOCKED BY SHORT CONC. WALL AS SHOWN IN 2.

La Breche

WALL & DITCH

Division. 185 Brigade was to land next, form up at Hermanville in the bridgehead seized by 8 Brigade, and then thrust down the axis Beuville-Bieville-Lebisey to secure the high ground just north of Caen, and if possible Caen itself. Finally 9 Brigade was to strike down the axis Mathieu-Cambes-St Contest, and hold the ground on the right between 185 Brigade and 3rd Canadian Division.

The beach defences that 3rd Division was to assault — the Atlantic Wall — had been constructed with Teutonic thoroughness under the dynamic supervision of Rommel, Commander of Army Group B. Although not as extensive as in the Pas de Calais, they were daunting nonetheless. The beaches were covered down to low water mark with steel stakes and 'hedgehogs', tipped with shells and mines, and the gaps between were covered by machine-gun nests. There were deep shelters in the strongpoints to protect the defenders from preliminary bombardment, and further strongpoints and batteries were sited in depth up to three miles inland.

The enemy defending 'Queen' beach was 736th Regiment of 716th Coast Defence Division, while 21st Panzer Division was stationed south of Caen and near enough to intervene on D-Day. It was imperative that 3rd Division, with its supporting tanks from 27 Armoured Brigade, should secure a sizeable bridgehead before the panzers could reach the battle. The rapid enlargement of the bridgehead depended on the speed with which troops could be landed and cleared from the beaches, and the clearance of both beach obstacles and beach exits was fundamental to the success of the landing programme. H-hour had been set for 7.25am — half flood. This timing was a compromise; it allowed a minimum period of time for the sappers to work on beach obstacles before these became submerged, while minimising with the width of open beach to be crossed by assaulting infantry. The sappers were also responsible for opening exits from the beach, through which would move the vehicles of many types planned to land at an astonishing rate after the initial assault.

Below: D-Day, 0600 hrs. LCAs carrying the assault companies of the East Yorkshires and South Lancashires past HMS *Largs* (left background) towards Queen Beach./*Imperial War Museum*

The Battle of the Beaches

So much for the plan. By 5.30am the soldiers who were to execute it were grouped on the boat decks of the LSIs, hove-to at the Lowering Position. A and B Companies of the East Yorkshires and A and C Companies of the South Lancashires climbed into their LCAs and were lowered into the heaving sea. They were followed by reserve companies and battalion headquarters, and as they headed for the shore past HMS *Largs* a bugler of the East Yorkshires sounded the General Salute, which was acknowledged by Rennie and Talbot. Ahead of them, in the LCA of A Company Headquarters of the East Yorkshires, Major C. K. King, known throughout the Division as 'Banger', held the attention of his men by reading moving extracts from *King Henry V* over the craft's Tannoy system.

While the infantry could only wait, huddled in their LCA until the moment of beaching, the gunners following behind were able to land on Europe the Division's first shells since May 1940. Major Hendrie Bruce, Battery Captain of 9th (Irish) Field Battery, 7th Field Regiment, describes his view of the landing:

'By this time the big LSIs had hove-to at the Lowering Position and had launched the 30-odd LCAs carrying the assault companies of the East Yorkshires and South Lancashires. These small craft were making their way, pitching and rolling, towards the distant shore which was now clearly visible in the light of a grey stormy day and appeared absolutely deserted. We could see the long row of villas and boarding houses on the sea front and identified the mouth of the River Orne by the lighthouse at Ouistreham but had not positively identified Strongpoint 'Cod' as yet.

'Meanwhile the LCTs carrying the DD tanks of the 13th/18th Royal Hussars and the AVREs of 5th Assault Regt RE kept steaming steadily on. It was planned that the former should heave-to at 7,000yd and launch the DDs but owing to the heavy sea running they closed to 5,000yd. We were quite close when some time after 06.00hrs we saw them swing round with their bows down-wind and lower their ramps, allowing the extraordinary amphibious tanks with high, inflated bulwarks to crawl down into the water and set off for the shore looking like a lot of rubber dinghies. We were

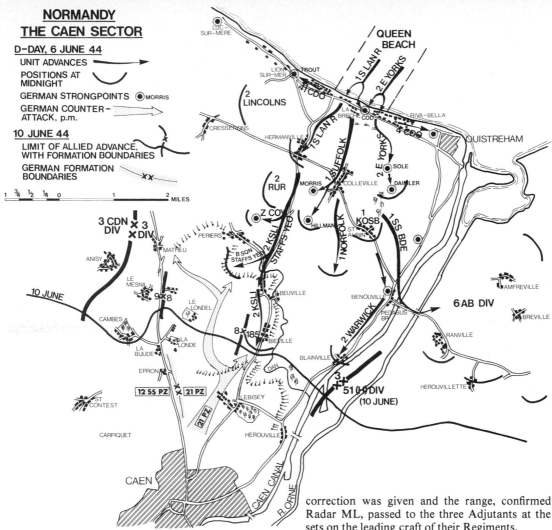

NORMANDY
THE CAEN SECTOR

D-DAY, 6 JUNE 44

UNIT ADVANCES ➤

POSITIONS AT
MIDNIGHT

GERMAN STRONGPOINTS ⦿ MORRIS

GERMAN COUNTER-
ATTACK, p.m. ⟹

10 JUNE 44

LIMIT OF ALLIED ADVANCE,
WITH FORMATION BOUNDARIES

GERMAN FORMATION
BOUNDARIES ×× ××

content to cruise along in their wake, scanning the coastline constantly with our special-issue Naval binoculars until we were satisfied that we had identified 'Cod'.

'We had now closed the shore to about 3,000yd. Further out to sea came the group of 18 LCTs carrying the Divisional Artillery and at about 06.30hrs, when they were about 15,000yd from the shore, they began to change formation in readiness for the 'Run-In-Shoot', as it was called. Led by LCT 331 (A Troop, 7th Field Regt aboard), the craft adopted an arrowhead formation in three groups of six each with 7th Field Regt in the centre and 33rd and 76th (Highland) Field Regts slightly to left and right rear respectively. In close attendance was a Motor Launch (ML) equipped with radar to calculate the opening range. The radio links were working perfectly and all was now ready for ranging to begin at H-42 (06.43hrs).

'At 06.44hrs (1 min late) the first ranging rounds were fired by A Troop, 7th Field Regt, a section salvo of white Phosphorous Smoke, Fuze 48, Delay. These rounds were unobserved as was the second salvo a few minutes later.

'To my great satisfaction, the third salvo hit the foreshore about 400yd to the right of the target. The correction was given and the range, confirmed by the Radar ML, passed to the three Adjutants at the control sets on the leading craft of their Regiments.

'The bombardment of shore targets by Naval gunfire from battleships, monitors, cruisers and destroyers had already begun and promptly at H-35 (06.50hrs) the seventy-two 105mm SP guns of 3 Div Arty opened fire at just over 10,000yd, firing HE, rate 3. The Field Artillery was now playing a unique naval role in the softening-up of the defences by firing from the decks of their LCTs which maintained a steady speed and course with their bows aimed at the target. The guns had been embarked side by side in sections with 2 guns forward, 2 right aft, and other vehicles in between. Over 100rds per gun had been stacked on the tank decks to be expended solely on the run-in: mostly HE but some Smoke also, if required. At rate 3, over 200rds per minute were arriving on the target which was seen to be well covered with burst both on the foreshore and among the buildings behind, and by the end of the bombardment some 6,500rds, all HE, had been fired. The steady rate of decrease in range was calculated by an instrument called the Coventry Clock with which each GPO, (Gun Position Officer) standing on the bridge of his craft, was equipped. A stream of range corrections, dropping 100yd at a time, was given out over the Tannoy loudspeakers.

'The din down in the tank decks was deafening and not only the gunners, but all personnel — drivers, signallers, cooks etc — were kept busy passing the ammunition and throwing the empty cartridge cases overboard. The 105mm ammunition came packed in large cardboard cylinders and these, floating in their thousands in the wake of the LCTs, laid a clear trail to the beach for those who followed.'

The LCT closed the shore and his account continues:

'The enemy had now wakened up with a vengeance and the sea around the leading craft was peppered with splashes. Several LCTs took evasive action, causing confusion in general and some casualties among the DDs in particular and although many of the splashes could be attributed to enemy fire, some of our own rounds appeared to be falling short. We were particularly concerned at the fact that the pitching of the Div Arty LCTs in the unusually rough sea might be lengthening the zone of the guns so, as the first assault wave was nearing the beach, I gave a correction of "add 600". The trouble persisted on the right of the target so I stopped the 76th to try and sort things out. It was immediately apparent that the culprit was an LCT(R) whose salvoes of rockets were falling short so I immediately gave "Go on" and the 76th resumed at an increased rate to catch up. It was now H-5 when all the guns lifted 400yd, the assault then went in at 07.25hrs, the run-in shoot terminated, and my first task of the day was over.'

As the assault companies of the East Yorkshires and South Lancashires swept towards the shore, the first desperate minutes of the Division's landing are described by Major A. R. Rouse, of the South Lancashires:

'The boat crews had been ordered to go in at 4 knots and hit the beach hard. During the last 100 yards of the run-in everything seemed to happen at once. Out of the haze of smoke the underwater obstacles loomed up. We had studied them on air photographs and knew exactly what to expect but somehow we had never realised the vertical height of them, and as we weaved in between iron rails and ramps and pickets with tellamines on top like gigantic mushrooms we seemed to be groping through a grotesque petrified forset.

'The noise was so continuous that it seemed almost like a siren. The seamanship was magnificent. The LCAs weaved in and out of the obstacles and we almost had a dry landing. I have very little recollection of wading ashore, there was too much going on above and around to notice it. It was, however, apparent from the beginning that it was by no means an unopposed landing. Mortar fire was coming down on the sands, an 88mm gun was firing along the line of the beach and there was continuous machine-gun and rifle fire. Immediately ahead of us a DD tank, its rear end enveloped in flames, unable to get off the beach, continued to fire its guns.

'In planning the operation the Commanding Officer, Lt-Col Richard Burbury, had tried to visualise some of the difficulties of command in the event of the battalion not being able to get off the beaches. He therefore had a hand flag made in the battalion colours. The idea was that this would be a rallying point and he could be identified. He carried this in his hand as he landed. Unfortunately it made him far too conspicuous and he was killed by a sniper as we reached the beach wire. The Second in Command, Major Jack Stone, took over command.

'A and C Companies had landed almost simultaneously with the DD tank. They immediately came under heavy fire. Major Harwood, commanding A Company was mortally wounded. One of his subalterns was killed crossing the beaches. Lieutenant Pierce took command of the company and moved off to the right clearing fortified houses. He himself was later wounded and before their task had been completed the company was left with only one officer.

'C Company were more fortunate, they crossed the beach with only light casualties and Major Eric Johnson directed them to the left towards strongpoint 'Cod'. B and C Companies were to have landed exactly behind A and C but they hit the beach well to the left with battalion headquarters almost exactly opposite the western end of 'Cod' Major Harrison, B Company Commander, was killed immediately and one of his subalterns, Lieutenant Bell-Walker took command. He moved a platoon to the left to attack a concrete pillbox which was firing with devastating effect to our right along the beaches. We saw Bob Bell-Walker deal with it in classic battle school fashion. He crept round behind it, lobbed a grenade through a gun port and then gave it a burst of sten-gun fire. He himself was killed instantly by a burst of machine-gun fire from strongpoint 'Cod' over on our left. He had, however, opened a way for the rest of his company to get off the beach. They had landed almost exactly opposite the strongest fortifications of 'Cod' and began immediately to attack frontally.

'A good deal of confused fighting followed with platoons and sections taking on their own targets. There are many acts of individual heroism. The orders were that as soon as the beach task had been completed the battalion should rendezvous at Hermanville. The silencing of the concrete pillbox at the western end of 'Cod' by Bob Bell-Walker enabled battalion headquarters to work round to the right and begin to move towards Hermanville. The confused fighting on the beaches lasted for a considerable time. The anti-tank platoon coming in at H + 30 even had their share with a corporal bringing one of the battalion six-pounders into action on the sand to deal effectively with a machine-gun post.'

While the infantry and DD tanks were overcoming the enemy beach defences the tide, much increased in height by the strong wind, was rapidly covering the sand behind them and it was now time for the engineer gapping parties to clear exits from the beach area. The sappers had already suffered heavily from enemy fire; several had been drowned while working on the half submerged beach obstacles, the Commanding Officer of 5 Assault Regiment RE, Lt-Col Cocks, had been killed while disembarking from a LCT, but the work went ahead. 246 Field Company cleared an exit on the right but on the left, where roads were blocked by damaged tanks, it took nearly two hours to open up further exits. To get clear of the beach, vehicles had to move laterally to the right before meeting the road to Hermanville which formed the nearest causeway over the marshy land behind the dunes. As the morning progressed, queues at the exits built up, and meanwhile more and more vehicles were landing on the ever decreasing strip of sand. The congestion was extreme. In addition to vehicles waiting to move forward

there were some 50 SP guns firing from the beach — and eventually these were standing on some feet of surf. At midday it was decided to suspend beaching for half an hour to allow the congestion to subside.

While his assault troops were fighting their way ashore, General Tom Rennie was observing operations from HMS *Largs* and assessing the proper moment at which to land and follow them. Captain A. C. Duckworth RN was at the time Staff Officer (Plans) to Admiral Talbot. He remembers that 3 Div's GOC was a great inspiration to them all, and recalls that at the time of the landing Rennie and Talbot were on the bridge, and were engaged in a heated argument as to when the General should be allowed to land:

'Rennie insisted that he should embark in a landing craft forthwith, while Talbot stated firmly that he was in command and the General would land at his discretion. Meanwhile, a Polish destroyer had been sunk on our port bow by German E-Boats, and the spread of their torpedoes narrowly missed sinking us while this frustrating argument continued. Fortunately, the Captain of HMS *Largs* took the necessary avoiding action on his own and Rennie was allowed to land shortly afterwards.'

Left: An amphibious tank of the 13th/18th Royal Hussars 'drowned' in the surf on Queen Beach. These tanks played an essential part by 'shooting in' the assault infantry and engineers./*Imperial War Museum*

Below: The congestion on Queen Beach at high water on D-Day. Troops of 3 Div dig in while queues of vehicles wait in the surf. The waterproofing of all vehicles and radios was one of the major responsibilities of 3 Div's Royal Electrical and Mechanical Engineers; REME had been formed as a new Corps in 1942. /*Imperial War Museum*

Enlarging the Beach-head

By 8.30am 8 Brigade had cleared the beach area of enemy and within half an hour the South Lancashires had pushed south and secured Hermanville. The East Yorkshires moved east towards strongpoint 'Sole', while the Suffolks landed and struck south to enlarge the beach-head. They cleared Colleville and strongpoint 'Morris' by 1pm with little trouble; but Captain (later Colonel) Sperling who was Regimental Signal Officer with the Suffolks recollects that the attack on 'Hillman' was a very different proposition:

'The area covered was approximately 600 yards by 400 yards containing three steel cupolas, deep concrete shelters, infantry guns, machine-guns etc, very well dug in and camouflaged; it was the local Coastal Bn HQ, surrounded by wire, anti-tank mines and anti-personnel mines. It showed no sign of softening up from the air and of course aerial photographs did not reveal the depth and complexity of this defensive position. To make matters worse, cruiser fire was not available as the Forward Officer Bombardment had been wounded. Cruiser fire in my experience was terrifying to an enemy in its effectiveness.

'D Company and the Sappers breached the wire with bangalore torpedoes. PIATs were fired at the cupolas to no effect whatever — and the same situation arose later when the 17-pounder armour-piercing shot from the tanks also made no impression on the cupolas. During the day A Company Commander, Captain Ryley, was killed and also Lieutenant Tooley, and the leading section

Above right: Priest SP guns of 7 Field Regiment RA in action near Hermanville. At the conclusion of the Normandy campaign these were replaced by 25-pounder towed guns, as the US Army could no longer supply 105mm ammunition to the British./*Imperial War Museum*

Right: D-Day. The first prisoners are brought in through Hermanville./*Imperial War Museum*

Left: D-Day pm: HMS *Ramillies* and HMS *Warspite*, having bombarded the beaches in support of Force S, wait offshore. Overhead, gliders carrying follow-up elements of 6th Airborne Division are towed in by aircraft of 38 Group RAF, with whom 3 Div was to form close links 16 years later. /*Imperial War Museum*

Right: 9 Brigade landing on Queen Beach, pm on D-Day. The beach is under enemy mortar fire, wounded are being helped away, and the Beach Group Marshal in the foreground is directing units clear of the beach./*Imperial War Museum*

commander Corporal Jones, among others. It became quite clear to the Commanding Officer that Company and Battalion fire-power resources were quite inadequate against this strongpoint. Flails*, and tanks of the 13th/18th Hussars were called for; Lt-Col Dick Goodwin made a first-rate plan and the position was taken about 20.00 hours with many prisoners. The German Colonel commanding 736 Coast Defence Regiment surrendered to us from the depths next morning, the first time we had consolidated on live Germans.

' My memory of all this is of almost continuous enemy fire, bullets whistling very close, and the total saving of a highly dangerous situation by the utter coolness of Lt-Col Dick Goodwin's planning and orders under continuous fire.'

While 8 Brigade fought their way inland 185 Brigade landed and formed up at Hermanville, and by 11am it was ready to start its thrust for Caen. The KSLI had been ordered to lead on the axis Beuville-Lebisey, carried on and supported by tanks of the Staffordshire Yeomanry. However, the Yeomanry were still queuing up at the beach exits and Lt-Col Maurice, commanding the KSLI, waited until midday and was then given permission by his Brigade Commander, Brigadier Smith, to advance on foot. At that moment 7th Field Regiment, just clear of the beaches, roared through Hermanville past the KSLI and went into action in fields south of the village, to become the foremost troops on the axis.

The KSLI started off and before long the Staffordshire Yeomanry caught them up. Near Periers they came upon a howitzer battery against which a company/squadron attack was mounted. The enemy fought doggedly, but eventually a Pole among them was captured who showed Major Wheelock, commanding Z Company, a route in

*Flail tanks were equipped with chains on revolving drums fixed to the front of the tank. These chains detonated mines forward of the tank, thus creating a gap in the minefield.

through the wire at the back of the battery position. The assault went in, and by late evening the position was secure. Meanwhile the main body of the KSLI/Staffordshire Yeomanry group had pushed on and secured Bieville by 4pm. The reconnaissance troop of the Yeomanry then reported a squadron of panzers approaching fast from the direction of Caen, and the number of tanks reported rapidly increased to a total of 40. This was the expected intervention by the leading battle group of 21st Panzer Division. The KSLI and Yeomanry deployed rapidly to meet the threat. Around Bieville was A Squadron of the Yeomanry, together with the KSLI's anti-tank platoon, and an SP troop of 41 Anti-tank Battery RA, and in depth at Periers was B Squadron of the Yeomanry.

The panzers hit Bieville head on. Two were knocked out by the Yeomanry and two by KSLI anti-tank gunners. The remainder swung to the west, followed by two troops of A Squadron who knocked out four more enemy tanks, and a further two fell to No 4 Gun of 41 Battery. The panzers continued west and ran into B Squadron who were waiting for them hull-down behind Periers ridge. As the German Mark IV (Specials) came into the Yeomanry's sights three were quickly destroyed and the rest withdrew having lost a total of 13 tanks to the admirable British gunnery.

The KSLI pushed one company forward from Beuville towards Lebisey, where it became involved in a heavy fire fight, losing the company commander, Major Steel. It was then ordered to withdraw and consolidate for the night. The enemy in Lebisey were newly arrived panzer grenadiers of 21st Panzer Division, who were energetically digging in on the high ground north of Caen. Meanwhile the Norfolks had reached a point between Beuville and Benouville, having suffered 150 casualties on the way, and the Royal Warwicks had cleared the route St Aubin-Benouville-Blainville, mopping up snipers as they went. As midnight approached the weary units of 185 Brigade dug in.

9 Brigade had landed at 1pm and as Brigadier Cunningham went forward to Hermanville to contact 8 Brigade, he describes the scene:

'On reaching the northern outskirts of Hermanville I was amazed to see standing inside the wall of an orchard not only Tom Rennie but John Crocker, in their red hats. I said I had never before been beaten into action by my Divisional and Corps Commanders and we had a good laugh about it.

'These two highly responsible and competent men realised that the moment was an extremely critical one, and they deemed it necessary to be in a position where they could be given an immediate decision on any matter, perhaps affecting the whole course of the battle.

'They told me to cancel my original role of going straight down on the right to get Carpiquet and if possible Caen, and instead to get across to Pegasus Bridge to help the Airborne who were hard pressed. This was disappointing as 9 Brigade had their run down the right flank all buttoned up. However, these two officers would not have taken a major decision of that nature if they had not considered it essential. They knew it would have the effect of Carpiquet not being taken that night, unless 9 Canadian Brigade managed to get it alone.

'It cannot be emphasised too strongly that they were on the spot to make their decision, it must have been a very hard order to give knowing what it all entailed.

'My armour had not then landed, and they said I had better wait for that before moving, so on the way back to the beach I did no more than warn the KOSB that we had to get across to assist 6th Airborne at Pegasus Bridge. My armour was still trying to find a place to land when I viewed it from the shore, so I returned to my Brigade HQ. On arrival there, I left my carrier and went towards my armoured command vehicle. My anti-tank gunner and my intelligence staff moved to join me there. At that moment a stick of mortar bombs landed on us killing six and wounding six. I was unable to convey the new instructions to my staff. Colonel Dennis Orr late of the

Scots Fusiliers had gone over with me as my second-in-command but between my leaving my Brigade HQ and returning to it he had been ordered to go over to Pegasus Bridge to (I think) report on the situation, certainly not to take command. When I was wounded he was not present to take over, and in fact I was told it was a very long time before he managed to get back. The result was a long hiatus when the Brigade should have been moving and nothing happened. In short, if a number two is considered worthwhile, do not use him for some other job instead.'

In the event the Lincolns were left at Cresserons to secure the right flank, the RUR dug in north east of Periers while the KOSB moved across and occupied St Aubin and the high ground overlooking Benouville, where 17 Field Company were working furiously to build rafts and relief Bailey bridges across the Caen Canal and River Orne. Sapper operations had been hampered by delays in clearing equipment from the beaches and heavy casualties, among the latter being the CRE, OC 17 Field Company and two reconnaissance officers. Fortunately the original bridges remained intact throughout.

So ended the 'longest day'. Casualties had been heavy, and although the immediate objective — Caen — had not been taken, a breach 5 miles deep by 4 miles wide had been made in the Atlantic Wall. As they wearily dug in for the night, the men of 3rd Division knew that although they had accomplished much it was only the beginning. D + 1 would soon be upon them.

During this short, tense night the enemy were working hard to seal off the beachhead. The newly arrived grenadier battalions of 21st Panzer Division were fortifying the ridge Lebisey to La Londe which dominated the approaches to Caen — and hurrying into position on their left was the 12th SS Panzer Division (*Hitler Jugend*). 3rd Division was to find these two formations an altogether different proposition from 716 Coast Defence Division. Their soldiers were the elite of the German armed forces, and they were as well organised for defence as for attack.

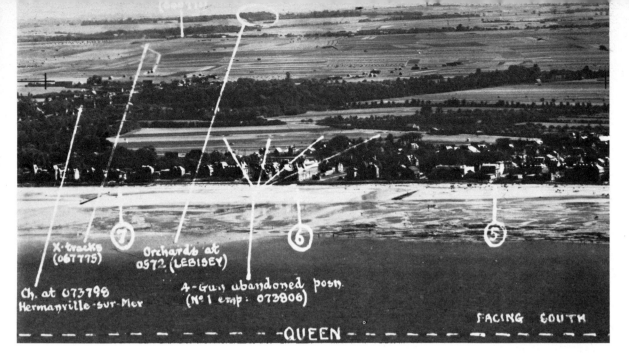

X-tracks
(067775)

Orchards at
0572 (LEBISEY)

Ch. at 073798
Hermanville-sur-Mer

4-Guns abandoned posn.
(No 1 emp: 073806)

FACING SOUTH

-QUEEN-

Above left: The Royal Ulster Rifles assembling in Hermanville, pm on
D-Day in preparation for 9 Brigade's thrust to Carpiquet, which was
subsequently cancelled due to the enemy threat to the Orne bridges.
/*Imperial War Museum*

Above: 3rd Division's intended D-Day objectives. In the middle distance
is the long wooded feature Lebisey-La Londe-Cambes, on which
21st Panzer and 12th SS Panzer Divisions consolidated during the night
6/7 June 1944. Behind this feature lies Caen, and in the foreground is
Lion-Sur-Mer./*Imperial War Museum*

Standard Wehrmacht panzer divisions comprised two
tank battalions (total of 160 tanks) and four grenadier
(infantry) battalions while SS divisions had three tank
battalions and six grenadier battalions; both types of
division were lavishly equipped with artillery, mortars and
anti-tank guns.

Lebisey and Cambes

The fighting on D + 1 started early, with 185 and 9
Brigades thrusting respectively left and right at Caen, but
it was a day of bloody fighting, frustrating setbacks and
little progress. On the left, the Royal Warwicks were
ordered to attack Lebisey wood from Blainville with H-
hour at 8.45am. Lt (later Lt-Col) Kingston Adams was a
platoon commander and he remembers that: 'It was a
terrible rush to get through our recces, orders etc, and
when H-hr arrived only our company seemed to be on the
start line and none of the supporting fire promised had
started. We later found, I believe, that H-hr had been
postponed.'

H-hour had in fact been postponed an hour and the
gunners informed, but two companies were out of radio
contact and crossed the start line at 8.45 as originally
ordered. The Commanding Officer, Lt-Col Herdon, had
an agonising decision to make and he decided to commit
the whole battalion rather than leave these two companies
to go on alone. Adams continues:

'I have recollections of advancing up a corn field and
coming under heavy fire from Lebisey wood. When we

were about 100 yards short of it my platoon was unable
to make directly for its objective, so I tried to work my
way round to the right flank. We were heavily engaged
from that direction also but we eventually got into the
wood where control became very difficult, and as I was
trying to consolidate our position, I was hit by a
phosphorous grenade and burst of machine-gun fire from
a hidden position in front of me. This put me out of the
battle, but the company held on to the edges of the wood
until the rest of the Battalion came up and joined in the
attack, but they also were unable to move further
forward.'

The battalion was pinned down in front of Lebisey wood
and Lt-Col Herdon was killed while moving between his
companies. A further disaster followed. The battalion's
F Echelon vehicles and anti-tank guns were making a
wide detour through Bieville to reach the objective on
reorganisation. Having been delayed en route and
expecting the objective to be secure, they pressed on to
Lebisey and drove straight into an enemy ambush. They
were virtually annihilated but some men were able to take
to the cornfields and filter back.

By 4pm the rifle companies were very nearly out of
ammunition and under tank attack. The Royal Norfolks
were now ordered forward to take Lebisey and restore the
situation. Up they went across the cornfields on the right
of the Warwicks but they in turn could make no progress
into the wood which was very strongly held by tanks and
infantry. Casualties mounted and further progress was
impossible. When darkness fell both battalions were
withdrawn back to their starting points.

Brigadier Harry Illing, later Deputy Colonel
(Warwickshire) of the Royal Regiment of Fusiliers, and at
the time commanding A Company of the Warwicks, puts
his battalion's battle into perspective:

'The first battle of Lebisey was lost and it was galling that
the great prize of Caen had not fallen into our hands.
Lebisey could in all probability have been captured if a

properly coordinated brigade attack had been put in instead of battalions being committed piecemeal — but this is mere hindsight — for the atmosphere within the battalion, brigade and division at the time should be appreciated. Troops were immensely fit, morale was terrific, they were probably the best trained, battle inoculated and rehearsed troops the world has ever seen, but for nearly all of them it was their first time in battle apart from a few who were at Dunkirk. There was a desire to 'Seek Glory' — a term well known in the Regiment from its Peninsula days. There was the doctrine of "getting on", "taking risks" and "staking a claim". There was real determination to succeed or die in the attempt. The atmosphere was heroic.'

Meanwhile 9 Brigade had started their advance on D + 1 under constant shelling, with the RUR and KOSB leapfrogging up the axis Periers-Mathieu-Le Mesnil. Late that afternoon D Company of the Ulster Rifles advanced on Cambes, a small, thickly wooded village surrounded by a 10-foot high stone wall. The company was met by a hail of fire. Major Aldworth and many of his men were killed, and the remainder were ordered to withdraw to Le Mesnil and reorganise. It was clear that the capture of Cambes would require a full-scale battalion attack.

D + 1 drew to a close with the enemy determined to prevent the capture of Caen at all costs. However already 21st Panzer and 12th SS Panzer Divisions had been committed to battle, and thus Montgomery's concept was developing as planned.

On 9 June the Ulster Rifles returned to the attack on Cambes, making a right hook from Anisy, supported by the fire of the divisional artillery, the cruiser HMS *Danae* and tanks of the East Riding Yeomanry. As the leading companies reached a point 1,000 yards from the village they were struck by mortars, shellfire and machine guns, but despite mounting casualties, they pressed on in perfect formation. Major (later Brigadier) 'Digger' Tighe-Wood, the platoon commander at Louvain in 1940 and now commanding A Company on the left of the attack, describes the action:

Above: Lebisey — the scene of the destruction of the Royal Warwicks' F Echelon on D + 1, an abandoned 17-pounder anti-tank gun in the foreground. Photograph taken when the Royal Warwicks captured the village a month later after a massive aerial bombardment. */Imperial War Museum*

'Bullets started to fly and some men were hit but the advance continued with the encouraging sight of a tremendous weight of artillery fire falling in front of the objective. The attack continued until we were close up to the barrage which, by now, should have lifted. The truth suddenly dawned that our own artillery was firing on the objective and this was the enemy defensive fire coming down where our own concentrations had started. There was nothing to it but to continue the advance as fast as possible and get to the other side of it. The air was thick with whistling splinters and one remembers the sound made by fragments of shells cutting through the green corn which was about a foot high. Once through the belt of DFs the spandaus opened up but their fire was not very accurate and the remainder of the company reached the wall round the wood safely but out of breath. The casualties had been very heavy, all the platoon commanders killed or wounded, one platoon commanded by a corporal, and only one sergeant and one lance-sergeant left in the company. Some enemy could be seen pulling out from the area of the chateau in the wood and it was pleasant to get one's own back and have a bang at them.

'B Company had come through the fire with not quite so many casualties and were advancing into the village.

'A Company having reorganised behind the wall now advanced on to their final objective near the chateau driving a few Germans out of their position in the trees. Near where we finally consolidated there was a group of about ten Ulster Riflemen and six Germans all lying dead in an area of about 10 × 10yd. The fighting had been hand to hand. This was the remnants of D Company's attack on D + 1 and their Company Commander, Major Aldworth, with his runner had advanced further into the wood than anyone. He lay at the head of his men opposite

Above: Montgomery with 'Bolo' Whistler as a Brigadier commanding 160 Brigade, 53rd (Welsh) Division, shortly before being appointed to command 3 Div. After commanding 131 Brigade in Italy, Whistler had been 'held' in UK with 150 Brigade, in readiness to take over the first vacant divisional commander's appointment in Normandy. */Lady Whistler*

Left: The gateway to the Chateau at Hermanville where 3 Div Headquarters was established on D-Day. The memorial tablet was designed by Major Graham Lewis, late of 17 Field Company RE, and was erected by the 3rd Division Officers Association after the war./*Lady Whistler*

a dead German officer. The enemy all had the SS insignia with the legend *Adolf Hitler Jugend* on their sleeves; they were from the 12th SS Panzer Division.

'C Company with three AVRE tanks now passed through A Company and captured the far edge of the village and wood. The task of the RE tanks was to deal with pill-boxes which it was believed were located in the village. This was not so but instead they took on a German Mk IV tank and knocked it out with their bombards. They behaved with the utmost gallantry and advanced beyond the village where they were all destroyed by 88mm guns. B Company now having a firm grip on the village the remains of D Company were passed through and consolidated on the forward edge in line with C.'

The enemy now drenched Cambes with artillery fire. The Ulsters' affiliated battery commander and an FOO were killed, as was the CO of 33rd Field Regiment, Lt-Col Hussey, and the company commander, his 2IC and CSM of the supporting Middlesex machine-gun company. The battalion dug in among the woods and shattered cottages and waited for the counter-attack, but astonishingly it never came. The KOSB came forward to reinforce them,

unclear as to the degree of success in the village. It was an excited reunion. When enemy shells fell, a Borderer jumped into the nearest trench and put his arms heartily round two dim figures with the words 'Well, Paddy you old b———! I didn't think we'd see you again!' The two individuals so greeted turned out to be Brigadier Orr, now commanding 9 Brigade and Lt-Col Harris commanding the Ulster Rifles.

By 10 June 3rd Division was holding a line from Blainville on the Caen Canal to Cambes. From this line the infantry patrolled continuously and each night there were fierce encounters in No Man's Land, which in places was only 150 yards wide. The Germans were dug in with many tanks in close support and with their artillery and mortars imposing a continual threat to movement in the open. Under such conditions of stress, personal leadership is essential. General Tom Rennie set an outstanding example of this by frequently visiting forward units. He made a point of including recently wounded soldiers in his rounds, and on 13 June he was being driven by Lt-Col Wood, RAMC, commanding 9th Field Ambulance, to visit the Regimental Aid Post of the Ulster Rifles in Cambes. Unknown to the visitors a small and very recent change in forward positions had resulted in mines being laid on the track they were following. Their jeep was blown up, Rennie sustaining a fractured arm and Wood a badly injured foot. It was extreme ill fortune that the GOC should have been wounded by one of our mines, but it is understandable when one considers the close proximity of our own and enemy positions, and the degree of leadership 'from the front' exhibited by senior commanders. Rennie hoped that a few days' rest and treatment about HMS *Largs* would enable him to return to command the Division, but his wound was too serious, and on 18 June he was evacuated to England. Brigadier Cass of 8 Brigade took over temporarily until 23 June when Major-General L. G. Whistler DSO arrived to take command.

General 'Bolo' Whistler had already made a name for himself as being, in Montgomery's words, 'probably the finest fighting Brigadier in the British Army'. Commissioned into the Royal Sussex Regiment, he had won his DSO commanding their 4th Battalion during the retreat to Dunkirk, and his first and second bars commanding 131 (Queens) Brigade in North Africa and Italy.

A big man in every sense of the word, his dominant personality and sense of humour electrified every soldier and officer under his command. He had earned a selection of nicknames, the oldest and best known — 'Bolo' — originating from his service with the Archangel expedition of 1919 against the Bolsheviks or 'Bolos'. In 1940 he was described as the 'Man who went back to Dunkirk', for when he was evacuated with 4th Royal Sussex on 30 May, he found that one of his companies was missing, so unofficially he went back, had a good look round the beaches and port, and finally returned with a battalion of the Manchester Regiment on 1 June; his missing company had meanwhile found its own way home. While commanding 131 Brigade he was known by his soldiers as 'Private Bolo', from his habit of seeing the situation at first hand by going out on patrol dressed and equipped as any other patrol member. Like his gallant predecessor he commanded from the front, and he and 3rd Division were to be together for 2½ years.

La Londe — 'The Bloodiest Square Mile in Normandy'

The day before Whistler's arrival, 8 Brigade had launched a fresh attack in the centre. The Germans held a salient around the Chateau of La Londe, and it was here that some of the Division's costliest fighting took place. The terrible irony was that initially La Londe fell quite easily to a silent night attack by the South Lancashires on 22 June. The enemy fled or were captured; amongst the latter was a FOO with marked maps. But disaster followed. The battalion's anti-tank guns were slow in joining the rifle companies and the Germans reacted very quickly. Just before dawn extremely heavy and accurate artillery and mortar fire fell on the battalion culminating in a dense box smoke screen. Through this screen came tanks which overran B Company, many of whose members were crushed to death in their hastily dug foxholes. A Company fought gallantly on and remained in position throughout the day, but were ordered to withdraw on the 24 June. The episode illustrates well the effect of tanks in an immediate counter-attack against

infantry who have not yet consolidated. 5th Company, 192nd Panzer Grenadiers, who had lost the Chateau in the first place, were put back in, reinforced by over 30 tanks, a platoon of engineers and Headquarters company of 22nd Panzer Regiment — both fighting as infantry — and told to 'hold it to the death'.

On the evening of 27 June the South Lancashires, supported by the divisional artillery, returned to the attack, and discovered the strength and the determination of the enemy's defence. Lt (later Lt-Col) Jones was commanding 8 Platoon of A Company in the attack, and he recalls:

'About 50 yards from the Chateau wall there was a cross bank at right angles, enclosing a medium sized field on our right, in front of the Chateau wall. I myself, with a few of the leading men of my Platoon had barely got beyond this point, when we were subjected to intense MG fire from both flanks and the front, and at the same time we were heavily mortared. Many men became casualties at once, others took refuge in the ditch and crawled back, and I and two riflemen were cut off completely from the rest of the Company, the slightest movement on our part provoking the heaviest enemy fire. We were in a shallow ditch, blocked a few yards ahead by the bloated corpse of a cow, whilst the hedge-junction to our rear was continually raked by machine-gun fire. A heavy concentration of mortar-shells was falling to our left, on the other side of the hedge/bank, and a Crocodile (flame throwing tank) was burning there, with its turret blown completely off. One of the two riflemen with me was struck in the shoulder by a bullet which seemed to pass through his body and he died within seconds. The rifle of the other soldier was struck by a bullet which wedged across the barrel. I had the camouflage netting shot from my steel helmet. The fire seemed to come from every direction and it was impossible to locate its source. We

8 BRIGADE'S BATTLE FOR LA LONDE
22 – 28 JUNE 1944

1 S LAN R FIRM BASE **1**

SEIZED BY A COY 1 S LAN R 22 JUNE AND **2**
HELD UNTIL 25 JUNE

SEIZED BY B COY 1 S LAN R 22 JUNE; **3**
OVER-RUN BY C-ATTACK DAWN 23 JUNE;
RECAPTURED BY 2 E YORKS 28 JUNE

COYS OF 1 S LAN R PINNED **4**
DOWN 22 & 27 JUNE

CAPTURED BY 1 SUFFOLK **5**
28 JUNE

0   100   200   300   400   500
YARDS

kept expecting troops and tanks to follow us up in support and relieve the pressure, but none came. When dusk came on we were able, under cover of darkness, to return to Le Landel and report to Bn HQ where we learned that our attack had been called off and that a Brigade attack was planned for a few hours ahead.'

The brigade attack, by the East Yorkshires and the Suffolks, went in at dawn on 28 June. The determination of the assault is recalled by Major John Waring, commanding 454 Field Battery 76th Field Regiment:
'The spirited attack on the Chateau by the Suffolks started from a wooded farming area and continued over mainly open country covered in some 2ft to 3ft of growing corn in which many British infantrymen lay dead and wounded. As the advance reached the area of the Chateau the ground became rougher, there being ditches, hedgerows and walls. In this area the Suffolks met their stiffest resistance; all gaps in fences, hedgerows, etc and every conceivable place was booby trapped and mined and every yard of ground had to be fought for. Many men lost their lives or limbs pushing their way through hedges or climbing over ditches. I was proud to be an Englishman that day.'

The fighting inside the Chateau grounds was bloody and confused; and Colonel Sperling's memories of the attack were of:
'The most intensive enemy shell fire, machine-gun fire and tank fire. The whole 8 Brigade casualties were very heavy. Tigers of 22 Panzer Regiment were dug in the Chateau grounds. A possibly unique experience was when Captain Brown (a Canadian Officer) commanding C Coy requested fire support from a German tank. The hatch closed abruptly but Brown, resourceful as ever, escaped before fire could be brought to bear on him. I cite this as an example of the confusion caused when the enemy gets in amongst you.

Above: 'The Bloodiest Square Mile in Normandy' — the Chateau of La Londe, captured by 8 Brigade after six days' intensive fighting. A rifle section of the Suffolks consolidates in the foreground. /*Imperial War Museum*

'After the capture of the Chateau shelling was continuous until 7 July. First World War conditions prevailed in my view for more than one month after the landing; the whole battalion in slit trenches, 100 per cent dawn and dusk stand-tos, rations brought up under great difficulty, daily losses of officers and men by active patrolling and by enemy gunfire.
'I would like to mention three morale points sometimes overlooked. Our Padre (the Reverend Hugh Woodall) allowed no dead bodies to remain without burial, highly dangerous work since he personally saw to collection as well as to burial. The Medical Officer (Captain Robinson, later killed) had casualties collected by the stretcher bearers at the double, therefore all ranks had confidence in his casualty collecting procedure. The Quartermaster got the rations up somehow, usually on carriers, always at the time ordered, for as one of my five COs said "Feed them and you can do anything with them". All this I consider adds up to the vital maintenance of high morale.'

The Suffolks alone lost a total of 163 killed, wounded and missing on 28 June. By the same day, 3rd Division's total casualties were 3,508, which was one seventh of the casualties suffered by the equivalent of 17 British divisions engaged in Normandy. The Division had so mauled 21st Panzer Division that it was withdrawn from battle and replaced by 10th GAF (German Air Force) Division fresh from Holland — thus another German reserve formation was committed to battle.
Colonel Sperling's mention of a Canadian Officer in the La Londe battle is significant, for he was one of many serving in the Division under 'CANLOAN', a unique scheme which deserves a place of its own in this story.

109

CANLOAN

By 1943 when preparations for the invasion of Europe were in hand, the British Army found itself short of junior infantry officers due to the intense fighting in the Mediterranean and the Far East. At the same time the Canadian Army had a surplus of officers, due in part to the disbanding of two Home Defence divisions and to the fact that the Canadians were fighting on one front only, Italy. Many young officers were therefore cooling their heels in Depots and Reinforcement Units and the Canadian Government offered to loan some of these officers to the British Army on a voluntary basis, under the codename 'CANLOAN'. They were attached for all purposes except pay, and given special numbers with the prefix CDN.

Six hundred and twenty-three Infantry Officers, together with fifty Ordnance Officers, whom the Royal Army Ordnance Corps were anxious to have, volunteered and served under the Scheme. The majority were junior officers, but captains were included on the basis of one for every seven subalterns. Some officers with higher ranks reverted and some from other arms of the service transferred to Infantry, attracted by the chance of early action.

In the spring of 1944 volunteers were interviewed by a special selection board, and on acceptance were sent to the Special Officers' Training Centre, Sussex, New Brunswick, where they underwent a short refresher course while the necessary preparations for overseas service were completed. During this phase they were under the command of Brigadier Milton F. Gregg, VC, MC, who, because of his continued keen interest in the welfare of all CANLOAN, is regarded as their Colonel-in-Chief and became Honorary President of the postwar CANLOAN Army Officers' Association. They proceeded overseas in drafts of from fifty to two hundred, the first draft arriving on 7 April 1944. They were immediately posted to British Regiments, as far as possible to the Regiment to which their Canadian Regiment was affiliated.

A total of 39 CANLOAN officers served with 3rd Division during 1944-45. Their names, awards and units are as follows:

Captain Francis F. Andrew, 1st KOSB;
Captain William J. Ayers (MID), 1st Suffolk;
Lieutenant Lorne W. Ballance, 2nd East Yorkshire;
Lieutenant Albert H. Blackmore, 1st KOSB;
Lieutenant Norman A. Brown, 2nd East Yorkshire
 — died of wounds 14.8.44;
Captain Ralph M. Brown, 1st Suffolk;
Lieutenant Willard S. Caseley, 1st KOSB
 — killed in action 6.8.44;
Lieutenant Lawrence Cohen, 2nd Royal Warwickshire;
Lieutenant Alfred R. Cope, 1st South Lancashire
 — killed in action 18.9.44;

Lieutenant David E. Edwards, 1st South Lancashire
 — killed in action 27.6.44;
Captain Reginald F. Fendick, 2nd Middlesex;
Captain James R. Fetterley, MC, 2nd East Yorkshire;
Lieutenant Richard C. Fox, 2nd Royal Warwickshire;
Lieutenant Melville A. Guidotti, 2nd East Yorkshire;
Lieutenant Gerald D. Hebb MC, 2nd East Yorkshire;
Captain Harold J. Hihn, *Croix de Guerre,* 2nd Royal
 Ulster Rifles;
Captain Lloyd M. Huggan, 1st KOSB;
Lieutenant Harry F. Hughes, 1st South Lancashire
 — died of wounds 28.6.44;
Lieutenant Robert E. Inman, 2nd East Yorkshire;
Lieutenant Lawrence P. Kane, 1st KOSB;
Lieutenant Robert J. Keast, 2nd Royal Warwickshire;
 — killed in action 24.9.44;
Captain Sydney A. Kemsley, 1st Royal Norfolk/2nd
 Royal Warwickshire;
Lieutenant Laurent Laperriere, 2nd East Yorkshire;
Lieutenant John A. Laurie, MC, 1st Royal Norfolk
 — killed in action 16.4.45;
Lieutenant Francis A. McConaghy, 2nd Middlesex;
Captain James A. McGregor, 2nd East Yorkshire
 — killed in action 7.6.44
Lieutenant John C. Midwinter, 1st Suffolk;
Lieutenant Melbourne H. Neily, 2nd East Yorkshire;
Lieutenant Donald J. Oland, 2nd Royal Warwickshire;
Lieutenant Leonard V. Pattison, 1st KOSB;
Captain Walter A. Pilchar, 1st South Lancashire;
Lieutenant Stirling A. Reid, 2nd East Yorkshire
 — killed in action 13.7.44;
Captain Leonard B. Robertson, MC, 2nd East Yorkshire;
Lieutenant Robert Robertson, 1st KOSB;
Lieutenant Malcolm R. Rose, 1st KOSB
 — killed in action 6.8.44;
Captain Montague L. Tyrwhitt-Drake, 2nd East
 Yorkshire/HQ 8 Brigade;
Lieutenant Ritchie Walker, MC, 1st KOSB;
Lieutenant Kenneth J. Wilson, 1st Royal Norfolk;
Captain Allister M. Young, 1st KOSB.

These officers fought with distinction with 3rd Division throughout the North West European campaign, and quickly developed an intense regimental and divisional loyalty. In addition to those who lost their lives many were wounded, and this led to the formation of the CANLOAN Association. Colonel Rex Fendick writes: 'We served in most units of the Division's infantry, some being knocked out before others joined as reinforcements, thus few knew one another during the campaign. Our association was born with a small group who found themselves in hospital together in Colchester and was consolidated at home with reunions, first very ad hoc and then more organised, when we realised that we shared the common experience of British Service, and had relatively little in common with Canadian veterans.'

In June 1974 CANLOAN held its 7th National Reunion and celebrated the 30th Anniversary of D-Day. They invited Colonel Bill Renison of the East Yorkshires, accompanied by Mrs Renison, to represent the British officers of 3rd Division, 1944-45. The Renisons will never forget the warmth of the reception they received. As Bill Renison had no fewer than 12 CANLOANS under

Right: The CANLOAN National President, Lorne Ballance, who served in 3 Div with the East Yorkshires, presents a scroll bearing the Divisional insignia of 673 CANLOAN Officers to Ralph Manning of the National War Museum, Ottawa, in 1972. */Canadian Forces Photo*

Below: The 3rd Divisional Club, Luc-Sur-Mer. The club's amenities were greatly appreciated by units in the very short periods spent out of the line, and it followed close behind the Division throughout the advance across North West Europe./*Imperial War Museum*

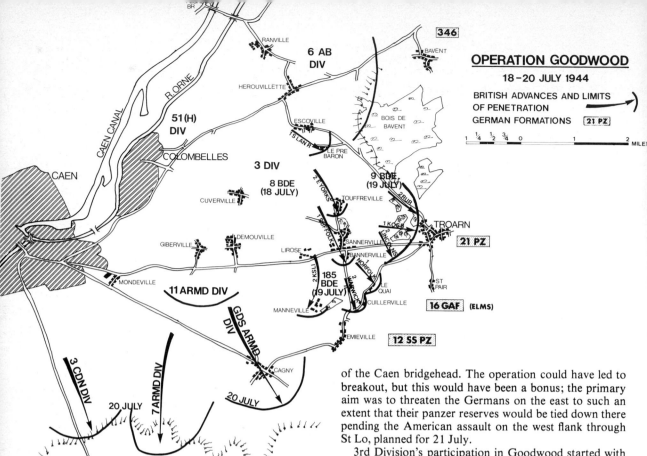

OPERATION GOODWOOD
18–20 JULY 1944

BRITISH ADVANCES AND LIMITS
OF PENETRATION
GERMAN FORMATIONS `21 PZ`

his command, his attendance was particularly appropriate. The CANLOAN Association, whose President, Lorne Balance, also served with the East Yorkshires is still very active and in Rex Fendick's words: 'the ones who are left are just as proud as ever of 3 Div and our Regiments'.

Operation Goodwood

After 8 Brigade's capture of La Londe 3rd Division continued patrolling vigorously until 7 July, when 450 Allied bombers struck Caen, pulverising the city and its approaches. Next day 185 Brigade advanced and took Lebisey — the scene of their repulse on 7 June — with little trouble. At dawn on 9 July 9 Brigade passed through and by midday had occupied all of Caen north of the Orne. Montgomery was now ready to launch a further offensive aimed at drawing in the last of the enemy's armoured reserves. The plan for Operation Goodwood was for 8th Corps with three armoured divisions (Guards, 7th and 11th) to move east across the Orne into the bridgehead held by 51st Highland and 6th Airborne Divisions, and on 18 July thrust southwards to Bourguebus and Vimot. 3rd Division was to protect the left flank and 3rd Canadian Division was to push south from Caen on the right. At the time there was considerable misunderstanding concerning the concept of Goodwood, the Press and certain members of Eisenhower's staff thinking that the aim was to break out

of the Caen bridgehead. The operation could have led to breakout, but this would have been a bonus; the primary aim was to threaten the Germans on the east to such an extent that their panzer reserves would be tied down there pending the American assault on the west flank through St Lo, planned for 21 July.

3rd Division's participation in Goodwood started with the artillery contributing to the Army fire plan on a scale of 750 rounds per gun. The area to the east of the Orne was already familiar to the gunners, as they were able to cover the front of 6th Airborne and 51st Highland Divisions and had already helped break up a number of enemy attacks. The fire plan for Goodwood was complementary to a massive aerial bombardment on the enemy who, under Rommel's direction, had formed a deep defensive zone manned by three infantry and two panzer divisions.

As the three British armoured divisions struggled to deploy in the restricted area east of the Orne, 3rd Division set off to secure its objectives, a complex of villages forming the triangle Touffreville-Manneville-Troarn. 8 Brigade was in the lead, and by late afternoon on 18 July had seized all its objectives. The South Lancashires and Suffolks were able to deal relatively easily with an enemy dazed and decimated by bombing but the East Yorkshires had to fight hard to secure Touffreville, which by chance had been missed by much of the air strike. 185 Brigade then pushed on south for Manneville. The KSLI, mounted on Shermans of the Staffordshire Yeomanry, took Lirose after a sharp fight, but a brigade attack on Manneville by the Warwicks and Norfolks was held up by a very determined enemy 200 yards short of the objective. The following morning they took it and repulsed a panzer counter-attack.

Already imprinted on the memory of each brigade was the name of a particular location where fighting had been singularly bitter. 8 Brigade remembered La Londe; 9 Brigade, Cambes; and 185 Brigade, Lebisey. Now 9 Brigade was to add Troarn to its list. By 19 July the

Germans had come to terms with the Allies' habit of preceding their attacks with saturation bombardment, so enemy tactics were to hold the forward positions thinly until the bombardment finished, when Tiger and Panther tanks and panzer grenadiers would hurry forward to occupy the position in strength. This is what 9 Brigade found at Troarn, which the enemy regarded as a key position, with determined infantry of both 21st Panzer and 16th GAF Divisions supported by tanks now holding it. By evening the Ulster Rifles had fought their way to within a mile of the centre of the village, with the Borderers moving up on their right. However next day when they returned to the attack they found the enemy contesting every yard and counter-attacking violently when given the opportunity. Troarn church provided the Germans with an excellent observation post; the Ulster Rifles fought their way up to it but were unable to secure the centre of the village and had to consolidate on its western fringe. On the extreme right the Lincolns mounted a costly attack to divert pressure, but by last light the brigade was still 800 yards from the centre of the objective, and the weary, grimy infantry dug in amidst a welter of shelling, mortaring and sniping.

20 July dawned with Troarn still to be taken, but 9 Brigade was ordered to consolidate where it was. Though the village itself had not been secured, the ground that 3 Div had seized was sufficient to protect the left flank of 8th Corps' corridor. But that day the rain poured down, and the British armoured assault slowed to a halt on Bourguebous Ridge, cut short by a combination of German anti-tank defence and the weather. If the achievement of Goodwood is questioned, the answer is provided by the Germans themselves, for by 25 July they had concentrated 645 tanks against the British sector, compared with 190 facing the Americans.

3rd Division spent a further 11 days holding the flank and confronting the enemy in Emieville and Troarn. It was a grim existence, subjected constantly to counter-attacks, shelling, and *Nebelwerfer* multi-barrelled mortars, living in ground reduced to quagmire by rain and shellfire, and with units seriously weakened by casualties. The Germans fought hard and skilfully, and it was remarked that they also fought cleanly. On one occasion they helped a Borderer's stretcher-bearer find his wounded, and on 23 July both sides held their fire while British and German soldiers collected their dead from No Man's Land. These 11 days of close contact under appalling conditions were some of the most trying of the Normandy Campaign. Officers ran a particular risk from the attentions of German snipers. Lt-Col Douglas Wilson had assumed command of the Lincolns on 20 July and when the time eventually came for 3 Div to be relieved, he recalls that the CO of the battalion taking over was killed by a sniper's bullet while standing beside him.

On 31 July the Division was relieved and moved back across the Orne to take part in the breakout from Normandy bridgehead. So ended eight weeks of gruelling fighting since D-Day, during which the infantry brigades of 3rd Division had been out of contact for only seven days. It had been a period when the spirit and skill of the infantry soldier had been employed and tested under classic conditions.

Normandy: the Breakout

On 25 July Bradley launched the 1st US Army offensive, Operation Cobra, and by 30 July had taken Avranches. Montgomery appreciated that the Germans would swing back pivoting on the high ground between Caen and Vire, and he instructed Dempsey, commanding 2nd Army, to drive southwards to destroy this hinge (see page 94).

The armoured divisions of 8th Corps relieved from Goodwood were transferred to this sector; but as the country they were entering was 'Bocage', a maze of woodland, sunken lanes and small fields and ideal for infantry defence, 3rd Division joined 8th Corps to provide the assault infantry necessary to assist the armour. The Division was to advance on the axis Beny Bocage-Vaudry-Tinchebray-Flers with 11th Armoured Division on the left; on the right was 5th US Corps with whom 3 Div was to strike up a happy liaison and rivalry.

On 9 August the Division moved off with 185 Brigade left, 9 Brigade right, and 3rd Recce Regiment probing ahead and on the flanks, unleashed at last in its mobile role. By 11 August the Vire-Conde road had been reached, after sharp fighting through close country defended by remnants of two German parachute divisions. In 9 Brigade 1st KOSB found a determined enemy holding the river Alliere. After fighting their way across, the Borderers were counter-attacked but held on until a troop of 44th Royal Tanks were able to get over the river and drive the enemy off. On their left C Squadron of 3rd Recce Regiment worked two troops across and pushed boldly foward. They met an enemy parachute battalion and, although forced to pull back to the river after fierce fighting, the armoured car troop under Lieutenant Shelley held the bridgehead against repeated counter-attacks.

Further left 185 Brigade faced an equally active enemy. The Norfolks were in the process of relieving the 3rd Monmoths of 11th Armoured Division at Sourdevalle, when 10th Panzer Division counter-attacked. The combined British force, nicknamed the 'Normons', beat the enemy off and it was during this battle that 3rd Division's first VC of World War II was won by Corporal Sidney Bates of the Royal Norfolks, whose citation reads:

'The attack in strength by 10th SS Panzer Division near Sourdevalle started with a heavy and accurate artillery and mortar programme on the position which the enemy had, by this time, pin-pointed. Half an hour later the main attack developed and heavy machine-gun and mortar fire was concentrated on the point of junction of the two forward companies. Corporal Bates was commanding the right forward section of the left forward company which suffered some casualties, so he decided to move the remnants of his section to an alternative position whence he appreciated he could better counter the enemy thrust. However, the enemy wedge grew still deeper, until there was about 50 to 60 Germans, supported by machine-guns and mortars, in the area occupied by the section.

'Seeing that the situation was becoming desperate, Corporal Bates then seized a light machine-gun and charged the enemy, moving forward through a hail of bullets and splinters and firing the gun from his hip. He was almost immediately wounded by machine-gun fire and fell to the ground, but recovering himself quickly, he got up and continued advancing towards the enemy, spraying bullets from his gun as he went. His action was now having effect on the enemy riflemen and machine-gunners, but mortar bombs continued to fall around him.

'He was then hit a second time, and much more seriously and painfully wounded. Undaunted, he staggered once more to his feet and continued towards the enemy, who were now seemingly nonplussed at their inability to check him. His constant firing continued until the enemy started to withdraw before him. At this moment he was hit for the third time by mortar-bomb splinters and sustained a wound that was to prove fatal. He fell to the ground but continued to fire his weapon until his strength failed him. This was not, however, until the enemy had withdrawn and the situation in this locality had been restored.'

Sidney Bates died of his wounds two days later.

By 11 August the enemy's defence was weakening. 'Bolo' Whistler told Brigadier Cass of 8 Brigade to press on down the axis of the main Vire-Tinchebray-Flers road the following day with 3rd Recce Regiment leading. At 7pm that night Cass was giving out his orders when a stray shell wounded nearly every member of the 'O' Group other than himself. His simple reaction — 'Send for the Seconds-in-Command' — was admired for its sang froid as well as its expediency. From 12 to 18 August 8 Brigade and 3rd Recce pushed ahead quickly towards Flers, but the enemy showed that he could still fight for on 13 August B Company of the Suffolks lost all three platoon commanders, the CSM, and a platoon sergeant, killed by enemy defensive fire. However resistance was crumbling and on 15 August C Squadron of 3rd Recce Regiment entered Tinchebray ten minutes ahead of their rivals, the US 102nd Mechanised Cavalry. That night the East Yorkshires and South Lancashires crossed the river Noireau, and next morning the Suffolks and 3rd Recce resumed the pursuit. Most of the enemy encountered were willing to surrender and at midday 16 August C Squadron of 3rd Recce occupied Flers. The divisional intelligence summary recorded: 'A rare honour has this day fallen to the Division. It has captured a town ahead of the BBC'.

Below: Brigadier E. E. E. 'Copper' Cass CBE, DSO, MC, (late KOYLI), Commander 8 Brigade, is decorated with the US Silver Star by General Omar Bradley, commanding 1st US Army. */Imperial War Musuem*

8.
Victory in the West

Right: The Distinguished Conduct Medal. Awarded to Warrant
Officers, NCOs and Soldiers for bravery in the field.

'Follow the Sapper' 17 Fd. Coy. R.E.
Venrai, October, 1944.

Right: General 'Bolo' Whistler in characteristic form with the Staff of Headquarters 1st Corps. Left to right: Brigadier Gerald Mears (CCRA, formerly CRA 3 Div), Brigadier 'Nipper' Pike (CE), Brigadier Philip Balfour (Chief of Staff) and Brigadier Joe Childs (CSO). Photograph taken early in 1945./*Lady Whistler*

THE LOW COUNTRIES AND RHINELAND

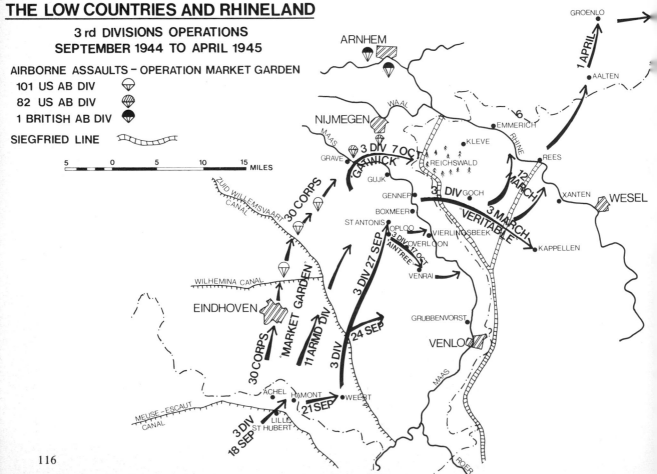

3rd DIVISIONS OPERATIONS
SEPTEMBER 1944 TO APRIL 1945

AIRBORNE ASSAULTS – OPERATION MARKET GARDEN

101 US AB DIV

82 US AB DIV

1 BRITISH AB DIV

SIEGFRIED LINE

5   0   5   10   15 MILES

After capturing Flers 3rd Division halted with the remainder of 8th Corps, while other formations continued the pursuit of the defeated enemy. Then on 3 September the Division moved to a concentration area at St Andelys, 50 miles north-west of Paris, where it was to train and refit in readiness for Montgomery's intended narrow but concentrated thrust into the Low Countries and Northern Germany.

3 Div had been continuously engaged in operations for 10 weeks following the D-Day landings, and the task of refitting facing the Division's administrative services was a particularly heavy one. The RAOC and REME set to making good the damage and losses of the Normandy battles, 10 vehicles a day being overhauled in each field workshop. Improvisation enabled inventive skills to flourish; German tanks were converted to armoured recovery vehicles, mortars were mounted inside 3rd Recce Regiment's half-tracks, and the CREME, Lt-Col Biggs, made the most of a visit to Paris by obtaining a large quantity of canvas for penthouses. The RASC Column was under extreme pressure as the Division was providing 14 transport platoons for third line duties, moving 120,000 gallons of fuel per day from the Maintenance Area at Bayeux to a forward 'Army Cushion' at Arras, a distance of 220 miles. Their drivers, two to each vehicle, kept this up for three weeks, during which they had only one major traffic accident. On 10 September a major logistic problem arose when the Division was warned for a 300-mile move forward which was to start within six days. This move would require over 40,000 gallons of petrol, but only 7,000 gallons were readily available, and the vehicles that would normally collect the balance were committed to the 'Bayeux Bash'. Accordingly 'Gadforce' was formed, under Captain Gadsby of the Divisional RASC, to collect the petrol from Bayeux. Lt-Col Yapp, the CRASC, described 'Gadforce' as the most unusual collection ever, consisting of stripped down office, workshop and stores lorries and captured German vehicles. Each towed a trailer, many of very unorthodox design, and drivers were found from headquarters clerks, batmen, and sanitary men. The result of their 24-hour foray to Bayeux was 40,000 gallons of fuel, without a single accident.

The reason for the move was that 3 Div was required to take part in Operation Market Garden in Holland. The Division was ordered to take with it four days' rations and a very large quantity of gun and small arms ammunition. In theory the quantity of combat supplies was far in excess of the lift available, which included eight extra transport platoons. However by overloading every vehicle by one ton, by using 25-pounder ammunition boxes as seats, and by devious other means, the equivalent of 660 3-ton loads were moved forward.

The prospect of action after a month's inactivity was welcomed by General 'Bolo', for a fortnight earlier he had recorded: 'It is almost unbelievable to be out of the battle to this extent. It feels hundreds of miles away . . . I cannot see the soldiers being anything but restive before very long'. However on 15 September he was able to say: 'We are off again, after what was a very long pause but now feels to have been a short one. The battalions are in very fine order indeed. I have never seen better men anywhere.

Well-seasoned, strong looking and very determined. I expect them to give a very good account of themselves.'

The admiration was clearly mutual for Lt-Col Tom Evill, who was CRE in the latter part of the campaign described his GOC as:
'A tall, scornful General with a twinkle in his eye, who knows more about fighting in this war than anyone I had previously met. 3 Div was a wonderful team of which to be a member, with everyone devoted to the master. I saw an infantry battalion on its way into battle. They were resting on both sides of the road when Bolo came back from the sharp end. He was driving himself, flag flying and his hat, as usual, on the back of his head. Every man stood up and waved to him as he went past, laughing and waving in reply.'

Operation Market Garden

The concept of this operation was to lay a carpet of airborne troops from Eindhoven to Arnhem, seize bridges over the major waterways and thus open the route into North Germany. This ambitious idea was Montgomery's, approved by Eisenhower, and it offered the possibility of ending the war by Christmas. Success depended on the early relief of the airborne divisions by Horrocks' 30th Corps, whose armoured divisions would thrust straight up the axis, protected on the right flank by 8th Corps, consisting of 11th Armoured Division and 3rd Division.

The airborne assault and 30th Corps advance was launched on 17 September, and next day 3rd Division's flank advance started with an assault crossing of the Meuse-Escaut canal by 9 Brigade, which had arrived in the area only 24 hours earlier. Major Glyn Gilbert (who was to command the Division 28 years later) was OC C Company of the Lincolns, and he remembers the operation well:
'At 16.30 hours on the 18 September, in an Assembly Area about 2½ miles south of the Escaut Canal, I had just received a warning order that we would be carrying out an assault crossing of the Canal at midnight that night; this came as a bit of a surprise as we had previously been told that the crossing would be on the following night. However, there it was, and we obviously had to get a move on.

'As the COs 'O' Group was not for another hour, I decided to do a quick reconnaissance of the canal and so I hopped in my jeep, went forward into Lille St Hubert, got into a house and had a brief look. The canal seemed to be about 40 yards wide and contained between banks, which were about 10 feet high on the near side with a concrete wall of about 4-6 feet sloping into the water. It was obviously going to be a brute to cross, and the handling of assault boats would present all sorts of problems. There was no sign of the enemy. On my return I just had time to call in at the company on my way to orders, and found the assault boats had arrived. A few quick instructions to George Bennett, my second-in-command, on 'dry' boating practice, and I was on my way. The CO completed his 'O' Group in under the hour, and I recall well the importance he placed on speed in relation to Market Garden. I then returned to find the Company embarked in the middle of a field lustily paddling and singing *The Volga Boatmen*.

'At this stage a word or two about C Company might not come amiss. There were about forty of us who had survived the fighting in Normandy from D-Day, and the remainder, including the other three officers, had arrived as reinforcements during the past fortnight, and so for many their first action was to be one of the most difficult of all, namely the opposed crossing of a water obstacle at night.

'The company 'O' Group was waiting, and I just managed to give the group a quick look at the Canal. We were to be the left hand assault company and the battalion was on the right of 2nd Royal Ulster Rifles with 1st Kings Own Scottish Borderers in reserve.

'My 'O' Group was followed by platoon orders, a meal and the collection of the boats by carrying parties from the Borderers. There was no time for section commanders to be shown the ground. By 23.50 hours we had moved forward, reclaimed and erected our boats, and were snug in the FUP immediately under the near bank. No sign of the enemy and so far so good.

'As so often happens in quick actions of this sort, we knew nothing about the opposition, except that they were there! I therefore selected four features within the Company objective which I reckon I would have held if I had been the enemy, and gave one to each platoon, and one to Company HQ which operated as a fighting sub-unit and not just a Command HQ. Sub-units were to make their own way independently to their objectives; there was to be no forming up on the far bank, the emphasis being on speed of crossing and exploitation. The one place not to be was in the area of the canal itself.

'Promptly at midnight that superb weapon, 3rd Division Artillery, came into action with concentrations on all suspected enemy locations, and up the bank we scrambled lugging our boats and easing them down the steep slope into the water. I thanked our lucky stars we had made sure they could be secured fore and aft and held beam on to the bank so that we could slide down and embark over the sides and not over the bows.

'In the meantime the enemy response had been immediate and fierce. Very heavy mortar fire opened up directed at the canal and village, and several machine-guns and a 20mm were firing on fixed lines down the canal. We immediately suffered heavy casualties crossing the bank, but once in the water the small arms fire was high, although there was no shortage of mortar bombs bursting around the boats, and the one on my right received a direct hit. The speed of the crossing would have done credit to Oxford and Cambridge, and in a matter of minutes we were across and over the far bank, leaving two sunken boats and many killed and wounded in the canal and on the banks.

'Without a pause platoons pressed on and took their objectives, which in the event were all held by the enemy. Privates Stell and Ollerenshaw the company signallers were told to report that C Company had seized its objective, but pointed out fairly sharply that the 18 Set had two bullet holes through it; however up went the confirmatory Very lights and that was that.

'The cost was heavy. George Bennett was badly wounded with most of his jaw shot off. Peter London and Denis Querky, the two platoon commanders, were dead and there were over 70 NCOs and men killed and wounded, mostly by small arms fire. Fortunately the third platoon commander, Sergeant Goddard, survived. The Germans had fought a good action at little loss to themselves, by employing small numbers of determined infantry armed with a high proportion of well-sited automatic weapons and well supported by mortars.'

Left: Soldiers of the South Lancashires (8 Brigade) examining a captured enemy sub-machine-gun during the advance into Holland./*Imperial War Museum*

Right: A platoon of the Royal Warwicks (185 Brigade) taking a few minutes rest during the advance to the Rhineland. /*Imperial War Museum*

By 10am that morning the Lincolns and Ulster Rifles had cleared the far bank of enemy, and immediately 246 and 17 Field Companies, RE started building a Class 9 and a Class 40 bridge respectively, their recce officers having already crossed with the assault companies. Despite casualties from mortaring and sniping, the sappers carried out their traditional work under the most traditional conditions — bridging under fire, waist deep in water, on a raw, dark night. The Class 9 was open at 7am and the Class 40 by 5pm, and for their efforts 17 Field Company received the personal congratulations of the Army Commander, General Dempsey.

8 Brigade crossed on 9 Brigade's right on the afternoon of 19 September and they also met stiff resistance. A company of the East Yorkshires found a group of SS officer cadets fiercely contesting a wood, apparently there to gain battle experience. 'See they get it' the company commander was told by his CO, and next morning 32 officer cadets surrendered.

On 20 September the KOSB and Suffolks pushed forward to Achel and Hamont. Enemy resistance was light, the welcome from the inhabitants overwhelming. A touching feature of the liberation of Hamont was the assembly of the entire population for the funeral of Private Hollis of the Suffolks, the only soldier killed that morning. He was buried with full civic honours, his coffin draped with the Belgian flag and covered with flowers. Next day 8 Brigade crossed the Dutch frontier, pushing east across the sandy wastes of Boshover Heide to seize Weert, where the Suffolks received a tremendous reception from the inhabitants. Thereafter, 3rd Division extended its front northwards, and by 27 September had reached St Antonis. However by then, 1st Airborne Division's epic battle at Arnhem, the Bridge too Far, had been fought to a finish, and the survivors withdrawn.

The Allied forces now retained a narrow corridor over the Maas as far as Nijmegen, with the US 82nd Airborne Division holding the eastern flank, against which the enemy launched violent counter-attacks from the Reischswald forest. Operation Gatwick was therefore mounted to clear the Reichswald, with 8th Corps crossing the Maas at Grave and turning east, and on 1 October 3 Div relieved the US 82nd Airborne. The congestion was extreme, with three British divisions being compressed into a seven-mile front. However after four days' vigorous patrolling up to the German frontier during which 3rd Division lost 10 officers and 80 soldiers, Whistler was told that Gatwick was to be called off as it would absorb too many troops. There were few members of the Division who did not welcome the news, for the Reichswald was a grim, dark, cold quagmire of a forest infested by a determined enemy fighting from prepared positions in the Siegfried Line. The Division came back over the Maas, and on 9 October concentrated in the St Antonis-Oploo area, and was immediately committed to a new operation. For the previous week the US 7th Armoured Division had been trying to clear a German pocket west of the Maas which included Overloon and Venrai, but had failed and had suffered over 450 battle casualties. 3 Div was now committed to this daunting task and the US 7th Armoured was withdrawn and moved south. Within nine days 3rd Division would be in possession of Overloon and Venrai having suffered three times the casualties of 7th Armoured.

The Liberation of Overloon and Venrai

3rd Division's task, nicknamed Aintree, was to attack south-east from Oploo, seize Overloon and Venrai, and thus draw in enemy reserves while 8th Corps cleared the remainder of the pocket.

The countryside was flat and suited the defence — thick pine woods and marshy ground with the Molen Beek flowing across it. It was clearly to be another close-quarter infantry slogging match. To make matters worse the rain poured down chilling Bolo's 'seasoned, strong-looking and determined' soldiers to the bone. In support the Division welcomed the 6th Guards Tank Brigade (4th Tank Battalions, Grenadier and Coldstream Guards), and to supplement the Divisional artillery, it was allotted the fire of the guns of 11th Armoured and 15th (Scottish) Divisions, of 8th AGRA (four medium regiments, one heavy regiment and one heavy anti-aircraft regiment), and the rockets and bombs of two wings of Typhoon ground-attack aircraft; and when 8 Brigade crossed the start line it was supported by every Vickers gun of 2nd Middlesex, firing as a battalion and with their 4.2in mortars adding to the artillery fire plan. The Middlesex fired 300,000 rounds of Mark VII Z and 3,800 mortar bombs on the first day alone.

8 Brigade captured Overloon on 12 October, and on the following day 185 Brigade cleared the pine woods to the south-east, while 9 Brigade fought through those to the south-west. Throughout these first two days the infantry and their supporting tanks faced an enemy who contested every inch of ground. In the small wood north of Overloon D Company of the East Yorkshires lost all its officers, the CSM, and several NCOs, and at one stage a corporal was acting as company commander. In the woods south-west of Overloon two junior NCOs of the KOSB distinguished themselves when their company was held up by crossfire. L Cpl Harmon stalked two Spandau posts in succession, killing the crews with grenades and sub-machine-gun fire. Then when Cpl Forrest saw an enemy section preparing to ambush one of the supporting Churchills, he ran forward, killed two enemy with his Sten, tracked the remainder to their foxholes and took them prisoner.

OPERATION AINTREE

THE LIBERATION OF OVERLOON AND VENRAI BY 3rd DIVISION 12 – 17 OCT 1944

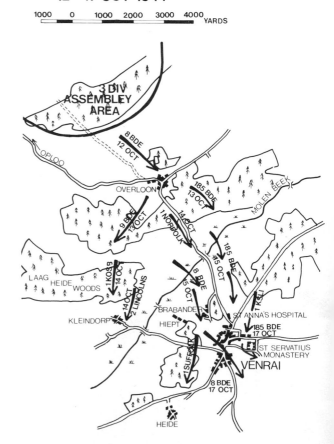

Above left: A Vickers detachment of 2nd Middlesex supporting the
8 Brigade attack on Overloon, 12 October 1944./*Imperial War Museum*

Above: A Churchill tank of 4th Tank Battalion, Grenadier Guards,
forming up with 1st Suffolk for the assault on Venrai.
/*Imperial War Museum*

On 14 October the Borderers went on to clear Laage
Heide Wood followed up by the Lincolns who fought
their way forward through heavy fire to Kleindorp, losing
two company commanders and suffering many other
casualties in the process. Their Commanding Officer, Lt-
Col Cecil Firbank, led the battalion in person, directing
and encouraging his men, and at times engaging the
enemy with his Sten. In the centre, the Norfolks pushed
up the axis of the Venrai road under continual artillery
fire directed from an OP in Venrai church, but after seven
Typhoon strikes the troublesome church started to burn,
and by the end of the day the battalion had consolidated
400 yards short of the Molen Beek.

This waterway was a more formidable obstacle than
appeared on the map, for although the water gap was
only 10 feet wide there were high sloping banks producing
a physical gap of 25 feet. The approaches crossed an
almost impassable bog, thickly sown with mines, and the
roads and tracks to Venrai had been broken up and
cratered. Whistler appreciated that crossing the Beek
would necessitate a two brigade operation, in which the
sappers under their CRE, Lt-Col 'Tiger' Urquart, would
play a major part. In addition to his Divisional companies
the CRE had AVREs of 617 Assault Squadron and Flail
tanks of the Westminster Dragoons under command. To
establish tank crossings two small box girder bridges were
quickly mounted on Churchill AVREs, and 210 feet of
floating Kapok bridging was obtained for the infantry.
The assault crossing was to be made with two battalions
'up' in each of 185 and 8 Brigades — from left to right

the Royal Norfolks, the Royal Warwicks, the Suffolks
and the East Yorkshires. 4th Tank Battalion Coldstream
Guards was to support 185 Brigade, and 4th Tank
Battalion Grenadier Guards 8 Brigade. That night orders
were issued in pitch darkness and pouring rain, platoon
and section commanders briefing their men as best they
could by torch under ground sheets, and little sleep was
possible as preparations for the complicated assault
crossing went ahead. The final loads of Kapok bridging
did not arrive forward until 4.20am, 40 minutes before H-
hour.

The assault on the left went well, against an enemy
obviously taken by surprise. The Norfolks and Warwicks
crossed the Beek on the Kapok bridges quickly, and beat
off a small counter-attack. However, 8 Brigade on the
right was not so fortunate. The infantry met heavy
crossfire and the COs of both the Suffolks and East
Yorkshires were wounded. The sappers had a particularly
gruelling time as under heavy fire and appalling ground
conditions, they brought up the box girder bridges and
fascines (large bundles of brushwood for gap filling) to
provide the tank crossings. Sergeant Finan of 617 Assault
Squadron drove his AVRE with girder bridge delicately
balanced in front down to the Beek, but found that the
release mechanism had been damaged by fire. One of his
crew climbed on his shoulders and released the bridge by
hand, dropping it neatly into position, and thus providing
the only tank bridge across the Beek for 24 hours. Over
went two troops of the Coldstream, but the bridge started
to collapse. More gallant work by the sappers using logs
resulted in a serviceable repair, enabling the rest of the
squadron to cross. Throughout the day in drenching rain
both brigades battled their way forward. By nightfall the
Suffolks were in Hiept, with the East Yorkshires between
them and the Norfolks in Brabander. Further left the
Warwicks fought they way into St Anna's hospital,
finding it to be a female lunatic asylum. A garbled radio

message from the Warwicks' FOO referring to 'two thousand bad women' caused speculation on the gunner net.

The leading brigades had now closed up to Venrai, which was strongly defended by a fresh German battalion rushed up from reserve. Meanwhile at the Beek the Sappers and REME recovery teams struggled under continual shelling to improve routes forward and that evening two further bridges were completed. The final assault on Venrai went in on 17 October. The KSLI led on the left, through thick minefields supported by tanks of the Coldstream. Here the battalion's Pioneer Platoon Commander, Lieutenant Aldridge, won the MC for personally prodding for mines under heavy shellfire and then leading the tanks forward. Colonel Thornycroft of the KSLI remembers Bert Aldridge as a 'superb character, commissioned in the field after having been pioneer sergeant for years. He was killed shortly after being awarded his MC — a sad loss, definitely one of the personalities of the battalion'. On the right the East Yorkshires entered the town and started house clearing while the Suffolks combed the woods to the west. The following day the South Lancashires, under cover of a 'Victor' shoot (every gun in range), passed through the East Yorkshires, and the operation was completed when the Warwicks secured the monastry of St Servatius.

Aintree was an operation in which the very special characteristics and capabilities of a British Infantry Division had been demonstrated to the full. For six cold, soaking days the infantry of 3rd Division had fought through forest, swamp, minefields and buildings to defeat a determined enemy and take all objectives. Every battalion had been engaged, all had suffered; in officers alone the Division had lost three commanding officers, and sixteen company commanders. Guards tank crews, gunner OP parties and sappers had fought as one with the

rifle companies, and their support, together with that of the RAF, had been essential to the success of the operation. 3rd Division had fought many close and bloody battles since D-Day; the six days of Aintree were as testing as any.

The welcome given by the people of Holland to the Allied armies was universally enthusiastic, and the people of Overloon took the men of the 3rd Division to their hearts. After the war they erected a memorial to the dead of the Division, and General Whistler returned to be presented with the 'Overloon Plate', which is now in the possession of Lady Whistler.

Winter on the Maas

During the month following the capture of Venrai, 3rd Division held the Maas from Gujk to Vierlingsbeek, from where the line swung south to rest on Venrai. The Division was in constant contact with the enemy, and it was a life of fighting patrols, minefield recces and shelling, in chilling rain and lashing gales. Fortunately one brigade at a time could be taken out of the line for a few days, as a welcome relief from flooded slit trenches, exhausting patrols and long periods on sentry. On 23 November intelligence indicated that the remaining enemy to the west of the Maas were pulling back, and the Division advanced its right flank to follow them up. In a series of sharp actions the KSLI, Suffolks and Ulster Rifles dislodged a determined enemy holding fortified buildings surrounded by flooded marshland. By 2 December the Division had cleared the west bank and taken over responsibility for the Maas from Boxmeer to Grubbenvorst, a front of nearly 20 miles.

A condition which can affect any soldier is 'battle exhaustion'. It is caused by fear, fatigue, shock or anxiety and now, in the wintry conditions on the Maas after months of hard fighting, it imposed a particular threat to

3rd Division's soldiers. Prevention of this sickness was the constant concern of every regimental, medical and staff officer, and although forward troops were thin on the ground, Whistler continued his policy of keeping one brigade at a time out of the line. The effectiveness of these measures can be judged by statistics. During the Division's six months on the Maas and in the Rhineland a total of 127 cases occurred, compared with 250 — a quarter of all wounded cases — during the eight days of Aintree.

The Division remained on the Maas until 5 February, with the routine of patrol and sentry being broken by a number of incidents. On 1 January the Germans 'celebrated' the New Year as part of the Ardennes offensive by attacking targets in Belgium with 800 aircraft, and 92nd Light Anti-Aircraft Regiment shot down 11 during their return journey. The following day the enemy counter-attacked across the Maas in 3rd Division's thinly held sector, and before they were thrown back, Lieutenant Baxter of the 2nd Middlesex won his MC and Pte Orme a GOC's Certificate for Gallantry, when their Mortar OP party of seven men beat off an enemy platoon during a 20-minute battle. An attack by the Suffolks on the same day is particularly remembered by Dick Goodwin as an example of how weather can affect operational plans. His battalion was

Above left: A Sapper field troop HQ of 3 Div Engineers moving through the outskirts of Venrai followed by a Flail tank of the Westminster Dragoons./*Imperial War Musuem*

Above: The 'Overloon Plate' presented to General Whistler after the war by the people of Overloon./*Lady Whistler*

Right: Commander 8th Corps congratulates 3 Div on Operation Aintree./*Lady Whistler*

SPECIAL ORDER OF THE DAY

BY

LT-GEN SIR RICHARD N. O'CONNOR, KCB,DSO,MC

Commander, 8 Corps

3rd British Division

    I would like to congratulate you all on the very fine performance you have put up during the recent operations against Venray.

    All of you have taken your share in this success, but I must particularly congratulate 185 Brigade on the magnificent performance of bridging the Beek north of Venray with all the elements against them.

    In this fighting you have shown grit and determination, and you have gained the knowledge that you are a better man than the enemy.

    It is probably the first action of a good many of you, and I feel that you have made a great start and have thereby gained my full confidence.

Lieutenant-General,
Commander, 8 Corps.

16th October, 1944.

Officers and soldiers of 3rd Division decorated for gallantry by Montgomery after operations in Belgium and Holland: *Top right: Front row:* left to right: Lt-Col Firbank DSO, Lincolns; Lt-Col Goodwin DSO, Suffolk; The GOC; The C-in-C; Brig Bols DSO, Comd 185 Bde; Major Bell MC, R Warwick. *Second row:* Lt Timbrell MC, Royals; Lt Bradstock MC, Royals; Lt Shaw MC, Royals; Lt Aldridge MC, KSLI; Lt Rourke MC, R Norfolk; Major Gilbert MC, Lincolns; Major Larkin MC, Lincolns; Major Clark MC, Lincolns. *Back Row:* Lt Bates MC, East Yorkshire; Captain Blaney MC, Middlesex; Captain Pacey MC, Lincolns; Major Crane MC, 92 LAA Regt RA; Lt Mavin MC, R Warwick. Three officers in this group — Lt-Col Goodwin, Lt-Col Firbank and Major Gilbert — became Commandants of the School of Infantry after the war. D Squadron of the Royal Dragoons, an armoured car regiment, operated under command of 3 Div during Market Garden./*Lady Whistler*

Centre right: Front Row: Gnr Miller MM, 7 Fd Regt RA: Cpl Harmon DCM, KOSB; the GOC; the C-in-C; CSM Leatherland DCM, Suffolk; CSM Hawley MM, Suffolk. *Second Row:* Cpl Carpenter MM, East Yorkshire; Tpr Kirwan MM, Royals; Pte Wooley MM, Lincolns; L Cpl Knight MM, South Lancashire; Sgt Finan MM, RE; L Cpl Clarke MM Suffolk; Cpl Tucker MM, Royals. *Back Row:* Cpl Forrest MM, KOSB: Pte Thomas MM, RAMC; L Cpl Green MM, RUR: Pte Everest MM, Suffolk; Unidentified Cpl, MM, RE./*Lady Whistler*

Left: Winter on the Maas — a Vickers detachment of 2nd Middlesex./*Lt-Col R. Fendick*

Left: In May 1940, during the retreat to Dunkirk, the drums of 1st Suffolk were left for safety in the homes of civilians at Roubaix. The French hid them in hat boxes in a factory. In December 1944 Lt-Col Goodwin sent a party under Capt Breach to recover the drums, which were then carried on Parade in Holland. Left to right: Drummer Day, Drummer Clark, Lt-Col Goodwin, RSM Tredini, L Cpl Hutchinson. Day, Clark and Hutchinson had all been members of the Corps of Drums in 1940 and RSM Tredini acted as Drum Major on the day of the parade./*Imperial War Museum*

Below: A welcome relief from winter on the Maas was the announcement that UK leave would start in January 1944. Members of 185 Brigade take part in the ballot for tickets./*Imperial War Museum*

mounted in Kangaroos (tanks converted to armoured personnel carriers) and before the attack Goodwin made a careful reconnaissance of the enemy's anti-tank minefield. Then before H-Hour it snowed — and all traces of the anti-tank mines disappeared. As fortune had it no mines exploded during the attack, although one went off when the Kangaroos reversed out after the infantry had dismounted.

On 5 February 3rd Division was relieved on the river by 52nd (Lowland) Division, having been in continual contact since the start of Aintree on 12 October. Eighteen days rest and training followed near Louvain, where the Division had fired its first shots of Hitler's war nearly five years earlier.

The Battle of the Rhineland

On 24th February 3rd Division crossed the Maas at Gennep to reinforce 30th Corps in Operation Veritable, which had been launched 14 days earlier with the aim of clearing the Rhineland. The Division entered the battle at Goch and was opposed by the 7th Parachute Regiment of 8th Parachute Division, one of eleven divisions facing the Allied offensive. It was tasked with punching through the Siegfried Line lay-back on the Xanten-Bonninghardt ridge to clear the way for a breakout by the Guards Armoured Division. For this operation 3 Div took under command its old friends, the 6th Guards Tank Brigade, plus a squadron each of Scorpion flail tanks, Crocodile flame-throwing tanks, and AVREs. Fire support included the divisional artillery of the Guards Armoured, 51st (Highland) and 53rd (Welsh) Divisions. Another dogged battle through close country thick with mines faced Bolo's men, hence the very generous allocation of supporting arms.

The axis of the assault followed sandy tracks through the wooded country south-east from Goch, taking the German paratroops by surprise, as they had expected the attack to come north-east from Weeze. Progress was therefore initially easier than in the battle for Venrai, with prisoners coming in fast, but before long resistance stiffened. The East Yorkshires were tasked with seizing

the bridge over the Muhlen Fleuth, and after hard fighting among farm buildings during the approach their CO, Colonel Bill Renison, takes up the story:
'I switched C Company under Reg Rutherford to take the bridge and in the face of heavy fire and across completely open ground they moved faster than I have ever seen troops move before. 'Sticky' Glew's platoon crossed the bridge unblown and at 1615hrs I received a signal from the Corps Commander, "Congratulations DONALD taken".

'I had moved Tac HQ up to Kampshof and was able to leave Burton Pirie my 76 Field Regiment battery commander in charge there, while I went over to Bussenhof to see how things were; unfortunately Laurens, my anti-tank platoon commander, was killed beside me on the way.

'For the moment all seemed quiet, but as darkness fell, Reg Rutherford reported movement in the woods on his

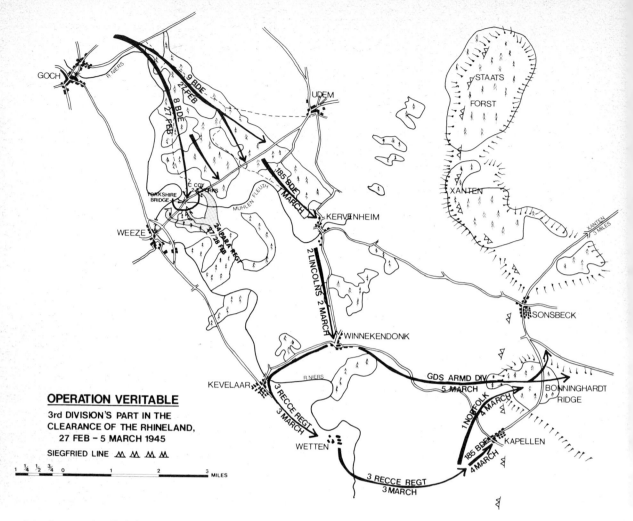

OPERATION VERITABLE

3rd DIVISION'S PART IN THE
CLEARANCE OF THE RHINELAND,
27 FEB – 5 MARCH 1945

SIEGFRIED LINE ⋀⋀ ⋀⋀ ⋀⋀ ⋀⋀

right front and called down the artillery SOS. This was the start of eight hours of counter-attacks on his company by paratroops and panzers. Soon he was almost out of small-arms ammunition; we discovered later that his carrier had been hit on the way up. His calls became more insistent and he was obliged to beg ammunition from his supporting arms, and at one stage we heard on the FOOs tank net "a hand will come through the hatch — fill it with .303."

'I went over to Bussenhof again and sent off B Company to reinforce C Company over the bridge on their right. Whilst there I heard the triumphant report "Bangers here". The ammunition had arrived, by courtesy of my second-in-command, 'Banger' King, who had broken through with his carrier.

'B Company got over the bridge as C Coy retracted their positions into the very cellars of Schaddenhof and the Gunners directed by John Ford, 76 Field's FOO, fired almost the whole of the Corps Artillery on the woods in front of C Company, and it was not until about 4 o'clock in the morning that the enemy counter-attacks started to subside. It had been what I think Wellington would have described as a 'close-run thing', but we had won and I suppose nothing will ever make me prouder than going round the battalion and reading General Bolo's personal

letter "Will you let all ranks know how moved' I have been by their very gallant action".

'It is difficult not to give C Company the lion's share of the credit, but it was a real battalion action with the greatest co-operation from all our supporting arms, whom we knew so well.'

As well as personally thanking C Company, Whistler ordered the sappers to erect a board on the bridge bearing the East Yorkshires' name and badge, and thereafter it was known as 'Yorkshire Bridge'.

The following day 185 Brigade assaulted Kervenheim, the KSLI on the left encountering bitter resistence. Private Stokes was with the leading section of 17 Platoon of Z Company, and the citation which earned him the posthumous award of the Victoria Cross read as follows:

'During the advance the platoon came under intense rifle and medium machine-gun fire from a farm building and was pinned down. The Platoon Commander began to reorganise the platoon when Private Stokes, without waiting for any orders, got up and, firing from the hip, dashed through the enemy fire and was seen to disappear inside the farm building. The enemy fire stopped and Private Stokes reappeared with twelve prisoners. During

Above: Private James Stokes, 2nd Bn, Kings Shropshire Light Infantry, winning the Victoria Cross at Kervenheim, 1 March 1945. Painted by Terence Cuneo, and reproduced by kind permission of the Regimental Trustees of the King's Shropshire Light Infantry. Painting photographed for this work by Studio 5, Richmond, North Yorkshire.

Lieutenant Banks comments on the battle as follows:
'Corporal Coles and Sergeant Evans were in the thick of things as soon as they reached the buildings; Corporal Coles was later awarded the MM for his part in the crossing of the Dortmund-Ems canal at Lingen, and was subsequently promoted Sergeant.

'The soldier who can just be seen apparently sitting left of the base of the concrete building was Private Field, who was well up front with us at that spot. He had been wounded soon after D-Day and had only recently rejoined the Battalion; regrettably he died from his wounds received at this point, doing as much as anyone to press home the attack.

'The Bren-gunner on Stokes's left, Private Devonport, was very badly wounded; he did extremely well and was still returning the enemy fire after he was wounded.'

The picture was painted by Terence Cuneo 'on location' in 1963, assisted by Major Read and Lieutenant Banks, Stokes's Company and Platoon commander respectively, and a party of soldiers from 1st KSLI, who were stationed in Munster and re-enacted the action. Mr Cuneo recalls that he found in a shop in Kervenheim a fly-blown photograph of the location, taken the day following the action and showing the scene exactly as it was. He was also able to talk to the widow of the German civilian who lies dead in the foreground, caught in cross-fire when he endeavoured to surrender.

Key:
A. Cpl Coles (Leading Section Commander)
B. Lt Banks (Platoon Commander)
C. Pte Field
D. Sgt Evans (Platoon Sergeant)
E. Pte Stokes
F. Pte Devonport (Bren-Gunner)

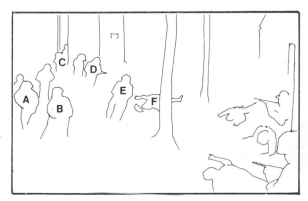

Above: Infantry of 185 Brigade mounted in Kangaroo APCs advance on Kervenheim, February 1945./*Imperial War Museum*

Above right: Through thick smoke, Bofors 2-pounder guns of 92nd Light Anti-aircraft Regiment RA bombard the east bank of the Rhine in support of 51st (Highland) Division./*Imperial War Museum*

this operation he was wounded in the neck. This action enabled the platoon to advance to the next objective and Private Stokes was ordered back to the Regimental Aid Post. He refused to go and continued to advance with his platoon.

'On approaching the second objective the platoon came under heavy fire from a house on the left. Again, without waiting for orders, Private Stokes rushed the house by himself, firing from the hip. He was seen to drop his rifle and fall to the ground wounded. However, a moment later he got to his feet again, picked up his rifle and continued to advance, despite the most intense fire. He entered the house and all firing from it ceased. He subsequently rejoined his platoon who, due to his gallantry, had been able to advance — bringing five more prisoners.

'At this stage the company was forming up for its final assault on the objective, which was a group of buildings, forming an enemy strong-point. Again, without waiting for orders Private Stokes, although now severely wounded and suffering from loss of blood, dashed on the remaining sixty yards to the objective, firing from the hip as he struggled through intense fire. He finally fell twenty yards from the enemy position, firing his rifle to the last, and as the company passed him in the final charge he raised his hand and shouted goodbye.'

The enemy paratroops holding Kervenheim fought suicidally. The Norfolks suffered heavily and an FOO from 7th Field Regiment, Captain George Haigh, took command of A Company which had lost all its officers. Eventually, with the help of the Lincolns from 9 Brigade, the town fell late that night. Next day the Lincolns, supported by tanks of the Scots Guards, went on to capture Winnekendonk, and on 3 and 4 March, 3rd Recce Regiment, followed by 185 Brigade, exploited to

Wetten, Kappellen and the Bonninghardt Ridge. German resistance had been broken, and on 5 March the Guards Armoured Division passed through the breach in the Siegfried Line created by 3rd Division's resolute fighting.

On the 12 March the Division closed up to the Rhine between Emmerich and Xanten. Spring was in the air, and with the feeling that the enemy were thoroughly beaten, 'Bolo' Whistler was able to record in his diary:

'It seems the hell of a long time since 24 February. I would say we have had our most successful battle. Down difficult country — centre line non-existent or on a mud track — yet we have done everything asked. We have captured 1,200 prisoners, nearly all paratroopers. We must have killed and wounded many more — I would say 9 Brigade under Denny have done best; 185 Brigade next under Mark Matthews. 8 Brigade have not had so much luck though E Yorks had a terrific night holding a bridgehead against repeated counter-attacks. The 7.2in Howitzer Mark VI which was only fifty feet from my caravan fired all night and the harassing fire of the field guns firing just over my tactical HQ was really a bit much.

'Where all have done well it is difficult to single out any, but the Gunners have been first-class as usual under Gerald (Mears) — the Sappers ditto under Tom Evill. The RASC, under the most trying conditions have kept us topped up with ammunition (and we have certainly shot off a bit!) — The Lincolns under Cecil Firbank are

probably the best battalion in the division. They have had hard fighting as any and have been most successful. The Suffolks, who I think highly of, have had less to do but have done it efficiently. The whole standard is very, very high.'

General 'Bolo' often recorded his views on the relative merits of brigades and units, but the final sentence places his opinions in their true perspective.

The Rhine Crossing

The Rhine Crossing operation was planned to start on 23 March. In 30th Corps sector, 51st (Highland) Division was to lead the amphibious assault, with 3rd Division in a vitally important supporting role — to hold the Rhine bank and provide the mounting facilities for the assault.

The infantry were to watch the enemy closely, denying him access to the west bank, while the sappers had the major task of constructing, signing and lighting the access routes for 51st Division to bridge and ferry sites. Meanwhile 3 Div Signal Regiment prepared 'beach' communications for this major amphibious assault, and using cable ploughs and bulldozers, they laid a hundred miles of 'quad' and fifty miles of heavy cable. The Divisional artillery was to support 51st Division, and the CRA, Brigadier Gerald Mears, took control of a 'Pepperpot' bombardment of the far bank, using three machine-gun battalions, a tank battalion, two anti-tank regiments and three light anti-aircraft regiments. Throughout the period of preparation the Allies masked their daytime activities with a massive smoke screen which although effective, was extremely unpleasant to work in.

On the evening of the 23 March the east bank of the Rhine erupted in smoke as the artillery barrage began; the Divisional sappers blasted access gaps in the west bank,

and the Highlanders commenced the crossing in amphibious Buffaloes. General Tom Rennie, recovered from his Normandy wound, was commanding 51st Highland and the men of his old Division were saddened by the news the following day that he had been killed by mortar fire during the crossing. The same afternoon 3rd Division Headquarters, situated at Schloss Moyland, some four miles from the River, had five minutes notice to react to a piece of more cheerful news — it was to be visited by the Prime Minister, Mr Winston Churchill. Captain (later Major-General) Tony Tighe was commanding a signal troop at the headquarters, and he recalls Churchill's visit:

'He arrived sitting on a looted red mattress on top of an armoured car, dressed in his uniform of Honorary Colonel of the 5th (Cinque Ports) Bn, Royal Sussex, in his hand a gold-topped cane. Having crossed the drawbridge and visited the Ops Room in the castle, he returned to the armoured car and was invited by General Bolo to say a few words to those of us assembled below him. "Who are they?" he asked. General Alanbroke replied "Headquarters 3rd Division, Sir". Churchill took up the cue immediately and told us that the last time he had spoken to us was just before we embarked for D-Day. This was apparently true and the older hands amongst us nodded wisely. After his few words the armoured car moved off down the drive to the entrance of the castle grounds. I followed behind in a jeep, since I was going on leave to UK and did not want to miss my connections in Brussels. We sped along at quite a pace and as we came out of the main entrance I realised that there was one telephone line we had not bothered to bury. It stretched across the road ahead of our little convoy and seemed perilously low. So it proved, since it clipped the top of Churchill's hat and knocked it flying into the air and under my vehicle. We all screeched to a halt. A

Above: The Prime Minister addresses soldiers of HQ 3rd Division. Left to right: Major-General Whistler, Mr Winston Churchill, and General Alanbrooke, the CIGS./*Lady Whistler*

despatch rider on a motorcycle who was behind me gathered up the hat in his hand as though he were tent pegging, pulled alongside the armoured car and placed the hat on churchill's proferred cane. Raising it aloft, he turned and addressed me and said with the familiar grin, "Better my hat than my head". I rose to my feet in my jeep and saluted, smiling back I suspect somewhat weakly. The Prime Minister's convoy moved off and I pulled away at the next road junction.'

3rd Division followed 51st Highland across the Rhine, passing through Groenlo on 1 April hard on the heels of the Guards Armoured Division which was heading for the Elbe. It was exhilarating to be moving fast through the enemy's homeland, but there was still hard fighting to be done. At Lingen 185 Brigade carried out an opposed crossing of the Dortmund-Elms canal on 4 April. Captain Graham Lewis, commanding 2 Platoon of 17 Field Company RE, was responsible for reconnoitring the crossing by night and he recalls:

'As we closed on the canal, flanked by buildings, we could hear the Germans snoring in their beds. We got to the water's edge and lay down. On our right we could see what remained of a bridge, a black silhouette drooping into the water. On our left we could see the sloping approach to the canal ferry, but the ferry boat had gone. We selected the "ferry site" for the bridge and "measured the gap". It was very dark and difficult to see, but taking a look around, found we were standing outside a pub.

'As dawn broke the KSLI were ready with their assault boats, and shooting from the opposite bank started in earnest. There was a whirl of paddles, the assault sections leapt ashore on the far bank, and swiftly making their way forward, merged into the landscape. Snipers appeared in the windows opposite us like a 'Jack in a box', but a Bren gunner, handling his weapon with masterly skill, kept their heads down. Guy Radcliffe, the KSLI's Adjutant arrived and pointing to a German soldier sitting on a bench outside the pub, yelled, "What's he doing there? Go on somebody, take him prisoner". Nobody took any notice. "Go on somebody, take him prisoner for God's sake". The German surrendered to Guy, who was delighted.

'The shooting had now stopped. It was a beautiful spring morning, and 17 Field Company were building a Class 9 Folding Boat Bridge, the sappers remarking that it was like Wallingford on a bridging exercise. Then promptly at 09.00, down the canal, flying low, came two Messerschmitt 109. "That's torn it", we muttered. It took a matter of minutes for the German gunners, alerted by the aircraft, to find the range. One of the folding boats was holed on the water line, but a Sapper took off his shirt, rolled it into a ball, and plugged the hole. At 09.45, in spite of heavy shelling, the bridge was finished, and the Warwicks crossed to pass through the KSLI. Armoured cars of the Staffordshire Yeomanry followed, ripping across, making waves on the water.'

At this stage Graham Lewis went ahead with the Warwick's CO, but was wounded in the hand. Returning to the Bridge he found his Company Commander, Major 'Scotty' Scott-Bowden, seriously wounded. He assumed command and then moved along the canal to classify a further but partially damaged bridge which the Warwicks had reported. Lewis inspected the bridge and reported back on the radio to the Adjutant of the Divisional engineers:

'It's a bow string with the top member blown on one side and the bottom member blown on the other. Possibly Class 9'.

'No good at all. Try again.'

'At best Class 21.'

'Still no good.'

'What do you want then?'.

'Class 45.'

'Is it important to the battle?'

'Yes! Crocodiles.'

'OK. Send them over one at a time; crews out, drivers only.'

'Soon after, the Crocodiles arrived, the bridge held, and these flame-throwing monsters were able to cross and help the Warwicks in their successful clearance of the town'.

After securing Lingen the Division covered 180 miles in three days and reached the Weser opposite Bremen, the scene of its final battle of Hitler's war.

Bremen — the Finale

The circumstances of the battle of Bremen were exceptional, for both sides knew that the war was almost over. The Germans could fight only with the blind fanaticism of despair whereas the British had everything to gain by remaining alive for a few more days. The outline plan for demobilisation had already been circulated to the troops and some reticence in taking risks would have been understandable, and here was a large built up area, defended in the main by young SS Trainees and elements of the *Horst Wessel* Division, against which a full set piece attack would have to be mounted.

Nonetheless every British soldier fought as hard as ever, knowing that the harder he fought the quicker the war would be over, and this feeling of purpose was hardened by resolute leadership at every level.

The battle took place in two phases. Between 13 and 19 April, the outlying villages south-west of the city were cleared, and from 25 to 27 the city itself was secured. The Germans used the villages as one of their main defence lines, and an 800-strong SS Training Battalion was distributed among them. 8 Brigade commenced operations on the 13 April with the Suffolks thrusting up the Fahrenhorst-Brinkum road, their objective being the crossroads 1½ miles short of Brinkum. The enemy determination is illustrated by the fact that after the Suffolks' leading platoons had been forced to withdraw by an enemy counter-attack, it took the battalion two days with the assistance of Crocodiles to recapture the crossroads. On the right the Warwicks cleared Erickshof and Leeste and on 10 April Brinkum itself fell to the Norfolks after an all-night battle which the battalion described as a 'model of co-operation of all arms'. Over 200 prisoners were taken.

9 Brigade on the left cleared the axis Heiligenrode-Mittelshuchting between 16 and 19 April. The village of Kirchuchting, defended by SS trainees, U-Boat and R-Boat crews, and Volksturm (German Home Guard), saw the heaviest fighting, but the Lincolns took it 24 hours ahead of the Divisional timetable, capturing the CO, Adjutant, two company commanders and the last 250 soldiers of 18th SS Training Battalion. The remainder fled over the causeway into Bremen, pursued not only by artillery and machine-gun fire, but also 'fifty rounds rapid'

THE CAPTURE OF BREMEN

OPERATIONS BY 3rd DIVISION

13 – 26 APRIL 1945

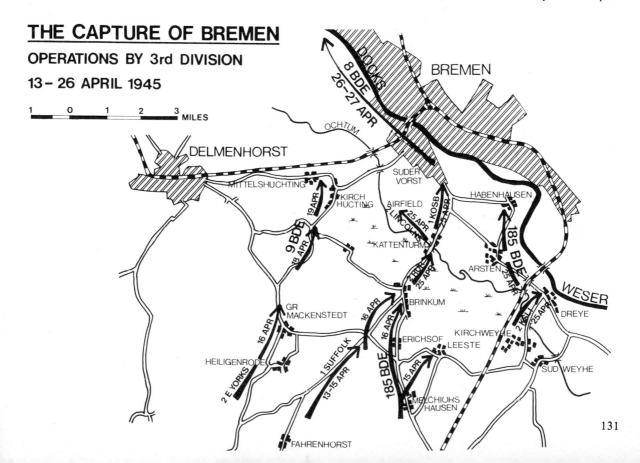

from the CO, Lt-Col Cecil Firbank, firing from an attic window. Colonel Firbank was always ready to contribute personally to the fire-fight, as his battalion had noted in the battle for Venrai.

These successes were overshadowed on 18 April by the death of Major 'Banger' King, second-in-command of the 2nd East Yorkshires. He died after being blown up by a mine while delivering rations to the forward companies at Mackenstedt. 'Banger' had become a legend in 3rd Division, since the time on D-Day when he inspired his company as they approached the beaches with readings from Shakespeare's *King Henry V*. He had won two DSOs and was universally loved and respected; 3 Div considered him invulnerable. To quote Norman Scarfe in *Assault Division,* 'the whole Division was proud of Major King and saw him as a representative of all that was best in themselves.'

3 Div had now closed up to the inundations bordering Bremen. The 30th Corps plan for assaulting the city involved three divisions — 3rd, 43rd (Wessex) and 52nd (Lowland). 3 Div's objective was that part of the city lying south of the Weser, and the initial assault was to be made in Buffaloes across the inundations from Brinkum and Kirchweyhe. Among the additional troops under command for the operation was 31st Armoured Brigade, consisting of the 4th/7th Dragoon Guards, 22nd Dragoons, Buffaloes of 4th Royal tanks, and Crocodiles of 7th Royal Tanks.

The attack started during the night 25/26 April. The Ulster Rifles crossed in Buffaloes and seized Kattenturm easily, while the KSLI advanced on foot and captured Dreye after sharp fighting. In this action Z Company made a bayonet charge along the railway embankment, the success of the company's attack being largely due to Private Wood, of the Intelligence Section, who went ahead shouting at the enemy in German to come out and surrender.

9 and 185 Brigade's tasks were completed by the evening of 25 April when they secured the line Sudervorst-Habenhausen, and during the next two days 8 Brigade pushed on to clear the rest of the city south of the Weser. The Germans were still full of fight, and nowhere more than on the KOSB's axis. One of their leading platoon commanders, Lt Peter Lloyd, recorded his experiences:

'The barracks had been badly damaged by shelling, and probably by aircraft. It was possible that it did not contain any enemy. I could not observe anything in the square. We pushed through the first block fairly quick, and I then decided to move into the open. It was an unwise risk to take, I suppose, and it was not really our job at all . . . we investigated and found two German soldiers hiding in a shelter with a girl . . . They said the SS Troops had withdrawn from the area.

'I was not very satisfied with the situation however. I sent Sergeant H out to see if there was a place suitable for an OP, and he came back leading a prisoner. This man said that he had some friends who were ready to give themselves up, so H set off again to see if he could bring them in. He came back fairly hurriedly with his patrol. Apparently the enemy had opened fire and proved to be in greater numbers than we were led to believe. He was all for taking a larger body of men out to 'get' this small

Above: 'He had become a legend in 3rd Division' — Major C. K. 'Banger' King DSO, Second-in-Command, 2nd East Yorkshire, killed on 18 April 1944. In this photograph he is supervising the evacuation of patients and nuns from St Servatius Hospital, Venrai, with the enemy 300 yards away./*Colonel J. D. W. Renison*

pocket and, as he was obviously in the right mood, I let him go. I did not think that there was much possibility of any large body of enemy. I was wrong. The patrol came back, having shot up some enemy, but they had also seen more movement at the end of the barracks.'

Lloyd was concerned that enemy had infiltrated back into the barracks — and this is in fact what happened. The enemy holding Habenhausen had withdrawn when the Norfolks attacked and were taking up positions in Lloyd's barracks, and he continues:

'Then suddenly we were sniped at from our right flank. We were completely exposed on this flank! I could hear the bullets whining very close and hugged the ground frantically. The terrifying thing was that we could not locate this solitary sniper. A man who was lying close to me was hit in the head and died shortly afterwards. Each of us tried to crawl as best we could to safety. Then another man was hit in the arm. Try as I could I was not able to locate the fire, and the platoon behind us could not pin it down. By now I was afraid to raise myself an inch off the ground. M's Piat man had been hit too. I wriggled as best as I could to a small wall in order to get protection from this enemy who was picking us off one by one. I could hear the ping of bullets all the time, and the shots seemed very close indeed! However I managed to reach the wall all right. Then a cry from H "They've hit me" and he went lunging past, clasping his arm and making a run for it. I then began my tortuous crawl back, hugging the ground desperately until I came into the open again. I got to my feet and ran, ran as hard as I could. Once back, I yelled for the mortar, hoping that I could put some smoke down to cover the rest in. However, as I got the mortar up, I saw that H and the other man had got through. We sent the casualties back and redistributed ourselves in the trenches.'

The enemy then counter-attacked, but with the help of fire from another platoon, Lloyd's men held on and when tanks were sent up by company headquarters the enemy were eventually driven off.

By the evening of 25 April organised resistance in Bremen was collapsing. The Lincolns had seized the Airfield, and Major Glyn Gilbert, still commanding C Company, recalls the closing scene:

'It was about 17.30 hours and I was standing beside a German U-Boat Commander outside the battered entrance to Bremen Airport Control Tower. This had just been captured by my Company after an exceptionally bitter little action, and the German survivors, mainly U-Boat crews, were being fallen in to be taken to the PW cage.

'Under a Petty Officer they then marched past us, carrying their wounded. The Commander called out the equivalent of "Well done", and received a spontaneous and tremendous cheer from his seamen. We then saluted each other and he followed them into captivity.

'I have never forgotten that incident, as this German naval officer and his men provided a perfect example of leadership and high morale at a time when their country was in ruins and their future quite unknown.

' "That's about it then", said my old friend CSM Sam Smalley. He was, as usual, right. We had fired our last shots in Europe. There were five of us left in C Company who had landed in Normandy on June last year, and I remember suddenly feeling very tired, and sad about the casualties we had suffered in the past few hours. I did not realise it at the time, but I was the only rifle company commander in the Division who had landed on D-Day and not been killed or wounded.

' "Japan next, I suppose", said Sam.'

Nine days later the war in Europe ended. In his summing up of the campaign, Eisenhower lists three episodes as being decisive in ensuring victory. They were the battle of the Normandy beaches, the battle of the Falaise pocket, and the battles west of the Rhine. 3rd Division had fought in all of them, a distinction shared with no other British division.

Below: The signal that everyone had waited 5½ years for — the Cease Fire, effective 5 May 1945./*Lady Whistler*

MSG FORM

From : Main 3 Br Inf Div   04?.?30 B

Action: 8 Br   9 Br   185 Inf Bde   RA   RE   Sigs   3 Recce Regt
         2 Mx   124 Mil Govt   ADC   G   Int   Infm   A/QMain
         A/Q Rear   APM   RASC   Med   Ord   REME   Pro   FS Sec   Camp

         Phantom

GG878. RESTRICTED. cancel ALL offensive ops forthwith and CEASE FIRE 0800 hrs 5 May 45. Further details later. all infm

This msg may be sent AS   This msg must be sent IN   Originators
WRITTEN by any means   CIPHER if liable to be   Instrs   TOR/
(excl) wrls.   intercepted or to fall   Degree of   TH
                           into enemy hands.   Priority.
      JD
                           D.J.?.?   *Emergency*
                           Capt   O??

24 June 1945

My Dear Bolo: -

Second Army Headquarters returns to England this week and I am leaving Germany tomorrow.

I am sorry that I have had no opportunity to come and say good-bye to you before I go.

I want to tell you how much I appreciate all you have done in Second Army from start to finish, and how grateful I am for the part you and your Division have played. Your successes have made my task easy.

I hope we shall meet again before long.

Yours ever

Major General L.G.Whistler,
Commander,   CB, DSO,
3 DIVISION.

Tributes from General Sir Miles Dempsey *(Right)* Commander 2nd Army, and *(Below)* from Lt-Gen Brian Horrocks, Commander 30th Corps./*Both Lady Whistler*

FROM: Lieut-General B.G. HORROCKS, CB DSO MC

HEADQUARTERS 30 CORPS

27th April, 1945

Dear Bolo,

I am writing to congratulate you on the very fine performance put up by your Division during the recent fighting. While fighting for the BREMEN approaches you met some very stiff opposition, notably in BRINKUM and LEESTE, but this was overcome thanks to the fine fighting qualities of your troops.

Your plan for the capture of BREMEN, South of the River WESER, was extremely well conceived and it was brilliantly carried out by the whole Division.

It seems to me that the Division has gone from strength to strength in the recent fighting, and I am certain that there is no better Division than the 3rd British in the British Liberation Army today.

During the capture of BREMEN the Corps as a whole took approximately ten thousand Prisoners many of whom came from your sector.

As I started the War commanding a Battalion in the 3rd Division nothing could give me greater pleasure than to see it in such fine fettle right at the end.

Well done 3rd Division!

Yours sincerely,

B.G.Horrocks

Major-General L.G. Whistler, CB DSO,
        Commander,
        3rd British Division.

Right: Special Order of the Day issued on General Whistler's instructions to every member of 3 Div who landed on D-Day. 'We were all very proud of this Order', said Mr E. J. Spinks, late Bombardier, 7th Field Regiment RA, 1939 to 1945./*Mr E. J. Spinks*

Middle Eastern Interlude: A Time for Farewells

Glyn Gilbert's sergeant-major was very nearly right, for after four months' occupation duties in an area stretching from Minden to Munster, the Division was warned to move to America to train for the sea-borne assault on the mainland of Japan. Then on 17 August Japan surrendered and instead 3rd Division became 'Imperial Strategic Reserve', at five days' notice to move anywhere. It was not long before the call came, for in November the Division moved by air, rail and sea to the Middle East. 185 Brigade went to Palestine and the remainder to Kassasin in the Suez Canal Zone. Bolo's comments were: 'Nothing ready for us and no plans made. This part of the world works on the principle of the Gippy flag which has three stars on it named Maleesh, Mafish and Baksheesh. In fact pretty sunsmitten and war weary'. However before long the Division followed 185 Brigade to Palestine to keep the peace between Jew and Arab. 3 Div was responsible for Northern Palestine with Divisional HQ established at Haifa. Its task was to support the police in operations against terrorists of the Irgun and Stern gangs, and in the prevention of landings by illegal Jewish immigrants. Internal Security duties occupied them heavily, but 'Bolo' Whistler ensured that as many of his men as possible took advantage of being stationed in the Holy Land, by organising a series of pilgrimages to the Holy Places. Conducted by the divisional chaplains, pilgrimages each catered for 40 soldiers, lasted three days, and were greatly appreciated by the 7,000 men who were able to take part.

SPECIAL ORDER OF THE DAY

BY

MAJOR-GENERAL L.G. WHISTLER, CB. DSO.

COMMANDER 3RD BRITISH INFANTRY DIVISION.

IT IS USUAL THAT UNITS OF THE BRITISH ARMY PUT ASIDE ONE DAY IN THE YEAR ON WHICH TO REMEMBER SOME GREAT HONOUR ACHIEVED IN BATTLE.

THIS DAY IS OBSERVED WITH CONSIDERABLE CEREMONY. IT BECOMES A PART OF THE LIFE OF THE UNIT AND THROUGH IT THE TRADITIONS OF THE PAST ARE BROUGHT HOME TO THE PRESENT.

IT IS NOT INTENDED THAT THIS PARTICULAR BATTLE ONLY SHOULD BE REMEMBERED. IT IS THE TOKEN OF THE FIGHTING RECORD OF THE UNIT AND IT REMINDS THOSE NOW LIVING OF ALL THE HONOURS WON IN BATTLE BOTH ANCIENT AND RECENT.

THIS THIRD BRITISH INFANTRY DIVISION, ONE OF THE OLDEST FORMATIONS OF THE BRITISH ARMY, HAS EARNED MUCH FAME. IN THIS WAR ALONE IT HAS FOUGHT WITH DISTINCTION IN TWO CAMPAIGNS IN N.W. EUROPE. IT WAS FOR A LONG TIME IN 1940 THE ONLY RESERVE IN ENGLAND AND IN FACT THE ONLY DIVISION PROPERLY EQUIPPED FOR THE BATTLE.

IT HAS HOWEVER, HAD ONE SPECIAL HONOUR, SHARED BY ONLY ENGLISH AND ONE CANADIAN DIVISION, THAT OF THE ASSAULT ON THE BEACHES OF NORMANDY ON THE REAL D DAY OF THIS PRESENT CAMPAIGN.

FIRST ON THE BEACHES OF NORMANDY ON JUNE 6TH 1944.

MANY NOW SERVING HAD NOT THE HONOUR TO BELONG TO THE DIVISION ON THAT DAY. ALL THAT HAVE SERVED, FOR HOWEVER SHORT A PERIOD, MUST BE PROUD TO HAVE HAD THE HONOUR TO DO SO.

ALL KNOW AND FEEL THE SPIRIT THAT GOES WITH THE D DAY DIVISION.

JUNE 6TH WILL THEREFORE BE CONSIDERED THE DIVISIONAL DAY.

IT IS HOPED THAT IT WILL BE POSSIBLE TO OBSERVE THIS DAY AS A HOLIDAY THROUGHOUT THE DIVISION EACH YEAR.

(signed) L.G. Whistler
Major-General.,
Commander.
3 Brit Inf Div.

25th May 1945

Divisional HQ returned to Egypt in April 1946, where it remained until moving back to Palestine in early 1947. It was a period of considerable change, for as wartime soldiers were demobilised with their release groups, they were replaced by young national servicemen conscripted in peace, in whom it was necessary to instil the standards set by their predecessors in war. Greater upheavals followed when, in accordance with peacetime 'arms plot' moves, entire units left the Division. There were sad partings after the six years comradeship forged in battle, and then in December, 'Bolo' himself left to become GOC British Troops in India. His comment was 'this is the third really serious parting of my soldier's life. The first was 4th Bn Royal Sussex, the second 131 Brigade — and now this one'. Before Whistler handed over, 3 Div was visited on 4 October, by its old commander, Field Marshal Lord Montgomery of Alamien, who as CIGS was touring the Middle East. He was received with a Guard of Honour from his own Regiment, The Royal Warwicks, and visited Divisional HQ and 7 Brigade, as 185 Brigade has been renamed on the recommendation of its commander, Brigadier (now General Sir Robert) Bray.

It was during this visit that Montgomery drafted the Special Order of the Day which appears on the first page of this book.

'Bolo' Whistler's sadness on leaving the Division was matched by those he commanded, and the impression he had made is summed up by Glyn Gilbert, who had served under him for 2½ years:

'I first met General 'Bolo' on Day 1 of Operation Goodwood. 2nd Lincolns were moving up to their objective near the town of Troarn. I remember it was a lovely summer's day marred only by numerous columns of smoke from the burnt out tanks on our right testifying to the skilful handling of a few 88mm guns by the Germans. Suddenly a Sherman tank overtook my Company, and I was hailed from the turret by a Senior Officer with an old SD cap well on the back of his head, a quizzical expression on his face leaving me in no doubt that he wanted to know the form but quickly. Having been given a worm's eye view he moved on, leaving a few words of encouragement, and a feeling that at least the Divisional Commander had seen a sticky situation for himself. I then noticed that the advance quickened noticeably, and it was clear that the whip was out.

'This was the first of many meetings I had with 'Bolo' during the remainder of the campaign and for fifteen months during the emergency in Palestine. As a Regimental Officer through and through he understood the weight which was taken at Rifle Company Commander level in war, and I believe he had a very special relationship with this level of command throughout the Division. He certainly enjoyed our complete confidence, and he had the knack of turning up at just the right time to see for himself, and have a laugh and a few words with all ranks.

'Bolo was ruthless with the inefficient, and the poor operator at Brigade, Battalion, and Company level disappeared at phenomenal speed, but at the same time he was tremendous fun militarily and socially, and I shall always remember his enjoyment of off-the-cuff parties after the war.

'Bolo's premature death in 1963 was a sad blow to his many friends. He was a proper fighting soldier, and that is the tribute I am sure he would appreciate most of all, because that in his opinion was what soldiering was all about. Khaki bureaucracy was not for him and never would have been.'

In January 1947 Major-General Jack Churcher assumed command of the Division, and within a few days Divisional HQ and two brigades had moved back to Palestine. They assumed control of a very large area which included Jerusalem, Tel Aviv and the southern half of Palestine and among their operations was the arrest of the total complement of an immigrant ship together with 500-strong reception party sent to meet it. Throughout this period the Division maintained its customary high standard of training and suffered no fatal casualties from terrorism.

At the end of 1946 the British Government had announced its intention of abandoning the UN Mandate in 1947, with the result that 3rd Division was disbanded in June of that year. Some units remained in Palestine under command of other formations, but the Division's proud title disappeared from the Army's Order of Battle after 44 years' continuous existence, including outstanding service in two World Wars.

Below: The 2nd Royal Ulster Rifles had served with 3rd Division since the outbreak of war; General Whistler issued this Order to the battalion exactly seven years later./*Lady Whistler*

Soldiers of the Royal Ulster Rifles, I have come this evening to break to you myself the news that you are leaving the Division.

You can probably imagine my feelings in saying goodbye to you, both from myself and from the rest of the Division whose representatives I have brought with me.

You know very well the position you have won in our hearts during the great days you have spent in the Division. You have won that position by your behaviour in and out of action since you joined many years ago.

The Division has a high reputation and you have played a great part in making that reputation.

The move of Regular Units to their proper peace positions is now beginning and there will be many other changes. In a way, perhaps, you are fortunate to be an early one to go, as you leave with the Division little changed from its fighting days.

Throughout your future history you will remember with great pride the feats of arms of these last six years. You will remember that you were a distinguished part of the 3rd British Infantry Division.

I am a very proud man to have had you under my command these last two years. I am very, very grateful for all you have done personally, so cheerfully and excellently.

You will always be remembered with great pride by all who have served with you.

Go on your way then with great confidence and with your own great spirit.

Goodbye — good luck — and God be with you.

L. G. Whistler.

EGYPT,
3rd September, 1946.

Major-General,
Commander,
3rd British Infantry Division.

9.
The 1950s:
Operations in the Middle East

3rd Division Reforms in 1951

Operation Roller

Return to the Middle East

The Suez Canal Zone, 1952 to 1954

Operation Musketeer and the Occupation of Port Said, 1956

New Thoughts and Fresh Emergencies

Right: The General Service Medal, 1952-1961.

'Two on, four off' - 1st East Surreys
Suez Canal Zone, 1953.

PRESENTED BY
THE 3RD DIVISION OFFICERS ASSOCIATION
1939-1947
TO MARK THE OCCASION OF
THE REFORMING OF THE DIVISION JANUARY 1951
AND TO COMMEMORATE ALL WHO SERVED IN THE DIVISION
DURING THE SECOND WORLD WAR

Right: The 'Bomber' statuette presented in 1951 by 3 Div Officers 1939-47 and displayed in the HQ 3rd Division Officers Mess. The model was sculpted by the late Colonel Tom Evill, CRE 3rd Division 1945-1947.

Below: Field Marshal Lord Montgomery with Major-General Sir Hugh Stockwell during the Field Marshal's visit to HQ 3rd Division, January 1951.

The disbandment of 3rd Division in 1947 was the result of the inevitable postwar decision to reduce forces and commitments in peacetime. However by 1950 the shadows cast by international Communism had already darkened many corners of the world. In February 1948 the Russians staged their coup d'etat in Czechoslovakia and followed this in June 1949 by the surface blockade of West Berlin.

In Malaya the Communist Malayan Races' Liberation Army had unleashed a murderous insurrection in 1948, and in June 1950 the war in Korea broke out. By August 1950 British soldiers were engaged in battle in two Far Eastern theatres and were placed on an operational footing in West Germany. The British Army was now widely committed, and in order to meet any future contingencies a strategic reserve was formed in the United Kingdom, the main component of which was to be a reformed 3rd Division of three brigades. 16 Parachute Brigade was also part of the UK Strategic Reserve but was to remain an independent formation.

3rd Division reformed in early 1951 under Major-General Sir Hugh Stockwell, with Divisional Headquarters and 19 Brigade at Colchester, 32 Guards Brigade in London District and 39 Brigade at Dover. The reformed Division was, like any other formation of the Army at the time, made up mainly of National Servicemen — the ever cheerful, lowly paid, quick witted youngsters to whom the country owes such a debt. While Britain endeavoured to administer and garrison worldwide commitments far beyond the scope of the prewar regular army, these young men in battledress, jungle-green and khaki-drill defied the Chinese masses on the Imjin, defeated guerillas in Malaya and Kenya, and dealt resolutely with mob violence and bombing in Middle Eastern town and village. In particular young NS Officers shouldered remarkable responsibilities, leading their men against skilled enemies after only four months' training at Eaton Hall or Mons. Regular officers were the first to acknowledge the benefits of working with, commanding and training these young men who were drawn from every walk of life, and included so many with a very high standard of aptitude and intelligence.

General Stockwell was instructed to have his new Division fully trained by the end of 1951. He recalls that in January 1951:

'We had hardly formed up when Monty rang me from Paris and briefly what he said was, "Ah — I am very glad to hear you have got command of the 3rd Division; now when I commanded it, it was a very good Division! I should like to meet all the Commanding officers." I replied, "what about a date in early April?" "What?" he said, "Next week, please". At that time battalions were scattered all over the UK! Anyhow he came and we had a dinner in the 19 Brigade Mess and he addressed all the COs for 50 minutes! He also said he wanted to see me in his room. "What do you think is the most difficult manoeuvre a Division can do?". "I don't know", I replied. "Well, I'll tell you" he said, "Move the Division 50 miles by night and be dug in at dawn ready to receive the enemy." This advice was reflected at a Divisional conference held on 22 February and as a result we took part in Exercise Hammer and Tongs, set by Gerald Templer (GOC-in-C Eastern Command) as a Divisional

Test Exercise. The basis was an advance to Stanford to meet the enemy, but by September we had got to know every lane and road in East Anglia, so we had practically only to clap our hands and the boys were off.

'To cut a long story short, by dawn I was in a slit trench at Div Tac HQ at Stanford when Gerald Templer turned up. "What the hell do you think you are doing?" he asked. I said, "What's wrong?" and he replied, "You are here and dug in before the bloody enemy has been positioned!!" I reckon that was the best test of our 9 months training.'

3rd Division went on to take part in Exercise Surprise Packet in the South of England. It manoeuvred with the newly formed 6th Armoured Division, then preparing for service in Germany. An exercise in UK on this scale, employing four infantry brigades and three armoured regiments, had never been held in peacetime before. It has never been seen since.

On 8 October the Prime Minister of Egypt, Nahas Pasha, abrogated the Treaty granting Britain the use of the Suez Canal Zone as a Middle Eastern Base, and announced that the British garrison must leave. Widespread mob violence followed, but General Erskine, GOC Troops Egypt, made it clear that the British had no intention of leaving and requested reinforcements. Those immediately available were 16 Parachute Brigade, which was already in Cyprus, and the brigades of 1st Division, spread between Cyprus and Libya. It was decided to reinforce the Mediterranean with 3rd Division but on Templer's instruction the news was withheld from the Division until Exercise Surprise Packet was completed.

Operation Roller

The first to move under Operation Roller was 19 Brigade (Brigadier Lipscomb) — 1st Devons, 1st Highland Light Infantry, and 1st Surreys — together with 48th Field Regiment RA. Within a week of completing Surprise Packet they were landing from Hastings aircraft in Tripoli, relieving 1 Guards Brigade (1st Division) which flew on to the Canal Zone. In November the remainder of 3 Div moved to Cyprus by courtesy of the Royal Navy. HMS *Illustrious* and HMS *Triumph* opened their cavernous hangars and cleared their flight decks to accommodate the men and vehicles of the Division, *Illustrious* sailing from Portsmouth with Divisional HQ, HQ 39 Brigade (Brigadier Tweedie), 1st Buffs, 1st Border and Divisional troops on 5 November, followed a few hours later by *Triumph* with 1st Inniskilling Fusiliers, 49th Field Regiment RA, 25th Field Engineer Regiment and Service units. Departing for operations in the 1950s by 'Grey Funnel Line' was done in a style missing in the 1970s; the Border Regiment's magazine describes the events of 4 and 5 November:

'At Portsmouth we were met by the Band and, together with the Drums, they marched us to the dockyard where the Commander-in-Chief Portsmouth, accompanied by General Sir Gerald Templer and the Divisional Commander, took the salute as we approached HMS *Victory*.

'Preceded by the Colours and Escort, the Battalion boarded *Illustrious* and were met by the Colonel of the

Above: Travel by 'Grey Funnel Line'. 3rd Division vehicles, and PT by the 1st Border Regiment on the flight deck of HMS *Illustrious*, November 1951./*Kings Own Royal Border Regt*

Centre right: Border Regiment National Servicemen enjoying Naval messing aboard HMS *Illustrious*./*Kings Own Royal Border Regt*

Bottom right: 2,000-odd hammocks of 32 Guards Brigade, slung on the hangar deck of HMS *Illustrious*, December 1951./*Brigadier D. Rossiter*

Regiment, who later in the evening came down into the hangar and amongst 2,000 hammocks bid us farewell.

'The hangar, which housed practically everyone for both sleeping and messing, had been converted by the Royal Naval Dockyards in five days. It was an immense undertaking which included welding to the steel floor some 300 army type trestle tables and 600 forms. In addition, steel hawsers for the slinging of 2,000 hammocks were fixed. Lashed to the flight deck above were 150 assorted vehicles of the Division.

'At 0915 hours on Monday 5 November, HMS *Illustrious* was towed out into the harbour, all troops were assembled on the flight deck, and as we left the quay our band, together with that of the Buffs, played incidental music and the Regimental Marches. At 0930 hours, with the ship under its own power, we all turned to starboard to salute the flag of the Flag Officer Submarines and so slipped out into the English Channel'.

On 12 November *Illustrious* and *Triumph* disembarked their cargoes at Famagusta, and within a few days *Illustrious* was back at Portsmouth to take aboard 32 Guards Brigade (Brigadier Heber-Percy) — 1st Coldstream, 1st Scots Guards and 1st Bedfordshire and Hertfordshire. The hospitality of the Senior Service is traditional and the C-in-C Portsmouth gave a farewell luncheon party aboard HMS *Victory* for officers of the Brigade and their wives. Lt-Col (later Brigadier) Denis Rossiter, commanding the Bedfordshires, remembers that the toast proposed by Admiral Sir Arthur Power was simple, direct and appreciated by all — 'God Damn Stalin'.

On arrival in the Mediterranean, 3rd Division was ordered to prepare for Operation Rodeo Flail — an amphibious landing at Alexandria with the aim of rescuing British nationals. This would be carried out in conjunction with Operation Rodeo Bernard, a thrust by 1st Division from the Canal Zone to Cairo. Planning for the former reached an advanced stage with Royal Marines carrying out a beach reconnaissance at Alexandria. On 26 January 1952 — 'Black Saturday' — Cairo erupted in flames as the mob first attacked British lives and property and then turned its frenzy on anything of European origin. Rodeo Bernard teetered on the brink, threatening Cairo with occupation by British troops, but the situation was redeemed by King Farouk who ordered the Egyptian army to clear the streets, which it did in quick time. Tension in Egypt eased immediately and both Rodeos were called off. Nevertheless there remained in the Canal Zone a security threat of vast proportions and early in 1952 HQ 3rd Division with 32 and 39 Brigades moved in from Cyprus to assume responsibility for the whole of 'Canal North' from inclusive Port Said to Ismailia. 3 Brigade was temporarily taken under command but was later replaced by 16 Parachute Brigade. At the same time 1st Division became the guardian of 'Canal South'.

The Suez Canal Zone

3rd Division's deployment was 32 Guards Brigade at El Ballah and Port Said, 39 Brigade at Tel-El-Kebir, and 16 Parachute Brigade at Ismailia. The task was to secure the numerous military installations, depots and barracks of the sprawling Middle Eastern base against organised thefts and sabotage by professional Egyptian thugs, reputedly advised and trained by German experts. It consumed a vast amount of manpower; for example, the Tel-El-Kebir base — TEK to those who served there — required a whole battalion to provide mobile patrols, in-lying picquets, gate guards, and the 100 men on the searchlights around the 17-mile perimeter. Thieves, paid £1 per night for their trouble, used every device imaginable including covering fire to gain entry, and a story going around when 3rd Division arrived was that of the armoured car, stored in the Base Vehicle Depot, that one day mysteriously started itself up and drove out of the gate, never to be seen again.

The patience and good temper of the British Soldier is legendary, but conditions in the Canal Zone during the Division's 2¾ year tour stretched these qualities to the limit. Guards and duties took up 80% of a unit's time, and when off duty the soldiers' home was an EPIP (Egyptian Pattern, Indian Produced) tent pitched on a hot, dusty patch of desert. If he was lucky his cookhouse and NAAFI canteen were in temporary corrugated iron buildings, redolent of DDT fly spray and dominated in the summer by the creak of antiquated electric Punka fans that stirred the stuffy, overheated atmosphere. His meals, cooked on spluttering oil-burning stoves, would

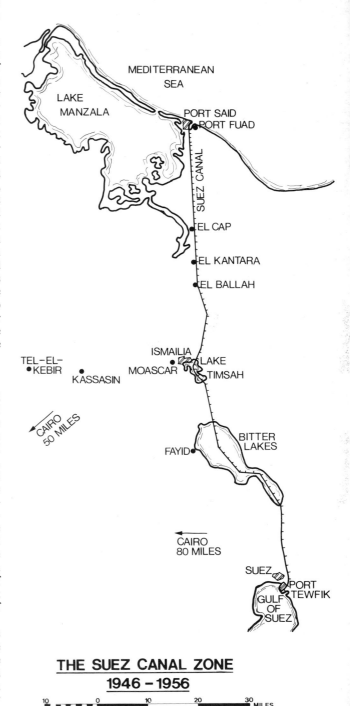

THE SUEZ CANAL ZONE
1946 – 1956

BRITISH FEMALES MUST NOW HAVE MALE ESCORT OUTSIDE STATION

ISMAILIA OUT OF BOUNDS

BRITISH OWNED PRIVATE CARS MUST NOW CONFORM TO MILITARY REGs

Above: A photograph that sums up life in the Canal Zone in the early 1950s; a check point manned by a sentry and Regimental Police of the 1st Bedfordshire and Hertfordshire. /*Lt-Col T. W. Stubbs*

Right: Training in the Sinai, 1952; Vickers section of 16 Parachute Brigade on exercise in the Wadi Pharan./*Lt-Col T. W. Stubbs*

Above: GOC 3rd Division's RMP Escort, 1953. Two Bren Light Machine-Guns and a wire cutter on the Landrover. The Royal Military Police are always in the forefront of Internal Security operations. */Major-General J. B. Churcher*

have made today's diploma-bearing ACC cook shudder. While the National Serviceman served 18 months under these conditions, the regular soldiers, most of whom were NCOs, faced them for nearly three years. The majority of married soldiers were unaccompanied for the whole of this period. Major-General (later General Sir Nigel) Poett, who had taken over from Stockwell in May 1952 recalls that after the first excitement of operations, the maintenance of morale was the most important task facing commanders at all levels: 'Most of the credit for the high state of morale which existed throughout belongs to the Regimental Officers which included many who were National Service. The very raw conditions brought out the best of everyone in the Division. Certainly the NS officers and men were a great strength and those I have met since admit in retrospect to having enjoyed their time in the Canal Zone.'

By late 1952 the security threat had eased sufficiently to allow unit and formation exercises to take place. These were thoroughly enjoyed despite the biting cold and sudden torrential rain that are a feature of the Egyptian desert in winter. The largest exercise, nicknamed 'Triangles', took place between 3rd Division and 1st Division (who sport the single white triangle sign) in the desert west and south of Suez in October and lasted six days.

In September 1952, HQ 19 Brigade, together with 1st HLI and shortly after 1st Surreys, rejoined 3rd Division in the Canal Zone. 39 Brigade then departed for UK prior to moving to Kenya, but left behind 1st Border, which became the third battalion of 19 Brigade.

During 1953 agreement was almost reached with the Egyptian Government whereby administrative troops only would be stationed in the Canal Zone, but discussions broke down when the Egyptians insisted that the troops should not wear uniform and that no British flag should be flown. The violence of early 1952 repeated itself and when Major-General Jack Churcher returned to

take over command from Poett in April 1954, he was faced with the same security situation as was his predecessor. Within days of his arrival a Scots Guards' vehicle was ambushed in Port Said, the Padre's driver and batman killed, and vehicle and weapons stolen. Churcher decided that drastic action was necessary and he informed the Egyptian Governor in Port Said that unless the bodies of the soldiers, the vehicle and weapons were returned that evening he would in his own words 'be forced to send the Scots Guards through Port Said'. Churcher's terms were complied with in full by 10pm that night.

Incidents continued to occur, but in July an agreement was finally reached with President Nasser, the Egyptian Government's new leader. Under this agreement British troops would evacuate the Canal Zone Base, which instead would be administered by British civilians. 3rd Division was released from its duties at the end of the year, and by early 1955 had rid itself of the dust and smell of the Canal Zone and was back once more in Colchester. The words of Lt-Col Robert Senior to his battalion, the 1st Bedfordshire and Hertfordshire, summarise the life and achievements of 3rd Division during the years in Egypt: 'There is no excitement to look back on, of battle in Korea, or jungle fighting in Malaya or Kenya, but rather of arduous and monotonous duties in sand, flies and heat, with living conditions and amenities much to be desired. Such tasks called for greater fortitude, high morale and strong discipline; these you displayed and maintained in the highest degree throughout.'

Above: Examined with interest at the CIGS's conference but thoroughly disliked by the FVRDE — 3rd Division's provocative Armoured Personnel Carrier — a commercial tractor and one-ton trailer modified by REME, 3 Div, in 1956./*Major-General J. B. Churcher*

Throughout 1955 and 1956 Churcher's task as GOC was to reform the Division as the UK Strategic Reserve and bring its training up to date. Divisional headquarters and 19 Brigade were based at Colchester, 29 Brigade (as 32 Guards Brigade had been renamed) was at Dover and Divisional artillery was split between both locations. One and sometimes two armoured regiments were based on Salisbury Plain as Divisional troops, and 1 Guards Brigade, located at Shorncliffe, joined in May 1956.

During this period the Division was expected to train for nuclear as well as limited war; however armoured personnel carriers, so essential for infantry in nuclear warfare, were not then available. Churcher therefore arranged for his REME workshops to design an APC, which was of sufficient interest to be shown at the CIGS's conference. The Fighting Vehicles Research and Development Establishment thoroughly disliked it, but nonetheless the project drew attention to the urgent need for a proper design.

Operation Musketeer

Under the terms of the Anglo-Egyptian agreement of 1954, British troops evacuated the Suez Canal Zone in June 1956. Six weeks later Nasser seized the Suez Canal Company, and that August Bank Holiday weekend the first members of a hastily reassembled Planning Team started work in the War Office; Operation Musketeer had begun. For over 20 years the political background to the Port Said landings of November 1956 has provided a lush pasture for military and political commentators, armchair strategists and journalists. This history will therefore confine itself to the story as it affected the soldiers of 3rd Division.

On 1 August 1956 the Division was ordered to mobilise, and Churcher recalls:
'At that time I was with the divisional artillery at Otterburn at annual practice Camp. Needless to say this was brought to a swift close and the artillery returned that night to their locations and myself back to Colchester. The mobilisation of the Division was a complicated business. We only had five infantry battalions out of nine, therefore four had to be brought in from outside. Our armoured regiment, the Greys, were removed from our command, the 1st and 6th Royal Tank Regiments were put under command, both of them on Salisbury Plain. 1st RTR had not fired its main armament for two years, I discovered, and I therefore refused to allow it to embark until it had done so. In order to train the Division and its new intakes we were given very nearly carte blanche of available areas. The drawing of all the mobilisation equipment went reasonably well but, as this was the first time anybody had mobilised since the end of the war, there were some sticky moments.'

19 Brigade faced the most complicated mobilisation task, for other than the 1st Argyll and Sutherland Highlanders, due to join from Berlin in mid-August, the brigade possessed no infantry! This shortfall was hastily corrected by the 1st Royal Scots in Elgin and the 1st West Yorkshires in Ulster being moved rapidly to join the Brigade in East Anglia. Soon reservists started appearing at unit guard rooms and the drawing of stores and equipment went on at a feverish rate.

On 27 August vehicles and equipment were despatched to South Wales for loading in a variety of hired transports. Only small parties of drivers stayed aboard the ships, and everyone confidently expected to get under way soon after. Instead the transports swung at anchor for two months, during which time radios and vehicles deteriorated. Units continued to train hard, but the problems of separation from equipment and documents led to many frustrations, and inevitably the two to three hundred reservists in each battalion grew restless. Where, they wondered, was the compelling emergency that had dragged them from their jobs and homes?

Initially the Musketeer plan had envisaged a landing at Alexandria and thrusts to Port Said, Suez and Cairo. In October when information of the Israeli intention to attack was received, the plan was revised; a joint parachute and commando assault on Port Said would be followed by occupation of the Canal Zone by the 3rd Division. In overall command was Lieutenant General Sir Hugh Stockwell, who had led 3 Div to the Canal in 1952. On 29 October the Israelis launched their attack — to the surprise, it would seem, of their friends. The following day news of the 'flap' they had caused filtered through to units of the Division. By 7am on 1 November, troop trains were pulling out of Dover and Colchester for Southampton and that evening the troopships *Empire Fowey*, *Empire Ken*, *Dilwara* and *Asturias* sailed into the channel with 3rd Division (less 1 Guards Brigade) on board. A day ahead of them steamed the transports carrying their vehicles and the tanks of 1st RTR. On 10 November the troopships arrived off Port Said, having overtaken the slow moving transports. The town was already in the secure grip of 16 Parachute Brigade and 3 Commando Brigade while Centurions of 6th RTR, in support of 2 PARA, had advanced 25miles south to El Cap, where they had halted in compliance with HMG's Cease-Fire order.

The Occupation of Port Said

After three days of uncertainty, 3rd Division disembarked on 13 November and relieved the Parachute and Commando Brigades. 19 Brigade (Brigadier Grimshaw) took over responsibility for Port Said town, and 29 Brigade (Brigadier Deakin) the causeway running south including the 'sharp end' at El Cap. In 19 Brigade's sector the Royal Scots had the trickiest area — Arab Town — to control, but they were reasonably well accommodated in permanent buildings, and did not envy the Argylls their beach-hut living quarters at Gamil. The latter had a particularly varied 'parish' which included the Airfield (the objective of 3 PARA's parachute assault on 5 November), the approaches across Lake Manzala, the Manzala Canal itself, and 'Shanty Town'. The West Yorkshires looked after the dock area and business quarter.

In 29 Brigade, the Royal West Kents faced the Egyptian Army at El Cap, where at battalion head-quarters in the railway station the commanding officer, Lt-Col Peter Buckle, dealt with a constant swarm of visitors and reporters viewing the 'front line'. The remaining battalions of the brigade — the Royal Fusiliers and York and Lancasters — patrolled the 20 miles of causeway leading north to Port Said.

3rd Division's tasks at Port Said were to prevent interference by the Egyptian Army, to maintain internal security among the population, and to assist the restoration of normal life and facilities in the town. The

PORT SAID 1956

Egyptian Army maintained the Cease-Fire very properly, the major threat to security being posed by professional thugs and urban guerillas paid, trained and led by the Police Special Branch, and known as the 'Black Hand'. Large quantities of arms had been distributed to civilians before the Allied landings, and attempts to smuggle them across Lake Manzala continued. Life for units in Port Said followed the routine well known to so many British soldiers — street patrols, curfew enforcement, cordon and search, checking of vehicles and watercraft, and interminable guards. Major (later Brigadier) Eddie Fursdon, who was DAA & QMG of 19 Brigade, wrote a vivid account of operations in Port Said*, and the extracts that follow depict the atmosphere well:

'In a remarkably short space of time our soldiers adjusted themselves to a life of constant patrol and guards. They learnt to be suspicious, cautious and extremely observant. I shall never forget watching one Royal Scots patrol working its way slowly along the wide street that separates Arab Town from Shanty Town. It was a patrol of seven, operating in the rough shape of a diamond. The rear Jock walked slowly backwards, his loaded bren gun, slung from his shoulder, was held at the hip; slowly and continuously the barrel traversed the street, but I am sure it was his expression that made for the perfect behaviour of the crowd. His bonnet was back a little on his head; his young sunburnt face was set; it was quite clear to everyone, "There will be no nonsense here". There wasn't.

'The success of the occupation was largely due to the high standard of junior leadership. It was the young corporal, sometimes just a private soldier, who led the patrol and got to know his area as well as the village policeman does at home. A grenade on a cafe table in Arab Town was seen by a passing Royal Scot. The printing press that produced most of the anti-British leaflets was discovered down a side street by Lance

* Published in Maurice Tugwell's 'The Unquiet Peace'.

Gamil Airfield   Manzala Canal   Coast Guard Barracks   Arab Town   Business Quarter

Shanty Town

Lake Manzala

Railway

Sweet Water Canal
Canal Road

To El Cap

Suez Canal

Above: Port Said, looking North, photographed by a French reconnaissance aircraft during the airborne assault, 5 November 1956. The Coast Guard Barracks burns after being struck by Fleet Air Arm aircraft; it had been used by the Egyptian army as a strong point to delay the advance of 3 PARA from Gamil airfield.
/Major-General M. J. H. Walsh

Corporal Furniss of the West Yorkshires, all because he spotted that only two out of four shops' shutters were padlocked. Corporal Armour of the Argylls became suspicious of two Arabs carrying baskets from a rowing boat. He gave chase and, as result, unearthed a large dump of ammunition and explosives smuggled from the Nile Delta into the fishing village of El Qabuti. Sometimes it was the junior officer, like Tony Moorhouse, who, by keenness, patience and observance captured seven Egyptian commandos in a house on the day before his tragic abduction.'

The abduction on 10 December of Lt Moorhouse of the West Yorkshires by the 'Black Hand' occurred when this young officer made a short journey in his vehicle, unescorted, to visit one of his outposts. On his way Moorhouse is believed to have seen an Egyptian youth posting an anti-British propaganda poster. He stopped his 'champ' with a view to arresting him. An altercation ensued and a small crowd collected. Lt Moorhouse drew his pistol but later placed it on the dashboard of his 'champ', still fastened to him by his lanyard, and then glanced round preparatory to backing his vehicle away from a lorry behind which it was parked. A man in the crowd seized the pistol and there was a scuffle. At this stage three men drove up in a large black car, bundled Moorhouse into it, and drove off. The car was soon found abandoned on the edge of Arab Town. Despite widespread searches and discussions between Stockwell, United Nations officers, and the Egyptian authorities, Moorhouse was never seen again.

Fursdon's account continues:
'It was interesting to watch the reactions of the Egyptians as the time of our occupation lengthened. For the first few days, the streets were practically deserted, and the majority of shutters were closed. Gradually young men appeared, mostly, we suspected, Egyptian Army soldiers in civilian clothes and Intelligence agents sent out to pick up every available scrap of information about us. They would hang about outside unit billets, with the persistence of flies. If you drove them away, within two minutes they, or others, would be back. One map we subsequently captured showed most of our Brigade positions, so they did their work well! Many of them posed as traders, and carried stocks of wallets and necklaces. The more traditional ones had the famous postcards. As all the shops were closed through fear of intimidation and reprisals, their trade was quite brisk. A little later, in an effort to get the shops open, it was arranged that the soldiers could draw some of their pay in Egyptian currency. For a brief few days the real traders came out in force, and a roaring trade was established. French Parachutists, British sailors, Jocks in kilts were soon buying up every souvenir there was. Camels, pouffles, wallets, watches, Spanish fly — the whole repertoire of Port Said was displayed. One Lance Corporal even fell for the old trick of buying a sealed bottle of gin for £1, finding to his dismay on opening it, that it was just water!

'After about three weeks the women appeared. The gay dresses and often alluring figures of the younger westernised girls brightened the dusty pavements and relieved the general look of khaki drill everywhere.

'The English Church was re-opened, and Sunday morning services were held there, taken by the Senior Chaplain. It always seems strange to me, to kneel and pray carrying a loaded revolver, but there are times when such a precaution is wise! The sheer simple beauty of the dome-shaped interior of that cool church was really

146

lovely. There are few soldiers, I am sure, who are not comforted by the familiar prayers and hymns of the Morning Service, wherever overseas they may be serving.'

Danish and Norwegian companies of the UN Peacekeeping Force — authorised early in November — started arriving on 21 November. By December there were sufficient UN troops to start taking over from 3 Div. Divisional headquarters and 29 Brigade (less 1st York and Lancaster) embarked for England on 6 December, and two days later the York and Lancasters handed over El Cap to UN troops. This left 19 Brigade as the sole fighting formation in Port Said. In addition to its own battalions the following units were placed under command: 6th RTR, 33rd Para Field Regiment RA, 3rd Light Anti-Aircraft Battery RA, 3rd Field Squadron RE, 15th Field Ambulance, 7th Infantry Workshops REME and a Field Security Section. The Brigade answered direct to General Stockwell's headquarters aboard HMS Tyne.

With the arrival of UN troops, and fortified with the knowledge that the British would soon, once more, be homeward bound, the Egyptians opened an intensive campaign of grenade and sniping attacks. By 15 December these attacks reached their peak, one victim being Major David Pinkerton commanding B Company of the Royal Scots, who died of wounds received when leading a patrol. An entry that day in the personal diary of Major Bill Fargus, commanding the Royal Scots D Company, reads:
'Grenades were going off all day in Arab Town. Ian Jeffrey and Corporal Irvine were sharing the patrolling there, on alternate patrols. They had some very lucky escapes from grenades which were being thrown with unpleasant regularity. One grenade thrown from a balcony scored a direct hit on Ian Jeffrey's ankle and exploded a few yards away without hurting anyone. I took out the curfew patrol, and another grenade was thrown at Irvine just as he was coming up the street to meet me. The patrol was a bit nerve-wracking. The latest game of the Egyptians is to gather in a small crowd so as to attract the patrol to disperse it, and then roll a grenade into the patrol. We moved pretty carefully — clearing the street for about 50 yards ahead of us and allowed no one on balconies. No nonsense about not having magazines on Stens! Everything was cocked!'

By nightfall on 15 December most of A Company of the Royal Scots supported by two Centurions of 6th RTR were deployed in subduing the 'Black Hand' in Arab Town, which they did with a sharp and accurate display of automatic weapons. The UN troops suggested that the reported Egyptian casualties — 27 killed and 60 wounded — were excessive, but it is significant that these included no women or children, and that for the remainder of its stay, 19 Brigade was left well alone by the Egyptians. On 21 December UN troops took over the town, and 19 Brigade withdrew to a close perimeter round the docks ready for embarkation. This took place on 22 December and went without serious incident, the Argylls leaving first, followed by the Royal Scots and the West Yorkshires. The 'Black Hand' clearly regained a little courage when they saw the British embarking for Fargus's diary records, 'we had a quiet night apart from a few minutes when someone fired a burst at a W Yorks sentry in the next building. The W Yorks gave him two magazines in retaliation'. By 8.15pm the last troops of 19 Brigade had left by landing craft for the troopship Dunera waiting in the outer harbour. Other than the marine who cast off, Brigadier Grimshaw was the last man on shore, and the troopship cleared the canal to the strains of 'Farewell to Port Said' played by pipers of the Royal Scots. On 2 January 1957 19 Brigade disembarked at Southampton, the Royal Scots leaving the brigade and returning home to Elgin, while the West Yorkshires and Argylls went back to Colchester and Bury St Edmunds respectively.

New Thoughts and Fresh Emergencies
Military as well as political heart searching followed the Suez expedition, for the confusion that had accompanied the ponderous sea move of 3rd Division, and the many other supporting elements, showed that radical improvements were necessary if the services were to react quickly to events overseas. Then in April 1957 Mr Duncan Sandys, Minister for Defence, announced that the call up of NS men would cease by 1960, resulting in smaller but all-regular forces by 1963. He also stated that the reduction in size of overseas garrisons would be redressed by strengthening the UK Strategic Reserve and providing sufficient transport aircraft to make it airportable. A new chapter in the history of 3rd Division was about to start; however the detailed measures to implement the new policy were to take some 18 months to put into effect. In the meantime 3 Div was caught up in a fresh Middle Eastern drama. One day in July 1958 Major-General Gordon-Lennox, who had assumed command of the Division in the spring of the previous year, was accompanying General Sir Gerald Templer, the CIGS, on an inspection of 29 Brigade at Dover. He recalls the events of the day:

Above: For 3rd Division, the shape of things to come — in this case the unmistakeable outline of the Blackburn 'Beverley'. Grenadier Guardsmen of 1 Guards Brigade emplaning for Cyprus, 1958. The Beverley was then the largest RAF aircraft in service and could carry 94 troops or 70 paratroops./*By courtesy of Central Press Photos*

'We were staying with General 'Willow' Turner at Dover Castle when General Templer's ADC came down to breakfast and told us that the King of Iraq and Nuri Said (his PM) had been murdered. General Templer said he couldn't believe it: He knew Nuri and he was well able to look after himself. We continued on our visit to the Gordon Highlanders.

'Half way through the Inspection the CIGS was recalled to London and a helicopter arrived to take him there.

'By chance that evening we had a Divisional Officers' dinner party at Colchester, which some 60 or more officers attended. The atmosphere in our Strategic Reserves circles was by then electric and I remember that at the end of the dinner I wrote a message to the CIGS on a paper napkin and told my ADC to telephone it through to him. It "hopefully anticipated" his orders to move etc. I heard nothing for a week, during which time I put the whole Division at 72 hours' notice. I then got a charming letter from General Templer, saying he had shown my message to the PM (MacMillan) in the middle of the night, and it had cheered them.

'I was then called to the War Office, to be told how unnecessary it was to put my Division at any notice, let alone 72 hours'. I returned to Colchester and put them at 24 hours' notice. I had not been a soldier for 25 years without learning how hopeless some Staffs are at judging time factors, or knowing how soldiers much prefer to stand-to in plenty of time, even if it is unnecessary in the event, than to be hustled and bustled out of their pace by panic orders.

'Shortly after, we were invited to move to Cyprus within 17 hours.

'Of course, we all hoped to have a glorious "swan" through the lava belt of North-East Jordan, to effect the rescue of British and other residents from the by then revolutionary situation in and around Baghdad. I took my HQ and two Brigades to Cyprus and took over the Parachute Brigade on arrival. But already the situation was quietening down.

'We arrived at Episcopi without most of our kit, including our all important vehicles and wireless sets. They arrived a week or so later by aircraft carrier, when we were at last able to undertake exercises.

'I was told one had to obtain permission from the Cyprus Government before we could carry out exercises with troops on the already heavily garrisoned Island (There were some 37,000 troops in Cyprus at that time under General Joe Kendrew, all chasing Grivas).

'The situation was, however, too urgent — or so we thought — to waste time on obtaining training rights through Staff Channels and so we carried out non-stop exercises for almost four months from one end of the Island to the other to ensure we were adequately prepared for any long range operation through Jordan that we might have to undertake. No one objected, least of all the local population, whom we found entirely friendly.

'Unfortunately, from our point of view, an operation in Iraq did not materialise and we were ordered back to the UK, which we reached about 12 November.'

The Division's return brought to a close a period of seven years during which time it had relied primarily on movement by sea. The years that followed were to see radical changes in its operational style, and the start of its close co-operation with 38 Group, Royal Air Force.

10.
The 1960s:
Airportable Strategic Reserve

The Airportable Concept

38 Group Royal Air Force

Joint Force Training

Kuwait Emergency, 1961

Berlin and the Cold War

United Nations Force HQ — Cyprus, 1964

Borneo, South Arabia and the New Professionals

Right: The United Nations Service Medal, Cyprus 1964.

'Ubique' - 2nd Regt. R.A.
'Triplex West' - 1963.

Above: The Chief of the Defence Staff, Admiral of the Fleet Earl
Mountbatten, visits HQ 3rd Division in Libya on Exercise Starlight,
1960, to see the new concept in operation. With him are left, Major-
General Charles Harington, GOC 3 Div, and right, Lieutenant-General
Sir Nigel Poett, GOC-in-C Southern Command./*Army Public Relations*

By 1959 the measures forecast in the 1957 Defence White Paper were ready for implementation. The first step was to nominate a divisional headquarters to command and train all UK-based field units allotted to the Strategic Reserve (less 16 Parachute Brigade) and one RAF Headquarters to co-ordinate support for the Army. HQ 3rd Division was selected as the army headquarters and in October 1959 it moved from Colchester to its traditional home, Bulford Camp, displacing HQ 1st Division which reformed in BAOR. It occupied a good building alongside that of HQ Salisbury Plain Sub-District, with whom it shared an officers' mess, and the happy working relationship established with their 'Landlords' has existed ever since.

3rd Division's brigades were widely spread — 1 Guards Brigade Group was now at Figsbury near Salisbury, 19 Brigade Group at Colchester, and 2 Brigade at Plymouth. Artillery and divisional units were distributed between Salisbury Plain, Colchester and Plymouth. 22nd Special Air Service Regiment, stationed at Malvern and later Hereford, also came under command. The interests of the Division were worldwide, for it was required to train and organise the Strategic Reserve so that any element of it, from a company to a brigade group, could move by air anywhere overseas for a variety of operational tasks ranging from internal security to conventional war. The new term 'brigade group' meant that 1 Guards and 19 Brigade Groups now included integral close support artillery, sapper and administrative units. 2 Brigade however was not designed to operate as an integrated group, but its individual units and headquarters were tasked with overseas reinforcement. Meanwhile Divisional Headquarters was to organise and train itself either to move abroad complete as a Force Headquarters, or to detach staff and logistic control elements to reinforce existing headquarters overseas.

When Major-General Charles Harington and his GSO1, Lieutenant-Colonel Hubert Penrose, took over their appointments at Bulford in the autumn of 1959 it was clear to them that it was extremely unlikely that the Division would ever be required to fight as a conventional infantry division, complete with three brigades and supporting arms and services. Instead, in Penrose's words:

'We were to be a great military supermarket, from which the planning staffs could select any combination of units and sub-units with which to meet a variety of overseas emergencies. Many people found it difficult at first to grasp the ramifications of the new role, for example the idea that supporting and logistic units should be capable of splitting themselves up into small self-contained elements, which don't normally appear on unit establishment tables. However we contrived to get everyone thinking the right way, and once they understood the concept and its challenges and interests they pursued it with vigour.

'Although there was a large number of troops directly under command — three brigades with normal supporting arms and services — there were many other units and resources who would support us or work with us on operations, and we had to build the closest possible relationship with them in peacetime. These included 16 Parachute Brigade, who might be required to seize landing grounds ahead of the force; fighter ground attack aircraft of both the RAF and Fleet Air Arm; Naval gunfire support, and indeed the full resources of Commando forces and naval assault ships. While not in any way attempting to take over any of these agencies, we had to establish with them joint operating procedures and in particular a quick method of getting things done. I think we were successful for in this type of situation it is personalities that count, and we all got on very well together.

'Of course, the Service which we were to rely on most, not only to support us during operations but indeed to lift us to the scene, was the Royal Air Force, and concurrent with 3rd Division assuming the Strategic Reserve role, Headquarters 38 Group was formed at RAF Upavon to command and train the appropriate air force units. We worked hand in glove with Air Vice Marshal Peter Wykeham and his SASO, Group Captain Charles Winn, from the start, and things couldn't have been better. In fact we tried to get them to share our headquarters building at Bulford but because it seemed traditional that an RAF headquarters should be on an airfield, they finally moved to Odiham which had just been rebuilt. It was a pity they were 40 miles away, but our excellent working relationship remained as good as ever.'

The coming together of 3rd Division and 38 Group was a most effective and happy event, for the bonds forged in 1960 are as strong, if not stronger, in 1977. 38 Group RAF therefore has a place of its own in this history.

Developing the Airportable Concept

Among the many subjects jointly studied by 3 Div and 38 Group were two of particular importance; one concerned the command and control of a force operating in an undeveloped country, the other was that of equipping the force so that it could initially move and be maintained by air. The size of the force could never be specified; it might be as large as two brigade groups but could be one brigade or even smaller. Even if one brigade only was committed, it would often be necessary to deploy the GOC and Force Headquarters to deal with political and strategic problems, both with the UK and the 'host' nation, and to provide all facets of support for the brigade group. Together HQ 3rd Division and 38 Group RAF would form a Joint Task Force Headquarters, with the Air Officer Commanding and his staff acting as the forward agent for the long range air maintenance of the force from UK or theatre base, commanding the medium and short range aircraft allotted to the force and allocating available close air support sorties.

An integrated and complex communications system for command and control of the force was provided by the divisional signal regiment and brigade signal squadrons, the Tactical Communications Wing RAF and 244 Signal Squadron (Air Support) for all air support links, 55 Signal Squadron (Volunteers) for logistic communications, and detachments from UK signal regiments for rear links back to the United Kingdom.

To plan the integration of the UK-based force with overseas commands in whose areas it might operate, the commanders and staffs of 3rd Division and 38 Group made a number of visits to headquarters abroad, and Penrose comments:

'I can't say that we were greeted with open arms wherever we went, and the RAF staff who went with us were often treated with positive coldness by their opposite numbers. Again, I don't think people abroad had properly grasped what our role was and regarded with grave suspicion the idea of a UK-based Force Headquarters operating in their parish. An example of this lack of realisation came with the 1961 Kuwait crisis, when Middle East Command cobbled together an ad hoc force headquarters. It was an obvious task for us, a task for which we had trained and organised ourselves, and many of the problems subsequently experienced in Kuwait stem from this failure to make use of the expertise of 3 Div and 38 Group.'

Equipping the Division so that it could move by air presented many problems but also provided wide scope for ideas and inventiveness. 19 Brigade was tasked with studying the ultra light-weight role, and experimented with techniques and equipment to enable it to move into battle by any means from Britannia to Whirlwind, while 1 Guards Brigade prepared itself for the semi light-weight role, where means of transport and communications would enable it to use a heavier scale of equipment and vehicles. Trials started in late 1959 and quickly showed that the traditional bulky and soldier-proof hardware of the AF G 1098 was largely unsuitable. A mobility trials fund was authorised and staff and services trawled industry to find the items necessary to save weight and increase efficiency. Within the Division the ingenuity of REME, sapper, logistic and medical units flourished, with equipment modifications and novel designs under constant trial and development. Airportable shelters for command posts and workshops, lightweight stores-handling equipment, and the carriage of stretchers in

landrovers were some of the more important of a host of innovations.

The landrover was the natural answer for airportable transport, but care was taken not to request more than could be sensibly airlifted. The aim was to arrive at unit staff tables divided into three elements: essential personnel, vehicles and freight to go by air; those that would follow by sea, for no force could be expected to subsist for ever on air supply; and those that could be left out of battle. There were other interesting factors: for example, what equipment and resources would be available in the theatre of operations? Public Works departments and oil companies owned large fleets of vehicles, which would probably be loaned, so the Intelligence Staff set about preparing dossiers on facilities and resources overseas. As trials continued, traditional reliance on vehicles evaporated, and unit vehicle empires disappeared, all landrovers — gun-towers even — being pooled, sometimes at brigade level. Above all, the individual soldier was trained to adopt a flexible attitude to movement. He became entirely self-sufficient on what he could carry, relied on resupply by air, and learnt the drills for entering battle by any form of transport — aircraft, vehicle or foot. Physical fitness, always essential for the soldier but often not as good as it should be, was given a new dimension by the need to be ready to move direct from English winter to tropical summer. Experiments with pre-acclimatisation in hot-houses were carried out, but it was acknowledged that nothing contributes more to rapid acclimatisation than constant physical fitness.The greatest impact on the soldier was his degree of individual involvement, and General Harington recalls:

'During my visits to brigades and units I was struck by the soldiers' enthusiasm for their new role. They were given the chance to experiment with their own ideas, instead of simply being told what to do. This was a great tonic for them, and many excellent suggestions for stowing kit and improvisation came from the soldiers themselves. Added to this was the exciting possibility of being flown to any part of the world at short notice, and

Left: 'The High Wire Act'. In the search for lightweight bridging, this system was devised by 3 Div Engineers and 8 Infantry Workshops, REME. At a demonstration at Colchester in April 1961, Brigadier Jackson, Commanding 19 Brigade, has as his passenger the CIGS, Field Marshal Sir Francis Festing./*By courtesy of Essex County Standard*

Right: The Beverley, with a payload of nearly 22 tons, could carry a variety of loads; and, for the first time, 3-ton vehicles could be airlifted. Here a 3 Div 3-tonner is loaded by RASC Air Despatchers during mobility trials in 1959. /*Army Public Relations*

their enthusiasm was most gratifying. Most of our junior ranks and many junior officers were still National Servicemen, and I feel this country often takes for granted the absolute reliance we placed on them, and the excellent service they gave us.'

A spirit of adventure pervaded the Division, a spirit which remains to this day. The shock-waves of any emergency, large or small, travelling from the ends of the earth, invariably touched 3rd Division, resulting in the despatch today of a battalion group, tomorrow of a small party of Royal Signals, RAMC or REME specialists. Every member of the division was involved in world affairs, every soldier mattered.

Until 1959, the staff of a divisional headquarters and the signallers of the divisional signal regiment were on separate establishments and belonged to separate units; yet in practice they were thoroughly intermingled in one functional headquarters. In the search for economy and mobility, trials were carried out to test the feasibility of amalgamating into one unit these separate elements, and as a result an integrated Headquarters and Signal Regiments, and Headquarters and Signal Squadrons were formed respectively at divisional and brigade headquarters. This measure was subsequently adopted throughout the British Army. These units were commanded by a Royal Signals officer and contained multifarious cap badges. In view of the role of 3rd Division a Chief Signal Officer (Colonel) was appointed to the Divisional headquarters staff. He was made responsible for all signals contingency planning and co-ordination of international, joint and logistic communications for the force, leaving the CO of the regiment free to provide the communication system to the forward components of the force, and the administration of all elements of force headquarters.

So much for developments within the 3rd Division. It is appropriate at this point to recall the history of 38 Group, Royal Air Force, the 3rd Division's partner in the Joint Force concept.

38 Group RAF and the Transport Support Tradition
The history of 38 Group, RAF starts in 1943 when 295 and 296 Squadrons of 38 Wing took part in the Allied landings in Sicily. 38 Wing's creditable performance showed the potential of a larger British airborne force, and so on 11 October 1943 the Wing was accorded Group status with a subsequently increased strength of 10 squadrons. No 38 Group's first AOC was AVM (later Air Chief Marshal Sir Leslie) Hollinghurst CB, OBE, DFC, whose use of a Spitfire as his personal transport between the Group's airfields established a tradition of using a fighter ground-attack aircraft which is followed by his successors — in 1977 the AOC, AVM Peter Williamson CB, CBE, DFC, travels between airfields by Jaguar or Harrier.

During the early months of 1944, the new Group was engaged in joint Army/RAF exercises, in bomber operations, and, later, in dropping supplies to the resistance movement and landing agents in the occupied countries of Europe. Finally, in June 1944, its ten squadrons, with five Dakots squadrons of 46 Group, were tasked to transport the 6th Airborne Division to France during Operation Overlord. After dropping pathfinder and coup-de-main parties shortly after midnight, aircraft of the two Groups dropped 4,310 paratroops and launched gliders carrying 493 troops, 17 guns, 44 jeeps, and 55 motorcycles during the early morning of the 6 June. Later the same day the Groups' aircraft returned with the remainder of the 6th Airborne, towed in gliders and watched from the ground by 3rd Division, fighting to enlarge its D-Day beachhead.

In 1945, 38 Group played an important part in Operation Varsity, the largest airborne assault ever, when on 24 March some 14,000 troops were dropped between five and six miles east of the Rhine. The Group also took part in Operation Schnapps, the relief of Copenhagen on VE-Day, and in Operation Doomsday, the transportation of 7,000 troops and 2,000 tons of equipment to Norway on the following days. Sir Leslie's successor, AVM J. R. Scarlett-Streatfield OBE, who had previously been refused permission by Tedder to take part in Varsity, was killed together with his crew and passengers when his aircraft crashed in a wood in Norway on 10 May 1945.

But 38 Group's most historic action was Operation Market (the air phase of Market Garden) in September 1944. Together, 38 and 46 Group were tasked to drop the first paratroops, to tow all the glider-borne forces and then to resupply the ground forces in the Arnhem sector; 38 Group was also to tow the glider-borne British Airborne Corps' Headquarters to the Nijmegen-Graves area. The lift on the 17 September was successful, but the second lift, on the following day, was critically delayed by bad weather and the gliders met heavy opposition on landing. The aircrew flying the resupply missions pressed on to their dropping zones despite the heavy and accurate anti-aircraft fire — Flight Lieutenant David Lord, a 46 Group Dakota pilot, was awarded a posthumous VC for making a second run over the DZ in his burning aircraft — and on the first major resupply mission alone, of 163 aircraft, 13 were destroyed and 97 damaged. Operation Market involved 12,997 Allied aircraft, including fighters, and 2,598 gliders; 238 aircraft and 139 gliders were lost. 38 Group's casualties were 21 killed, 159 missing, and 12 wounded.

During the second half of 1945, the Group's aircraft were fully employed in their transport role, flying 415 million passenger-miles, and establishing a daily service to India. In 1946 the Group contracted, until by April only two squadrons remained, but in 1947-49, 38 Group with a strength of up to two squadrons, was involved in several joint Army/RAF exercises, with relief operations during the harsh winter of 1947/48 and in the Berlin Airlift of 1948/49. Two of the more important exercises presaged its future role: in September 1947, in Exercise Longstop, the AOC, AVM A. L. Fiddament CBE, DFC, commanded the air forces in a mock war, and in Exercise Oil King in October 1950, the Group dropped the 16th

Parachute Brigade on to DZs in Norfolk. Later in that year, its Headquarters' functions were transferred to Transport Command, and on 1 February 1951, 38 Group disbanded.

38 Group's Reformation in 1960

With the emphasis placed on air transport and mobility by the new British strategy that evolved during the late 1950s, Transport Command's fleet and responsibilities grew. To shoulder the burden of controlling the tactical air support forces and providing tactical air mobility for the Army, and 3rd Division in particular, 38 Group was reformed on 1 January 1960. Group Headquarters was re-established at Upavon, in two wooden huts which had been moved there from the Isle of Wight in 1919. With an establishment of 17 officers and 20 airmen, it commanded two squadrons: 230, flying Single and later, Twin Pioneers at Upavon; and 225, flying Sycamores and Whirlwind Mark 4 helicopters from nearby Andover.

On appointing AVM Peter Wykeman DSO, OBE, DFC, AFC, to command the new Group on 18 January 1960, Air Marshall D. H. F. Barnett, the AOC-in-C Transport Command, gave him the following directions: 'Firstly, to plan and order all flying by No 225 and 230 Squadrons; Secondly, to plan and order all flying by such Hastings and Beverley aircraft, as may be allotted for designated tactical transport tasks; Thirdly, in collaboration with formation commanders of the Army to plan and analyse all tactical support exercises and operations; and Fourthly, to co-ordinate the requirements of the Army for air strike and air defence support in United Kingdom exercises, and to revise continuously the doctrines and techniques of tactical air transported and airborne assault operations.'

Below: Watched by, on the left, the AOC 38 Group, AVM Peter Wykeham, and SASO, Group Captain Charles Winn, Single Pioneers of 230 Squadron take off from Upavon for Ex Starlight, February 1960./*MOD Rep S*

Growth and development

In May 1960, the Group's Headquarters and its two short range tactical transport squadrons moved to the better equipped airfield at Odiham, and on 1 April 1961, it was given full command of all the tactical transport stations. Finally, on 1 January 1962, the two Hunter squadrons which had previously provided ground-attack support for the Army, 1 and 54, were transferred from Fighter Command to Transport Command to form the offensive support element of 38 Group.

Whilst the Hunters remained in service with 38 Group until the end of 1969, the Group's transport support aircraft were all replaced during the 1960s. Whirlwind helicopters took the place of Pioneers in 1962, and from 1961 Belvedere helicopters were also operated, these being replaced by Wessexs in 1964. Of medium and long-range transport aircraft, Beverleys and Hastings were gradually replaced by Argosys, in 1962 and 1963, and by Hercules and Andovers in 1968. By 1969 the Transport Support Force totalled one squadron (No 230) of Whirlwinds, two squadrons (Nos 18 and 72) of Wessex, two squadrons (Nos 114 and 267) of Argosys, one squadron (No 46) of Andovers, and four squadrons (Nos 24, 30, 36 and 47) of Hercules.

Top right: 38 Group support for 3rd Division in the 1960s. Offensive support: Nos 1 and 54 Squadrons were equipped with the Hawker Hunter, and were based at West Raynham, Norfolk. In the Ground Attack role the Hunter carried 36 rockets and 4 x 3mm Aden cannon, with a radius of action of 300nm./*MOD Rep S*

Centre right: Short Range Transport: Belvederes training at Odiham with underslung loads, 1961. The only twin-rotor helicopter ever to see service in the RAF, this aircraft could lift 25 troops or 5,500lb of freight. It remained in service for only four years./*MOD Rep S*

Right: Long Range Transport: The Hercules can carry 92 fully armed troops, 62 paratroops, or a wide variety of vehicle loads which include three scout cars or two landrovers with Mobat anti-tank guns. /*MOD Rep S*

Left: Medium Range Transport: Argosys of 114 Squadron from RAF Benson. These aircraft could carry either 69 troops, 54 paratroops, 48 stretchers or 14,000lb of equipment and vehicles, and could operate from semi-prepared surfaces./*MOD Rep S*

Top right: On Exercise Starlight, a Brigade Group was resupplied entirely by air: Troops of 1 Guards Brigade Group airhead company RASC unload a Twin Pioneer of 230 Squadron at Tmimi./*MOD Rep S*

Centre right: Single Pioneers of 230 Squadron landing, taxi-ing and unloading at a forward airstrip west of Tmimi. Both types of Pioneer could operate from very short, unprepared, landing strips. /*By courtesy of* Flight Magazine

Joint Force Training

The first overseas test of the joint airportable strategic reserve came in March 1960 with Exercise Starlight in Libya. Its aim was to practise the air move of a brigade group to an undeveloped country, and to maintain it there by air during operations against a Middle Eastern aggressor equipped with modern weapons including tanks. The forces participating were:

HQ 3rd Division	**HQ 38 Group RAF**
1 Guards Brigade Group	*LRT Force*
2nd Scots Guards	99 Squadron
1st Duke of Edinburgh's	(Britannias)
Royal Regiment	*Strike Force*
25 Field Regiment RA	8 Hunters
B Squadron Royal Horse	*MRT Force*
Guards (Armd Recce)	12 Beverleys
Malkara Troop, Queens Own	4 Hastings
Hussars (Airportable	*SRT Force*
Anti-Tank Guided Weapon)	8 Pioneers
23 Field Squadron RE	12 Whirlwinds

Enemy were provided by 1st Welch and A (Ajax) Squadron, 2nd Royal Tanks, who were already stationed in Libya.

Above: A Whirlwind of 225 Squadron picking up an underslung load of vehicle fuel at the 1 Guards Brigade airhead, Tmimi, to be lifted forward to units in the Jebel Akdar. The Whirlwind was finally replaced by the Puma in the early 1970s./*By courtesy of* Flight Magazine

Left: The airhead at Tmimi quickly became a dustbowl as Beverleys maintained a shuttle service from El Adem with combat supplies./*MOD rep S*

Both logistically and tactically, Starlight provided unique experience for staffs and units, and the exercise area — the barren desert and rugged Jebel Akdar west of El Adem — gave them thorough practice in air movement and resupply. By the end of the exercise the brigade airhead at Tmimi was 60 miles forward of the Strategic airfield at El Adem, the fighting troops 50 miles beyond that, and a total of 3,550 personnel, 670 vehicles and trailers, 40 guns and 2 million pounds of freight were moved through the brigade airhead. Major-General Harington stated afterwards that the exercise was of enormous value, but perhaps his most significant conclusion was that a lightweight force operating in good tank country against a well-equipped enemy must have its own tanks. The Malkara (a defensive weapon) even when supplemented by Hunter FGA aircraft, could not provide the offensive anti-armour capability so essential to a force if it is to intervene successfully. He recommended that tanks should be stockpiled overseas in areas where they might be needed, and that suitable shipping should be earmarked, capable of transporting and unloading tanks at an unsophisticated port with its own derricks. He also sounded a warning against the danger of overloading the infantryman beyond his fighting capacity, which could result from the constant efforts to reduce transport.

38 Group also found Starlight to be of great value, and AVM Peter Wykeham considered that it was: 'The first realistic test of the Army support techniques that have been progressed during the last few years . . . This exercise was extremely successful from the Royal Air Force point of view both in providing lessons and practice, and also in proving that though many details need attention, the main concepts of Army/Air co-operation are sound and capable of withstanding the test of operations.'

38 Group develops its Techniques

The exercises of the early 1960s showed that there were three particular aspects needing attention. Firstly, to support the UK Strategic Reserve in tactical operations overseas, the Group needed the ability to move its aircraft quickly to the area of operations, for whilst other equipment could be stockpiled abroad, sophisticated and expensive aircraft could not; secondly, it had to be able to

drop equipment and troops, accurately and without damage in all weathers, and preferably by night as well as by day, in featureless country; and thirdly, it had to be able to operate in the field with the minimum of facilities.

The time taken to deploy short-range aircraft even to the Mediterranean area was a major problem. To arrive in Libya to begin operations by 21 March 1960 for Starlight, the first Whirlwinds had to leave Andover by road for Abingdon on 7 February, to be airlifted by Beverley to El Adem. For the major exercise of 1963, Triplex West, (described later) the main party of five Whirlwinds and two Belvederes flew from Odiham to El Adem, but most of the Whirlwinds, delayed by servicing problems, arrived after the exercise had finished. Even in 1965, the Wessex helicopters taking part in Exercise Dazzle in Libya had to fly from Odiham to El Adem in seven stages and had to allow three days to complete the journey. It was not until the Belfast entered service that the problem was solved; on 3 August 1966, a 53 Squadron Belfast carried two 72 Squadron Wessex helicopters from the UK to Akrotiri with a minimum of dismantling so that they were able to be flown within hours of the Belfast's landing in Cyprus.

The problems of dropping troops and equipment were two-fold. Those involving the malfunction of dropping equipment or the non-deployment of parachutes were solved by modifying existing equipment and introducing new parachutes and containers, developed by the Army Air Transport Training and Development Centre. The difficulties in finding DZs and dropping accurately in featureless country, at night or in bad weather were resolved by using the Calculated Air Release Point (CARP) dropping technique, the Argosy's more advanced navigation equipment, and by training the most experienced crews as a Pathfinder force.

In 1960, 38 Group's fixed wing short-range tactical transport aircraft, its technical and domestic equipment, and even the clothing of its air and ground crews were more suited to operating on permanent station rather than in the field. The limitations of Pioneers (which required landing-strips) and the limited capabilities of the Sycamore and Whirlwind Mark 4 helicopters were overcome by the introduction of the Whirlwind Mark 10

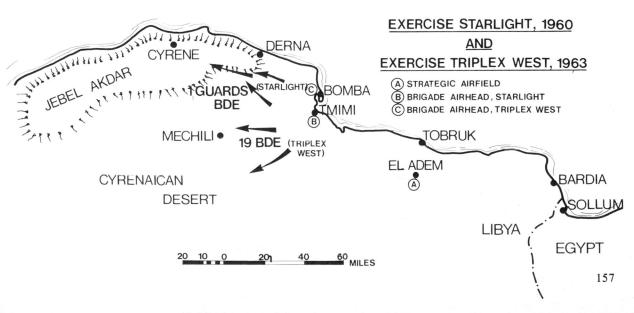

EXERCISE STARLIGHT, 1960
AND
EXERCISE TRIPLEX WEST, 1963

(A) STRATEGIC AIRFIELD
(B) BRIGADE AIRHEAD, STARLIGHT
(C) BRIGADE AIRHEAD, TRIPLEX WEST

and the Belvedere in 1961, and the Wessex in 1964. The communications, air traffic control and navigation problems that arose from operating in the field were solved in a number of ways. A new unit — 38 Group Support Unit — was formed, small airportable radio and radar equipments were designed and developed, and a series of joint communications exercises were held. Gradually a modus operandi was evolved which, with modification, was suitable for worldwide use. Finally, there were short-comings in the Group's field equipment that led the unnamed author of the 38 Group report on Exercise Stormy Petrel, held on Salisbury Plain in August 1960, to write:

'There was no lightweight tentage available from RAF sources, an Igloo tent was borrowed from HQ 1 Guards Brigade (for the officers), but the two airmen were unfortunately accommodated in one-man bivouacs; at best these could only be described as shelters. During bad weather the occupants chose to sleep in the landrover. The only dress available for airmen... was a suit of denim overalls. In order to improve the appearance and comfort of airmen... some form of combat clothing, preferably blue in colour, should be made available.'

By the end of the 1960s, officers and airmen wore camouflaged flying and combat suits, lived in purpose-made camouflaged tents, drove camouflaged vehicles and flew camouflaged aircraft. The Group's equipment had been completely adapted for operating in the field, and was virtually indistinguishable from the Army's.

Plans for Joint Training in Portugal

As soon as Starlight was over preparations started for the next exercise, scheduled to take place in Portugal in July - August 1961, and nicknamed Batalha, after the battle in which John of Gaunt's archers helped the Portuguese to free themselves from Spain. This exercise was to introduce a number of new aspects, including an assault river crossing and co-operation with allies. Forces taking part were to include Joint Force HQ, 19 Brigade and a Portuguese Brigade, while 2 Brigade was to provide the enemy. All concerned looked forward to a most interesting period of training, and 3rd Division was delighted to hear that their hosts were to be the 3rd Portuguese Division. Both formations recalled the bonds forged in battle when the 'Fighting Division' had included a Portuguese brigade in the Peninsular War, and a picture of the Battle of Bussaco and a silver statuette of a British soldier of 1809 were prepared for presentation to the Portuguese. But 1961 was to prove a turbulent year internationally. In June the first cloud appeared on the horizon when in Parliament the Opposition raised objections to the exercise on the grounds of Portugal's policy in Angola. The Government confirmed that the exercise would take place, but the seeds of doubt had been sown. Worse was to follow when, a few days before

Left: The statuette presented to the 3rd Portuguese Division in July 1961. It is now in the office of the Commander of the Independent Brigade at Santa Margarida; from 1979 this brigade will be the Portuguese Army's contribution to NATO.

the start of the exercise, President Kassem of Iraq announced his intention of annexing Kuwait with its oilfields. On 27 June Kuwait requested British aid and the airlift allotted for Batalha disappeared overnight to Kenya to move 24 Brigade, the Middle East reserve, to the Persian Gulf. Batalha was promptly cancelled.

Kuwait, 1961

The disappointment for 19 Brigade caused by cancellation of the exercise quickly evaporated when on 1 July it was put at short notice to move to Kenya to replace 24 Brigade. On 8 July the move started, and within four days brigade headquarters, 1st Duke of Wellington's and the brigade engineer squadron, field ambulance and administrative units had arrived at Kahawa Camp, near Nairobi. Other 3 Div units were also on their way — members of the 3rd Carabiniers from Tidworth were flown out to man Centurion tanks stockpiled in Kuwait, together with 29th Field Regiment RA from Plymouth who were to provide the close artillery support for 24 Brigade. 29th Regiment's CO was Lt-Col Terence McMeekin (who was to command 3rd Division in 1968-70) and he recalls that having occupied the Mutla Ridge in Kuwait before the Iraqis could advance 'it became a matter of survival in the heat, which reached 140° in the shade. Although the Iraqis never attacked, we were able to arrange effective and useful joint support exercises with the RAF and Fleet Air Arm, normally early in the morning when the heat was just bearable.' Meanwhile in Kenya 19 Brigade's minor units and the Duke of Wellington's were also able to train under rather more pleasant conditions.

Below: 3rd Division's mobility in the 1960s took many forms: The reconnaissance platoon of the 1st Grenadiers in the Cameroons in 1961 equipped itself with local Fulani horses. Small and hardy, these animals enabled the platoon to lift itself and its equipment through the mountains and bush to otherwise inaccessible parts of the territory.
/Mr C. T. Blackwood

The scattering of 3 Div units around East Africa and the Gulf during this emergency illustrated vividly the working of the supermarket concept previously described, and gave units excellent experience in the mechanics of reinforcement by air.

Meanwhile, 3 Div was fulfilling another little known overseas commitment — the provision of a security force for the Southern Cameroons in West Africa during the last six months of the United Nation's mandate before the territory became part of the Cameroon Republic in October 1961. The task was entrusted to 1st Grenadiers of 51 Brigade, as 1 Guards Brigade had been redesignated in November 1960. The Grenadiers flew out in May together with Sapper, Signals, RASC, RAMC, REME, and Pay and Postal elements all from 3rd Division. For six months Lt-Col (now General Sir David) Fraser and his men carried out perhaps one of the most remote and interesting tasks ever given to a battalion group. However, as one would expect from a battalion of the Foot Guards, they did not omit to celebrate the Queen's Birthday in traditional style. At Bamenda on 22 June led by the Queen's Company, the Battalion carried out a full ceremonial parade to the delight and wonderment of the local population. By the end of October the Grenadier battalion group was back in UK, as were the majority of units deployed during the Kuwait emergency.

Berlin and the Cold War

The year of 1961 continued to provide its share of surprises for 3rd Division. While attention was focused on Kuwait, the East Germans built the Berlin Wall and the Warsaw Pact nations indulged in a particularly noisy bout of sabre-rattling. Tension increased but even so the staff of HQ 3rd Division were taken aback to read in the newspapers on 25 August that 3 Div was being earmarked, with additional armour, to reinforce BAOR. This announcement, coming as it did without official confirmation, led to speculation to say the least. One

Above: The Officers of HQ 3rd Division, October 1961.
Back Row: Lt C. J. M. Haines, RB; Capt B. E. Samuels, Int Corps;
Capt D. J. Brind, RA; Capt M. C. C. Mogridge, Stafford; Capt
N. A. Gould, REME; Capt J. S. Bartholomew, GM, RE; Capt C. R. H.
Wells, RASC; Capt J. Gilmour, RA; Lt (QM) J. E. Edwards, East
Anglian; Capt W. E. Spreadbury, RASC; Capt B. W. G. Newby,
REME; Capt T. W. Evans, MBE, APTC.
Centre Row: Capt P. D. Mitchell, RAOC; Maj W. M. Allen, RASC;
Maj M. P. Dewing, 7 GR; Maj G. W. N. Obbard, RE; Maj
R. R. McNish, R Sussex; Maj G. B. Duckworth, R Tks; Maj
D. K. Neville, RA; Maj J. A. M. Flood, RAEC; Maj A. V. Burge, BEM,
RE; Maj J. M. Rogerson, REME; Maj H. F. Hutchinson, DCM, RMP;
Maj R. G. Davies, MC, RMP; Maj J. D. Stevenson ACC; Capt R. T. T.
Gurdon, BW; Maj E. L. Walker, RAOC.
Front Row: Lt-Col A. E. P. Joy, MBE, REME; Lt-Col T. A. K. Savage,
MBE, RASC; Lt-Col W. F. Cooper, MC, RE; Col J. M . S. Tulloch,
OBE; Lt-Col R. E. Worsley, RB; Maj-Gen V. W. Street, CMG, CBE,
DSO, MC; Brig J K. Greenwood, OBE; Lt-Col R. M. Somerville,
MBE, RA; Col W. M. Stewart, OBE; Lt-Col T. W. Baynes, MBE,
R Sigs; Lt-Col L. Brookes, RAOC. Lt-Col J. R. M. Gray, MBE, RAPC.
Brigadier Greenwood, the CRAC, assumed command of the Division in
1962 when General Street was admitted to hospital, and Lt-Col
Worsley, the GSO 1, was to return as GOC 3 Div in 1972-1974.

particularly puzzling aspect was the source of the
additional armour, for both the operational tank
regiments based in UK — the 3rd Carabiniers and
11th Hussars at Tidworth — were already part of
3rd Division. The Press announcement was followed on
1 September by a War Office letter which ordered the
reorganisation of the Strategic Reserve to meet BAOR
requirements, but without mention of additional armour.
The BAOR training instruction was received on
2 October, and on the same day Major-General Charles
Harington handed over to his successor, Major-General
Vivian Street.

The task facing the new GOC was formidable. He was
required, within six months, to train the Division for
nuclear warfare in North West Europe, while still
retaining the overseas limited war capability. Divisions in
1st British Corps (in BAOR) were fully equipped with
armoured troop-carrying vehicles, and organised on a
50:50 ratio of tanks to mechanised infantry. However
3rd Division was to receive no additional armour, and
had somehow to adapt its lightweight character and
tactics to defeat an enemy composed of tank and motor
rifle divisions.

Throughout the winter of 1961-62, 19. and 51 Brigade
trained hard for the new role, with Divisional
headquarters carrying out a series of command post
exercises based on 1st Corps procedures. A constant
stream of officers visited BAOR, attending exercises and
conferences, and planning went as far as selecting
barracks for the Division in Germany. By April 1962
when brigade test exercises took place, retraining was
complete, but the Division was dismayed to hear that
while directing 19 Brigade's exercise — Panther's Leap
— General Vivian Street had suffered a heart attack and
been admitted to hospital. The CRAC, Brigadier
Greenwood assumed command during the GOC's
absence, but Street was compelled to retire later in the
year as a result of his illness. This cruel disappointment
did not lessen his determination to make a contribution to
those less fortunate than himself, and he became
Chairman of the Save the Children Fund. In 1970 those
many members of 3rd Division who remembered his
dedication and charm while in command were saddened
to hear of his death.

The move to Germany never materialised for during
the early summer of 1962 tension eased, and although
3 Div retained a contingency task in Europe it was able to
re-apply itself to the airportable strategic reserve role.
Planning for an autumn Joint Force exercise in Northern
Ireland for 51 Brigade, named Winged Coachman, went
ahead. In May this Brigade underwent a radical change in

character when, for the first time in history, Gurkha troops were stationed in UK. HQ 63 Gurkha Infantry Brigade, 1/6th Gurkha Rifles, 68 Gurkha Field Squadron and 30 Company Gurkha ASC arrived in England and assumed the title and role of 51 Brigade, whilst retaining the Crossed Kukris sign of the Gurkhas. The bravery, discipline and good humour of Gurkha troops are universally acknowledged, and the splendid impression these units made on the Division and the British public confirmed this reputation. When Winged Coachman took place in November the Gurkhas displayed their traditional efficiency and hardiness under appalling weather conditions in the Mountains of Mourne, and the AQ staff at Force HQ scored well when they arranged release of 600 Parkas from an Ordnance Depot at 10pm on a Saturday night; the garments were airlifted to Ulster on the Sunday morning and on the backs of the Gurkhas by midday.

In September 1962 Major-General Michael Carver assumed command from Brigadier Greenwood, just as planning was starting for a further major Joint Force exercise, named Triplex West, due to take place in late 1963.

Exercise Triplex West

Triplex West was essentially a sequel to Starlight, taking place in the same area with a similar setting, but incorporating the lessons of the previous exercise. In particular the infantry element of the brigade group was reduced to one battalion, and a tank regiment and armoured car regiment included. One squadron of Centurions for the former had been stockpiled at El Adem as a result of General Harington's recommendations. The firepower of the force was greatly increased by the inclusion of an aircraft carrier, six frigates, a squadron each of Canberras and Javelins, and two of Hunters. A summary of forces taking part was:

GOC 3 Div and AOC 38 Group were joined by FOF (MED) as joint commanders, and the tri-service character of the force was reflected in Joint Force Headquarters, which included staff from HQ FOF (MED), and totalled 180 officers. This huge cuckoo's egg in the El Adem nest was viewed with misgivings by the Station Commander, but JFHQ pitched its marquees on the far side of the airfield and resisted the temptation to make free with the limited facilities of the station.

The build-up of the force in Libya took longer than for Starlight, for it included the activation of the Centurion stockpile at El Adem and the movement of the balance of the Inniskilling's tanks from UK by heavy lift ship. The tactical phase thoroughly tested the logistic support of the brigade group, for the distance from El Adem to the brigade airhead at Bomba was 65 miles, and forward troops advanced a further 50 miles. After the exercise, Carver emphasised the problem of anti-armour weapons for an airportable force, and his recommendations included the up-gunning of the Strategic Reserve Centurions from 20 pounder to 105mm, so as to be capable of destroying the Russian T54 at long range in the desert, and the replacement of the conspicuous Malkara anti-tank GW with Vigilant.

UN Force Headquarters in Cyprus, 1964

The headquarters staff had barely shaken the sand out of their bedding rolls on return from Triplex West, when ripples of trouble from that traditional cauldron — Cyprus — reached the United Kingdom. During Christmas 1963 the island erupted in voilence, with Greek and Turk at each other's throats in Nicosia and Larnaca. Under pressure from the Secretary of State for Commonwealth Relations, Mr Duncan Sandys, President Makarios accepted the intervention of a British truce force. Major-General Peter Young, GOC Cyprus

HQ 3 Div	HQ 38 Group RAF	HQ Flag Officer Flotillas Mediterranean (FOF (MED))
19 Brigade Group	*Bomber/PR Force*	
	20 Canberras	
5th Inniskilling	6 Shackletons	
Dragoon Guards (Tanks)		HMS *Hermes*, with embarked:
		10 Sea Vixens
14th/20th Hussars	*FGA Force*	9 Scimitars
(Armoured Cars)	8 Javelins	4 Gannets
	28 Hunters	4 Wessex (AS)
C Sqn, 2nd Royal Tank		2 Whirlwinds (SAR)
Regiment (Malakara	*LRT Force*	
Anti-tank GW)	6 Britannias	HMS *Surprise* (HQ Ship)
Troop, Life Guards		HMS *Rhyl*
(Scout Cars)	*MRT Force*	HMS *Undaunted*
	8 Argosies	HMS *Diamond*
2nd Regiment RA	4 Beverleys	HMS *Agincourt*
	14 Hastings	HMS *Lowestoft*
1st Foresters		HMS *Murray*
	SRT Force	
3rd Field Sqn RE	10 Whirlwinds	4 Coastal Minesweepers

Escort, Radar Picket, Air Defence and NGS Frigates

Above: Gurkhas on Salisbury Plain; Brigadier N. E. V. (Brunny) Short, Commander 51 Brigade, talks to soldiers of the 1st/6th Queen Elizabeth's Own Gurkha Rifles during a pause in training./*1/6 GR*

District. despatched the two battalions garrisoned in the Sovereign Base Areas (SBA) to carry out the task, and reinforcements from UK followed including 2nd Regiment RA from 3 Div, and elements of 16 Parachute Brigade. Cyprus Headquarters was too small to control the rapidly escalating situation and HQ 3rd Division was warned early in January for possible deployment to Cyprus to command the peace-keeping force. At the end of the month notice was reduced to 72 hours and after a series of conferences at the Ministry of Defence and a visit to Cyprus on 2 February, Major-General Carver, with his headquarters, took off from Lyneham on 14 February. On landing at Nicosia that evening the staff found themselves welcomed at the station mess in the middle of a St Valentines Day Dance, dressed somewhat incongruously in combat kit and pistols.

On 19 February, after quickly establishing his headquarters, Carver assumed operational command of all British Army units outside the SBAs, and became directly subordinate to the C-in-C Near East, Air Chief Marshal Sir Denis Barrett. GOC Cyprus District remained responsible for command of the SBAs.

For operational control, Cyprus was divided into three zones — Eastern, Western and Northern, the latter including Nicosia, Kyrenia and the 'pan handle' area, which was the responsibility of HQ 16 Parachute Brigade under Brigadier (later General Sir Roland) Gibbs, who became CGS in 1976. Carver called out from UK his HQ RA 3rd Division to command Western zone, and continued to command Eastern zone through Headquarters Dhekelia Garrison. The Western and Eastern zones each contained an infantry-role major unit, an armoured car squadron and a sapper squadron, while the particularly sensitive Northern zone was controlled by four infantry-role units, plus armoured cars and sappers.

In his first operational directive issued on 20 February, Carver gave as the mission the prevention of inter-communal fighting, and the reduction of tension to conditions in which free movement and normal life could be resumed. Greek and Turk remained as ever obdurate; neither side was prepared to abandon the use of force, regarding the task of the troops as being to assist them in disarming their opponents. Violence continued unabated, British troops being continually required to intervene. They saved many lives, particularly of women and schoolchildren.

On 4 March a United Nations resolution was passed establishing a UN peacekeeping force, with General Gyani of India as commander, General Carver as his deputy, and the headquarters of 3rd Division acting as Force Headquarters. There were to be five nations represented in addition to Britain: Canada, Sweden, Ireland, Finland and Denmark. The first contingent, from Canada, was scheduled to arrive on 14 March.

The UN announcement was followed by a series of requests from the contributing nations concerning their share of appointments in Force Headquarters — it would seem that each wished to be represented by a Brigadier at

CYPRUS, 1964

UN COMMAND ORGANISATION

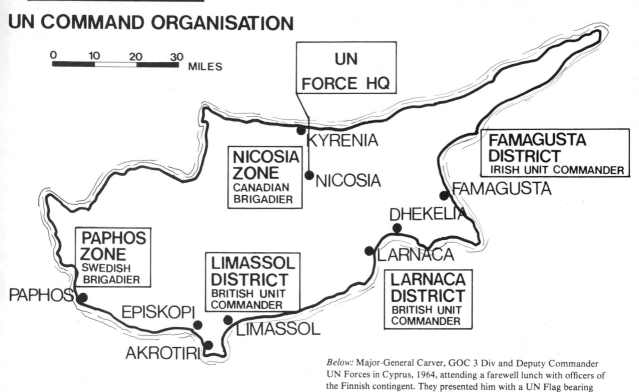

0 10 20 30 MILES

UN FORCE HQ

KYRENIA

NICOSIA ZONE
CANADIAN BRIGADIER

NICOSIA

FAMAGUSTA DISTRICT
IRISH UNIT COMMANDER

FAMAGUSTA

DHEKELIA

PAPHOS ZONE
SWEDISH BRIGADIER

PAPHOS

LIMASSOL DISTRICT
BRITISH UNIT COMMANDER

LARNACA

LARNACA DISTRICT
BRITISH UNIT COMMANDER

EPISKOPI

LIMASSOL

AKROTIRI

Below: Major-General Carver, GOC 3 Div and Deputy Commander UN Forces in Cyprus, 1964, attending a farewell lunch with officers of the Finnish contingent. They presented him with a UN Flag bearing emblems of all contingents represented./*Field Marshal Lord Carver*

least — and it looked as if HQ 3rd Division would rapidly become multi-national and top-heavy. Carver deftly avoided this situation while satisfying national aspirations by giving the Canadians and Swedes each an area of their own under a Brigadier, while the Irish provided a Colonel as MA to General Gyani. The Finns and Danes, each with smaller contingents, agreed to serve under the Canadian brigade headquarters, and on 27 March the UN force was officially established. Throughout this period the headquarters staff were kept busy dealing with the many novel administrative questions posed by a multinational force. Colonel John Tomes, who was the AA and QMG, remembers some of the problems:

'The first contingent to arrive was Canadian and since they were somewhat akin to ourselves I did not expect many problems. How wrong can you be! The battalion was from the R 22nd Regiment and was almost entirely French-speaking. So with 90% of the population of Cyprus speaking English, and with contingents from Finland and Sweden, very few of who could speak English, we also had the problem of a French-speaking unit as well.

'The Finns were a large contingent and after a period of settling in at Larnaca, were moved to their operational station in the north of the Island. They decided to move by bicycle. Cyprus is very hot and hilly but then Finns are very fit! We had problems with the Finns over food. They didn't really understand about compo and at first were inclined to empty the complete contents of the box — cigarettes, loo paper, boiled sweets and other items — into a large cauldron in order to make stew. We got over the problem by organising, with the help of Cyprus District, a small mobile catering team which went round each unit to advise on the best use that could be made of British field rations.

'The Irish battalion arrived next and was sent to Famagusta where the 2nd Royal Inniskilling Fusiliers were instructed to act as hosts. It was interesting to see units from the North and South alongside each other. It was also surprising to the Irish Army to find that the CO of the Inniskillings was a Roman Catholic. The two units also discovered quite quickly that they had a number of men in their respective ranks who had deserted from the other side and re-enlisted. However, they got on very well and the officers of the Irish battalion gave a special dinner to which only British officers were invited. This was a thank you for our help in getting them settled in. It must have been the first occasion on which an Irish regiment had drunk the Loyal Toast — we also drank to the President. This then became an occasion for the alternate singing of Loyalist and Republican songs — it was a few years before the present troubles started.'

By June the three-month mandate for the existing UN force was running out, and discussions opened on the composition of its successor. There were many arguments for reducing the British element — which had been vilified by Greek and Turk alike — to logistic units only, but it was difficult to see where the UN Secretary General could find sufficient acceptable troops to replace the British. However it was quite essential for HQ 3rd Division to return to UK and resume its Strategic

Reserve role. A compromise was reached whereby the British contingent would be reduced to one battalion and an armoured car squadron, and that Britain would provide aircraft, the majority of the headquarters staff (including a Brigadier Chief of Staff), signals and logistic support. Thirteen years later this contribution remains much the same.

HQ 3rd Division was reconstituted in UK by September 1964 and General Carver paid the following tribute to those who ultimately shoulder the burden in peacekeeping operations:

'Considering the strains and frustrations to which the soldiers of both the British and United Nations Force and their commanders were subjected, the fact that on no occasion did they lose their tempers or attempt to take revenge, and that almost invariably they acted with commonsense and balanced judgement in situations which could not be foreseen, is evidence of their high standards of discipline and sense of responsibility, for which I, as Commander of the British Joint Truce Force and Deputy Commander of United Nations Force in Cyprus, was always extremely grateful and shall ever remain so.'

Borneo, South Arabia and the New Professionals

The years that immediately followed HQ 3rd Division's return from Cyprus were dominated by the emergencies in Borneo and South Arabia. Although Divisional headquarters was not deployed to either theatre, its brigades and units played a full part in both campaigns. The first to go in 1964 was, perhaps naturally, HQ 51 Brigade with its large Gurkha element, and in Borneo it took control of the Central Brigade Area. Clearly 51 Brigade would be there for some time, so its place in 3 Div at Tidworth was taken by HQ 5 Brigade,

Above left: Peace-keeping at its best, as only the British soldier can do it; a Corporal of 16 Parachute Brigade in Cyprus, 1964. This photograph was used as the 3 Div Christmas card, inscribed 'Peace on earth, Goodwill towards men'.
/General Sir Cecil Blacker

Above: Troopers of the 22nd Special Air Service Regiment deploying into action in the Radfan, South Arabia, from a Wessex Helicopter. 22 SAS are specialists in deep patrolling and surveillance. Introduced in 1964 the Wessex is still in service; it is capable of lifting 12 troops or 3,000lb of freight, including an underslung landrover, close-support artillery, or anti-tank gun.*/22 SAS*

Right: In January 1966, Field Marshal Lord Montgomery visited 3rd Division to present the Headquarters with the pennant flown on his car in 1940.
/General Sir Cecil Blacker

Above: Air mobility training in UK, 1966. 72 Squadron of 38 Group, equipped with Wessex helicopters, lifts an infantry rifle company on Exercise Lifeline at Sennybridge, South Wales./*MOD Rep S*

which moved to UK from BAOR in June. That month HQ RE 3rd Division was sent on a 6-month tour to South Arabia, where it operated under the title of HQ Dhala Road Project. It controlled all engineer units building the road which ran northwards from Aden through the rugged mountains and hostile tribesmen of the Radfan, to Dhala on the frontier with Yemen.

During 1965 both HQ 5 and HQ 19 Brigade carried out an emergency tour in Borneo, and in the ensuing years units flitted backwards and forwards to Arabia, Malaysia, Cyprus, British Guiana, Gibraltar, and Thailand with remarkable rapidity. The soldiers of these units were the professionals of the new all-regular army, and during its early formative days Major-General 'Monkey' Blacker, who had assumed command of 3 Div in late 1964, paid particular attention to the problems of converting a National Service Division to a regular one. He found that in many instances NS training standards and ideas — necessarily simple in view of the requirement to train large numbers of men in limited time — still prevailed. Throughout his period in command, General Blacker emphasised the importance of imaginative, demanding leadership and individual tactical skill, for no longer could the army rely for success on 'mass tactics, mass support, and long lines of brave soldiers advancing in the open'. He also experienced manning problems as certain regiments had been initially slow to recruit regulars, and were therefore too weak to be used operationally.

The challenge posed by operations in Borneo and the Radfan was a fine test of the New Professionals, and the successes achieved by 1968 showed what could be done with a small, but well-trained service. But the pace of life brought complications. In March 1966 the GOC found

that out of 21 major units in the Division, seven were overseas on emergency tours and six due to leave within eight months. Turbulence had never been worse — family turbulence, regimental turbulence, formation turbulence. Commenting on the latter at the Infantry Conference in 1966, Blacker said: 'Commanders have to develop a Strategic Reserve mentality, the basis for which is the well known expression 'off the cuff'. I am often sorry for those like the freshly promoted brigadier, keen and dynamic and tingling with the desire to impose his personality on his command, who has arrived to find it consisting of one battalion just about to wave him goodbye on a trip to the Far East, and another just back from Borneo with only one desire — to be left alone by dynamic Brigadiers.'

In 1964, 16 Parachute Brigade became part of 3rd Division, having been independent for 10 years. There was no sinister significance in the change of command — simply a confirmation that the limited-war and counter-insurgency roles of 16 Para and 3 Div were the same. So for the three years that followed the Division consisted of three brigades — 5, 19 and 16. In 1967 Aden was evacuated, and home to Plymouth came 24 Brigade, which was also placed under 3rd Division. Thus Major-General Tony Deane-Drummond, who had taken over as GOC in Autumn 1966, commanded a Division with more units than ever before in its history. The total of 'teeth-arm' units was thirteen infantry battalions, six gunner regiments, one armoured regiment, three armoured reconnaissance regiments, one parachute armoured squadron, five engineer squadrons, and 22nd SAS Regiment. The Division continued to plan for many contingencies worldwide and this provided the opportunity to hold large annual airportable exercises and frequent unit exercises overseas, in conjunction with 38 Group RAF and its aircraft.

By 1968 both the Aden and Borneo emergencies were over and troops had been withdrawn to UK. A new era for 3rd Division was soon to start.

11.
The 1970s:
United Kingdom Mobile Force

A New Role within NATO

38 Group RAF in the 1970s

Reinforcement of Ulster

Overseas Emergencies Continue

A Tactical Concept for Europe

Restructuring and the Future

Right: The General Service Medal, 1969-1977.

Assigned to NATO — The European Concept.

Above: On the flanks of NATO: Scorpion reconnaissance vehicles of
C Squadron, The Life Guards, loading in Norway after Exercise Atlas
Express, March 1976./*The Life Guards*

The Statement on the Defence Estimates presented to Parliament in February 1968 announced the following policy decisions:

'It has been a fundamental principle of the current examination that reductions in capability, whether in terms of manpower or equipment, must be accompanied by reductions in the tasks imposed by the commitments that we require the Services to undertake. We have no intention of allowing a repetition of the situation which existed in 1964 when, because of the lack of balance between military tasks and resources, our forces were seriously overstretched.

'The major decisions which the Government has taken may be broadly summarized as follows:

'Britains defence effort will in future be concentrated mainly in Europe and the North Atlantic area .... No special capability for use outside Europe will be maintained when our withdrawal from Singapore and Malaysia, and the Persian Gulf, is complete.'

The effect of these decisions was that from 1969 3rd Division's primary role, together with elements of 38 Group RAF, was to form the 'United Kingdom Mobile Force'. The task of the UKMF was the reinforcement of NATO forces in Europe, and this was to take precedence over the capability of deploying a force of up to brigade strength elsewhere overseas.

Major-General Terence McMeekin had assumed command of 3rd Division in 1968. He and Air Vice Marshal Martin were determined that the benefits of the Joint Force concept, developed on overseas exercises during nine exhilarating years, should be fully used in the new role. They therefore travelled extensively in North West Europe with the aim of determining where the light weight air-mobile character of their joint force could best be employed — areas where natural obstacles would limit the effectiveness of enemy armoured forces. Two possibilities were examined and found suitable; firstly, the heavily wooded and hilly region of central Germany, and secondly Schleswig-Holstein — 'Jutland' — with its numerous waterways and extensive inundations. In these areas resolute, well-trained infantry, expert in the art of tank destroying and with the flexibility of transport helicopter support, could play havoc with enemy armour.

In the early days — 1969 to 1970 — both McMeekin and his successor, Major-General Glyn Gilbert, found that the concept of an airportable division was not easy to 'sell' to the armoured and mechanised experts in Europe; but Gilbert remembered his time as a company commander in 1944, when panzer grenadiers fighting in close country had opposed 3rd Division in Normandy. Confronted with vastly superior forces, subjected to incessant bombardment from massed artillery, naval gunfire, and aircraft, and with no air support, these highly trained and determined German soldiers had succeeded in confining the Allies to their beachhead for nearly six weeks. Surely this lesson could be applied to 3rd Division in the 1970s, with its much improved anti-armour weapons and air-mobile capability. Reason prevailed and the options of the Central area and Jutland were confirmed. In addition, alternative tasks for a brigade on the flanks of NATO were agreed.

Changes in Order of Battle were to follow. In 1968 the Division had four brigades — 5, 16, 19 and 24 — under command, and this had worked perfectly well for Strategic operations. However in 1970, since it was decided that the likely tasks of 16 Parachute Brigade in Europe would not necessarily be linked to that of 3rd Division, the Brigade was placed under the operational command of HQ Strategic Command at Wilton as part of the Joint Airborne Task Force; and as the role of 22nd SAS Regiment was also separate from that of 3 Div, this regiment left to become part of the newly formed SAS Group. Meanwhile 24 Brigade had moved from Plymouth, first to Barnard Castle and then in 1973 to Topcliffe, Yorkshire, and by 1970 the title 'Airportable' had been adopted by all three brigades in the Division.

The Division's European role, while geographically more limited than previously was just as challenging, and together with 38 Group RAF, and RN Carriers and Amphibious Ships, training was pursued with customary vigour. However, the outbreak of violence in Northern Ireland in the Summer of 1969 was to have a marked effect on 3rd Division's training and deployment, and this effect will be described later. Meanwhile 38 Group took steps to modify and develop its organisation and equipment to meet the new UKMF requirement,

38 Group RAF in the 1970s
The period from May 1969 was one of particular change for the Group. Firstly, it was committed with 3 Div as part of the UKMF to support NATO, and then in May 1972, the Group's Head-quarters moved from Odiham to Benson. In July, 38 Group became part of Strike Command, the RAF's single, home - based, front - line Command, and on 1 September Air Support Command, as Transport Command had been more appropriately named five years earlier, also became part of Strike Command as 46 Group. During this reorganisation, 38 Group relinquished control of the fixed-wing tactical transport fleet of Hercules and Andovers — the Argosy having been withdrawn from service as a tactical transport aircraft in UK in 1971 — but took over all home-based RAF Regiment units, including their Depot at Catterick.

Finally, in the Defence Review of 1975 it was decided that the two Groups should amalgamate, and 46 Group, the junior by three months, was disbanded on 10 November 1975. So, after 15 years, Headquarters 38 Group returned again to Upavon, to the purpose-built Air Support Command Headquarters block overlooking Salisbury Plain, only 10 miles from HQ 3rd Division.

This reorganisation in command and control was accompanied by equipment changes designed to fit the new defence policy. Of the strategic and tactical fixed-wing transport fleets, only VC10s of 10 Squadron and four Hercules squadrons — 24, 30, 47 and 70 — survived the defence cuts of 1975 and 1976; but although the size of the fixed-wing transport fleet was reduced, both the helicopter and offensive support forces were strengthened. By 1972 the Group possessed two Puma Squadrons (33 and 230) and one Wessex Squadron, No 72, and by 1977 the offensive support force consisted of three Jaguar (formerly Phantom) squadrons (6, 41 and 54), and No 1 Squadron equipped with the well-known vertical take-off Harrier.

Fulfilment of the Group's role in NATO with these new aircraft presented fresh challenges. Because of the speed with which an attack could be launched against either of NATO's flanks, 38 Group's squadrons had to be able to deploy rapidly for operations anywhere from Norway to Turkey. To meet this requirement vehicles and aircraft were modified for winter operations, new camouflage schemes were developed, and units equipped with servicing shelters, tents and clothing to allow them to operate in extremely low temperatures. Exercises were held in Greece and Turkey, and in-flight refuelling techniques practiced to enable Harriers and Jaguars to fly anywhere in Europe without landing — in June 1970 five Phantoms of 54 Squadron flew from UK direct to Singapore for Exercise Bersatu Padu, in support of 19 Brigade, with one pair completing the flight in a record-breaking 14 hours 8 minutes. Frequent 'no-notice'

Offensive Support for 3 Div in the 1970s:

Above and left: The vertical take-off Harrier, able to operate from dispersed, concealed hides, provides a new dimension in close air support. Armament includes two 30mm Aden guns, Sidewinder air-to-air missiles, plus up to 7 cluster or 5 × 1,000lb retard or freefall bombs. As well as supporting exercises in Europe, Harriers deployed operationally to Belize in 1975 and 1977./*MOD Rep S*

Top right: The Jaguar replaced the Phantom in 6, 41 and 54 Squadrons of 38 Group in 1974. Particularly suitable for fast, low-level penetration of an enemy's defences, the Jaguar is armed with two 30mm Aden Guns and can carry the 1,000lb retard or freefall bomb, or the cluster bomb, and it is planned to fit two Matra Magic air-to-air missiles./*RAF Conningsby*

Bottom right: A Phantom of 6 Squadron, refuelling from a Victor tanker, en route for Cyprus during a deployment exercise, May 1971. This aircraft was in service with 38 Group from 1969 to 1974, when it was transferred to 11 Group for Air Defence duties./*MOD Rep S*

exercises were held, to test the ability of stations and squadrons to operate under war conditions, and the speed with which aircraft can be deployed.

To meet the challenge posed by a highly mechanised enemy in Europe, large numbers of troops must be capable of being lifted quickly over long distances with their equipment, in all weathers, by day or night. The lift capability and advanced electronics of the Puma made this possible, and in 1972, a major exercise, named Sky Warrior was held at Otterburn to test the new techniques. In this exercise 5 Brigade, consisting of 1st Staffords, 3rd Queens, 25th Light Regiment RA, 3rd Field Squadron RE and brigade logistic units spent two months working up with 848 Naval Air Squadron and 18, 33, 72 and 230 Squadrons of 38 Group. In the final phase, the airportable element of the brigade — 913 men and 12 guns — was lifted 50 miles in 4 hours by a force of 23 Pumas and 20 Wessex support helicopters.

A third, and perhaps the most serious challenge, was that created by the need to counter an enemy equipped with many fighters and advanced anti-aircraft weapons. Offensive support aircraft need to be able to operate in an unfavourable air situation and to destroy their targets in single-pass attacks. 38 Group's Jaguars and Harriers are equipped with passive warning radar and self-contained inertial navigation and attack systems, laser range-finders and head-up displays, and are able to fly safely at very low altitudes, thus increasing their success rate in single-run attacks.

38 Group's 17 years of achievement

Whilst 38 Group's primary role since its reformation in 1960 has been to support the Army, and in particular 3rd Division, its aircraft and units have also been almost continuously engaged in operations or exercises to maintain law and order or to deter potential aggressors throughout the world. They have co-operated in exercises with the air and ground forces of all Britain's NATO allies, Australia, New Zealand, Singapore and Malaysia, other Army and RAF units and the Royal Navy. They have provided aid to civil communities in Britain and throughout the world, from flood, drought and earthquake relief operations, to placing the fleche on the top of Coventry Cathedral, and from dropping fodder, food and fuel to snow-bound farms, to delivering artificial kidney machines.

Perhaps the work of the Group can be best summed up by recalling the words of AVM Peter Wykeham's

Above: In 1970, 19 Airportable Brigade Group under Brigadier George Cooper was airlifted to Malaysia for Exercise Bersatu Padu the aim being to demonstrate Britain's ability to intervene overseas, despite the commitment of the UKMF to Europe. 19 Brigade carried out four months' jungle training, supported by aircraft of 38 Group. In this photo a 105mm howitzer of 7 RHA crosses a Class 16 Airportable Bridge erected by 34 Field Squadron RE; a considerable advance on the 'High Wire Act' of 1961./*19 Brigade*

greeting to the Group's new personnel on 1 April 1960: 'You are already familiar with the task; but I hope that together we will be able to improve and refine it, and also to enjoy what is, in my opinion, the most interesting role of any formation in the three Armed Services. In giving our very best to this job we will be making a major contribution to the security of our country and the peace of the world.'

3rd Division Reinforces Ulster

In 1969 the Northern Ireland garrison consisted of two infantry battalions and an armoured car regiment. There was no violence and soldiers stationed in Ulster lived a peaceful life, moving about freely, and enjoying the company of what seemed to be a vast surplus of charming, friendly girls. However in the Summer of 1969 sectarian violence flared up, flashing throught the slums of Shankhill and Bogside like a brush fire, and on 15 August troops moved in to restore law and order. The reinforcements that were called for inevitably came from 3rd Division, containing as it did the majority of field force units in UK. By 17 August HQ 24 Brigade was in Ulster, to be followed within three days by B Squadron of the Life Guards, 1st Royal Hampshires and 1st Royal Green Jackets. 2nd Light Infantry and 1st Bn, Parachute Regiment were despatched in September and October, by which time the garrison had reached a strength of 6,000. A month later they were followed by 1st Royal Horse

Artillery, reinforced by a battery of 47th Light Regiment RA, both operating in the infantry role. The infantry-intensive nature of operations in Ulster was to result in a succession of armoured, gunner and sapper units adapting their skills to hand-gun, shield and baton, and for 3rd Division the preparation of infantry role units for Ulster soon became a high priority, second only to its NATO role. It quickly became clear that the Ulster commitment might be longer than originally envisaged, perhaps the IRA thought it could outstay the British Army; if so, its judgement of history and the determination of the British soldier was wide of the mark.

Training for operations in Ulster took a form previously unknown in the army, despite its 25 years continual experience in peace-keeping throughout the world. The ingenuity of the IRA and the rapid development of sophisticated equipment was such that very specialised briefing and instruction of units was essential, and during 1970 and 1971 these were developed in UK and duplicated in BAOR. Measures included the formation of special Northern Ireland Training and Advisory Teams (NITATs), the construction of sophisticated marksmanship ranges, specialist courses on a variety of subjects ranging from Terrorist Recognition to Dog Handling, and provision of internal security and search-training equipment packs. Such was the complexity of the programme that units of the Division destined for Ulster were 'in baulk' for four months before deployment. Add to this the four-month tour itself and a month on return to UK for leave and reorganisation, and a tour took up nine months of a unit's time. At the height of operations units were deployed once a year, thus little time was left for UKMF training. The degree of centralisation of training would perhaps have surprised soldiers of the 1950s and 1960s who, when warned for the Near or Far East, would have simply looked up the pamphlet 'Keeping the Peace' and got on with preparation under their own arrangements; however it illustrates the care that is taken today in preparing troops for this highly complex operational task.

Headquarters 3rd Division itself was never deployed in Ulster, but between 1969 and 1972 the headquarters of 5, 19 and 24 Brigades all carried out four-month tours in the Province.

On 30 January 1972 security forces in Londonderry opened fire when attacked by hooligans and IRA gunmen during a civil rights march. This day became known as 'Bloody Sunday' and for some months afterwards the IRA established a so-called 'No-go' area in Londonderry's Creggan and Bogside. At the end of July it was decided to launch a major operation, codenamed Motorman, to regain control of these and other smaller areas in Belfast.

The IRA had frequently boasted that security forces would never be allowed to re-enter the Creggan or Bogside; it was therefore expected that Motorman would be opposed strongly. To ensure complete superiority over the terrorists many additional units were sent to Ulster, bringing the total of battalions to 18. 3rd Division already had HQ 24 Brigade and 3 RRF deployed there, and these were joined by B Squadron, Blues and Royals, 2 RRF, 1 Kings, 1 Argylls, and sappers of 6 Field Support Squadron.

At 4am on 31 July 11 battalions moved in to the IRA heartlands in Londonderry and Belfast simultaneously. 3 RRF were included in the Londonderry operation, and by 7am they had secured their objectives against only token opposition. Meanwhile 2 RRF and 1 Kings had taken part in the occupation of Andersonstown in Belfast, encountering no opposition. By afternoon security force domination was everywhere complete, and the 'lifting' of key terrorists was under way. The virtually bloodless nature of the operation — total casualties were two terrorists killed in Londonderry — fully justified the deployment of very strong forces.

Below: Training for Ulster: a Close-Quarter Battle (Urban) range, in which every type of incident from sniper-fire to bottle-throwing is simulated. Troops use sub-calibre live ammunition, the buildings being constructed of material that prevents ricochets. The patrol being exercised is filmed throughout on CCTV, and its actions are played back and discussed immediately afterwards./*Cpl Ingledew*

Above: 'Leeson Street Patrol', painted by Terence Cuneo and reproduced by kind permission of the Regimental Trustees of the Royal Green Jackets.

In 1971, a number of infantry battalions were reduced in strength to 'representative companies'. One of these was 'R' Company 3 RGJ. It formed at Netheravon on 2 August and was placed under the command of 5 Brigade and 3rd Division. Within a week of forming the company was warned for Northern Ireland, moving there on 11 August, and in the words of Major Christopher Dunphie, its commander 'It was entirely due to the personal efforts of the GOC and Staff of 3rd Division that we received our full scale of operational equipment in time'.

Throughout its tour — initially under command of 1 RGJ and subsequently under 3 Queens — 'R' Company was heavily engaged in anti-IRA operations in the Lower Falls area of Belfast. The painting depicts an incident on 13 September 1971 when the Company cleared a group of seven IRA gun-men from the Leeson Street area.

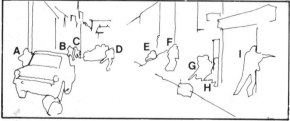

Key:
A. Cpl Harris (right hand section commander)
B. Cpl Hansford (Company Commander's escort)
C. Maj Dunphie (Company Commander)
D. Sgt Evans (Platoon Sergeant)
E. Rfn Horlock
F. Rfn Margrain
G. Rfn Draycott (Platoon Radio Operator)
H. 2Lt Puxley (OC 2 Platoon)
I. Cpl Thompson (Left hand section commander)

Awards for this action were: MC to Maj Dunphie; DCM to Cpl Thompson; and Mentions in Despatches to 2-Lt Puxley and Cpl Hansford. 'R' Company returned to UK on 10 December and became part of a reformed 3 RGJ, under command of 3rd Division.

Ulster — the Impact

After eight years of operations in Ulster, the impact on units is familiar throughout the Army of the 1970s. However for those readers who may not have witnessed this impact at close quarters, the comments of a unit commander will be of interest, perhaps of special interest if that unit consisted of gunners turned infantry. Brigadier Brian Davis was CO of 32 Light Regiment in 1972-1974 and he recalls:

'I brought my Regiment home to UK in December 1972 to join the Division in Bulford. It had been a Heavy Regiment (SP 175mm) in the same station in BAOR for nearly nine years and the withdrawal symptoms were acute. We were to convert to an airportable close support light regiment (105mm Pack How) for 5 Brigade, and this involved retraining on new equipment, and regimental reorganisation. We had six weeks in which to become "operational in our new role", at the end of which we were given a one day trade test from the GOC and CRA to prove it. The same night we put the guns to bed and were not to fire them again for over a year. The reason, of course, was Northern Ireland. We had about 10 weeks to totally reorganise the regiment into an infantry battalion and embark on a four month "rural" tour in Ulster. Although the regiment had already done a tour some eighteen months before from BAOR — one of the first Gunner regiments to do so — all the know-how had gone and we had to make a fresh start. The first task was to adopt a battalion organisation suitable for Internal Security, with Operations and Intelligence Officers down to Battery level, and Troops capable of being broken down into sections and four-man patrols. The selection of junior commanders was particularly important and highlights one of the problems that Gunners face in this context. Our junior NCOs, in the main, are not required, while on the gun position, to show much initiative. Fire orders come from the command post and are obeyed on the guns without question. These same NCOs in the IS situation must display initiative and quick decisiveness as an essential ingredient for success on patrol. They have to be alert, professional infantrymen and be able to give clear, concise and simple orders. This is quite a training hurdle to overcome.

'While the battalion organisation was being put together and leaders selected, the training requirement needed clearly defining. For me it fell into three main groups: First, Basic Military Skills — Simple radio communications for all, plus the three Fs — Fitness, Firing and First Aid, all of which had to be constantly worked at by all ranks even though we should already have acquired them. Second, Basic Infantry Skills — These we had no experience in, and we needed as much training as we could get from Infantry advisors on subjects such as use of ground, fire and movement and in particular the interdependence of one patrol member on another — the mutual thinking which is second nature to the trained infanteer; and third, Additional IS Skills — intelligence, rules for arrest, opening fire and using baton rounds (blue, yellow and white cards respectively), to name a few — plus the ability to work with the Press and come over sensibly to 5 million people watching TV. When we eventually reached Ulster each of our training

techniques was put to the test at some stage, and our decision to train for every situation paid off. We were involved on the Border, in the towns, in Long Kesh and in East Belfast and all those who went came back.

'After returning from Ulster we were faced with an intensive gunnery individual training programme to build on our earlier conversion. The same junior leaders whose initiative and quick thinking paid off in Ulster now had to return to the gun position routine, under No 1s who had been their equals as section and patrol commanders in action, and this was not an easy transition. Our gunnery had suffered severely but the benefits of participating as

Below: Armed helicopter in Northern Ireland: a Scout of 3rd Regiment Army Air Corps mounting a General Purpose Machine-Gun, manned by L Cpl Pike, 653 Squadron AAC. The armed Scout would be used to give covering fire, working in conjunction with patrols on the ground./*653 Sqn, 3 Regt, AAC*

Below left: 'Adapting their skills to hand-gun' — a gunner of 32 Light Regiment RA, under training for Northern Ireland in the infantry role, checks his SLR magazine before loading./*32 Lt Regt RA*

infantrymen far outweighed the disadvantages. Some two years later I came back to the Division as CRA to find my regiment had done yet another tour in "hard" Belfast and that the pattern I had known as CO was common throughout the Divisional Artillery. Since the present troubles started 13 Gunner Units from 3rd Division have aggregated 41 tours and gained over 50 awards — for gallant and distinguished service as infantrymen — ranging from the DSO to the Wilkinson Sword of Peace.'

Units of every arm and service required to take their share of duties in Ulster, were all faced with particular training problems. An example was that of the Life Guards, whose commitment to send each of their three sabre squadrons in succession throughout 1977 made it impossible for the whole Regiment to train together for its conventional NATO armoured reconnaissance role.

Lt-Gen Sir Richard Worsley, who commanded the Division while trouble was at its height in 1972-1974, sums up the effects of Ulster:

'Nothing will ever repay the fatal casualties both to officers and men that occur there, nor indeed will anything balance the large number of those who have been severely wounded; and the enforced separation of all ranks from their families is another adverse factor. However we would not be honest if we did not admit that there are certain advantages for the Army as a whole. The streets of Londonderry and Belfast, and the open country of South Armagh, are lonely places for the soldier. A very high standard of leadership, especially at the junior officer and NCO level is required, and much valuable experience in initiative and self reliance has been gained at all levels.

'Furthermore I do not believe that the army has ever been held in higher regard by the civilian population. This is probably because television has daily shown the sort of life that our soldiers lead in Northern Ireland and the pressures which are put upon them, and many people have commented that it is only the British army which could have succeeded in doing this very difficult task without fuss and with good humour.

'The drawbacks for 3rd Division were obvious. Training for our primary NATO role and joint training with the RAF, was affected both at the individual and at the formation level, and there is no doubt that brigade commanders found it very difficult to maintain a high standard of all arms training. Nevertheless exercises were held and despite all the difficulties, battalions and regiments have still been able to travel abroad and get a change of scene and of climate: it reflects great credit on the Division that despite the demands of Northern Ireland the standard of training has remained so high in all the other many varied aspects of modern soldiering.'

3rd Division's casualties, referred to by General Worsley in his first sentence, totalled 20 killed and 173 wounded during the period 1973 to 1977.

Overseas Emergencies Continue

Northern Ireland has provided for the units of 3rd Division the heaviest and longest emergency commitment ever. During the same period, however, there were numerous lesser known operations, now forgotten by many. In March 1969, for example, 2 PARA and 33 Field Squadron RE moved to Anguilla where the island's leader, Webster, was threatening to declare

Above left: Operations in Ulster: Outside a company base of the 1st Worcestershire and Sherwood Foresters Regiment in Crossmaglen, 1977. The sentry post and Saracen are protected against rocket attack by wire mesh. 1 WFR was a 19 Brigade unit, carrying out a four month tour in Ulster under command of 3 Brigade./*1 WFR*

Above: The 'Bessbrook Helipad' at Headquarters of the South Armagh battalion. Centre left, a 12-man patrol prepares to be lifted forward to the border area by a Wessex (top right) and a Puma (hovering). In the foreground are three Gazelles and a Scout; Gazelles are used for reconnaissance, while the Scout can lift four-man 'Eagle' patrols to remote sections of the border. /*1 WFR*

Right: In bandit country: two members of a 12-man patrol watching the border. Sergeant Hyde (standing) and Private Nottingham of the 1st Worcestershire and Sherwood Foresters./*1 WFR*

Left: A Scorpion crew commander of the Blues and Royals observing Turkish Army positions, Cyprus, 1974./*Army Public Relations*

Below: Cyprus, 1974; a patrol of 40 Commando, Royal Marines, under command of 19 Brigade, covering the approaches to the Akrotiri base./*19 Brigade*

Right: 3rd Division continued to provide units for the United Nations Force in Cyprus throughout the 1970s; Ferrets of A Squadron, The Life Guards, on patrol as Force Reserve Squadron, 1976. /*The Life Guards*

independence instead of federating with St Kitts. Settlement came after a few months political negotiation, during which time the soldiers won the hearts and minds of the inhabitants and withdrew leaving behind a number of long term improvements including a hospital, runway and harbour facilities.

In October 1970 Jordan erupted in civil war when King Hussein's army took action to oust Palestinian guerillas from his country. The capital, Amman, became the scene of fierce street fighting which resulted in many civilian casualties. Under the auspices of the International Red Cross, and wearing Red Cross uniform, a section of 19 Field Ambulance RAMC, under Captain Michael Heugh, (who in 1977 was DADMS of the Division), was flown to Amman as part of a field hospital formed from other medical units in UK, under the overall command of the ADMS 3 Div, Colonel Sandy Ferrie. Based on the King Hussein Military Hospital, the section's nursing orderlies received their first experience of treating real battle casualties, many of them civilians caught up in the crossfire of urban fighting. Over 200 operations were performed and 400 outpatients treated during their month's stay in Jordan.

Gibraltar, Belize (formerly British Honduras), and the United Nations' force in Cyprus continued to demand a contribution from 3rd Division during the 1970s, and as fortune had it, HQ 19 Brigade was training in Cyprus when the Turkish army invaded the island on 20 July 1974. The headquarters was on the point of returning to UK but was ordered to remain, and some members who were already airborne were turned round in midair. The brigade commander, Brigadier Jimmy Glover, was charged with protection of the western SBA at Episkopi/Limassol, and he took under command 1st Royal Scots (a resident battalion), 40 Commando Group Royal Marines (including 7 Commando Light Battery) from UK, 8 Field Squadron RE and 15 Squadron RAF Regiment. Also despatched from 3 Div in UK was a

composite armoured reconnaissance regiment under Lt-Col Richard Morris, CO of the 16th/5th Lancers. In addition to his own B Squadron he brought with him B Squadron, Blues and Royals (which joined 19 Brigade) and C Squadron 4th/7th Dragoon Guards. This composite regiment was deployed on a variety of tasks in support of the UN Contingent, including the surveillance of forward positions of the Turkish Army.

In the western SBA, Brigadier Glover's patrols, observation posts and checkpoints prevented any serious trouble, despite looting and threatening behaviour by the more unruly elements of EOKA living near the boundaries of the SBA. Brigadier Glover noted the benefits to his troops of experience in Northern Ireland, in particular the quiet decisiveness of section commanders, proficient weapon handling and the high standard of reporting and alertness. He singled out for praise the example of the OP of 40 Commando which came under fire within 30 minutes of deployment and suffered a marine wounded. In accordance with his orders the corporal in charge was entitled to return the fire, but displaying courage and presence of mind he forbore to do so, this defusing a potentially dangerous situation and setting a precedent which undoubtedly avoided other similar incidents. HQ 19 Brigade returned to Colchester after three months of patient peacekeeping, having confirmed its ability to react to the unexpected, though the task had rated only third priority among the many that units of 3rd Division were expected to perform.

A Tactical Concept for Europe

Despite the distractions of Ulster and other overseas commitments the Division, under the skilled direction in particular of Major-General Robin Carnegie, continually sought to perfect a concept of operations for Europe. The question was how to use to best effect the Division's nine airportable infantry battalions, lacking armoured personnel carriers but skilled in short-range tank-killing, in concert with its diminutive armoured strength — one tank regiment and two reconnaissance regiments — to destroy many times their own number of enemy tanks.

Detailed study of this problem was the task of successive Commanders Royal Armoured Corps 3rd Division, and in 1975 General Carnegie directed that a major exercise, nicknamed Bugle Call, be held on Salisbury Plain aimed at practising the Division's anti-armour tactics. The organisation, tactics and communications of a complete Soviet Motor Rifle Regiment were simulated, using 150 tanks and armoured personnel carriers drawn from RAC 3 Div and the School of Infantry, supported by helicopters of 3rd Regt, Army Air Corps and FGA aircraft of 38 Group RAF. Many valuable lessons were learnt concerning the capabilities and limitations of the potential enemy, and the exercise was repeated in 1976 with Bugle Call 2. In this a troop of Chieftain tanks of 4th/7th Dragoon Guards and infantry of 1st Bn The Duke of Edinburgh's Royal Regiment opposed the simulated enemy. 3 Div Engineers laid 7,000lb of explosive to represent the enemy artillery fire plan, together with 3,000 dummy pyrotechnic mines, and in the final stage, Scout helicopters of 3rd Regt AAC, equipped with SS11 anti-tank guided weapons, operated in conjunction with

179

Above: Exercise Bugle Call, 1975; a simulated Soviet Motor Rifle Battalion group prepares to deploy from the line of march. Leading are four T62 battle tanks represented by Chieftains; behind them are two rifle companies mounted in BMP armoured personnel carriers, represented by FV432s./*RAC 3 Div*

Right: UKMF Training within NATO. Maj-Gen Walsh, GOC 3 Div, with centre — Lt-Gen H. Schwiethal, Commander Land Forces, Jutland, and right — Maj-Gen I. Poeppel, Commander 6th (German) Panzer Grenadier Division. Photograph taken during Exercise Beacon Glare held in Schleswig Holstein, September 1976. General Schwiethal was the Corps Commander; and his corps was made up of 6th (GE) PG Div, 1st (Danish) Div and 3 Div./*Army Public Relations*

Scorpion armoured reconnaissance vehicles to defeat a simulated enemy break out.

The Bugle Call exercises taught the Division a great deal about countering the threat of massed Soviet armour. The lessons learnt were not wasted, for in 1976, as part of the restructuring of the British Army, confirmation was received that the 3rd Division was to become an Armoured Division in BAOR. The background to this restructuring was as follows.

Restructuring of the Army

In 1975 Great Britain's economic problems led to extensive cuts in public expenditure, and it was inevitable that Defence would suffer heavily. The problem facing the Army was how to absorb these cuts while maintaining an operationally viable contribution to NATO. Reductions in headquarter and administrative echelons would clearly be necessary and the following decisions were taken:

A. The Brigade level of command would disappear, and Divisions in BAOR would be reduced in size, each consisting basically of five Battle Groups, operating directly under Divisional HQs.

B. The Army in UK was to be organised into 'Field Forces', placed under the command and control of geographical District HQs. Field Forces would include Territorial Army as well as Regular units.

The effects on 3rd Division were extensive. Firstly, 3rd Divisional Headquarters and Signal Regiment was to be reformed as an armoured divisional headquarters and signal regiment, and would move to Germany to take command of a restructured armoured division based on the former 6th Armoured Brigade. Secondly, the airportable brigades in UK would, in the case of 5 and 19

Top: Restructuring in 1976 and 1977 took place at a time when many units were retraining on new weapons: for example, the 105mm Light Gun with which close-support artillery regiments in Field Forces will be equipped from 1978. This gun can throw a 35lb shell 11 miles, with a maximum rate of fire of 6rpm./*Central Office of Information*

Above: 3 Div's operational commitments continued throughout the Restructuring period; a Scimitar (left) and Scorpion of the Life Guards crossing a river in Belize, 1977./*Army Public Relations*

Right: Pair of decanters presented to 3rd Division by 19 Airportable Brigade on 29 July 1977 to mark the Brigade's departure from 3 Div after 25 years' service in the Strategic Reserve./*Photo/Litho Section, 38 Group RAF*

Above: The Officers, Headquarters 3rd Division, 31 July 1977.
Back Row: Capt J. E. C. Lewis RCT (SC 'Q'); Capt D. J. Perry RRF (SC 'A'); Capt R. G. Ginn RAOC (Adjt, Ord); Capt I. D. McNab REME (Adjt, EME); Capt A. R. Freer PARA (ADC); Capt C. K. Price 4/7 DG (GSO3 Trg RAC); Capt G. J. Widdows 15/19H (SC 'A' RAC); Capt M. C. De L. Gaillard RA (GSO3 RA); Capt H. C. Abela RA (GSO3 SD).
Third Row: Maj R. A. M. Mulligan R Irish (GSO3 Trg); Maj P. Wescott RE (OC 1 PCC Sqn); Maj R. J. Stringer AAC (Catering Advisor); Maj S. V. Durn REME (2IC EME); Maj C. J. Ahearne RAOC (DADOS C Sups); Maj J. P. Mordant RCT (Ops Tpt); Maj B. R. Willis RCT (2IC Tpt); Sqn Ldr B. A. Raphael RAF (Sqn Ldr Plans); Maj M. H. Hardy RA (SC RA); Maj B. J. Sanderson RE (GSO2 RE); Maj (QM) I. M. Lyall RE (SO2 RE); Capt J. L. Powell REME (Div AE); Capt G. C. Anerdi Italian Army (GSO2 Ex).
Second Row: Lt-Cdr A. G. C. Franklin RN (Retd) (Mess Sec); Maj M. C. Spence R Signals (DAQMG Man); Maj J. R. Andrew RA (DAQMG Ops); Maj P. H. Surtees MC RMP (SC A/DAPM); Maj D. J. Younger QOH (DAAG); Maj A. T. R. Shelley RGJ (GSO2 Int); Maj J. H. Keep R Anglian (GSO3 Ops/SD); Maj D. M. Chappel 4/7 DG (DAA&QMG, RAC); Maj B. S. McCombe RTR (BM, RAC); Maj

C. G. Deacon REME (BEME, RAC); Maj R. C. Letchworth RA (BM RA); Maj R. K. L. Jackson RA (DAA&QMG RA).
Front Row: Lt-Col D. J. Cornwell RAOC (CRAOC); Lt-Col R. Bell R Signals (CO, 3 HQ & Sig Regt); Col J. Edgington (ADMS), Col R. L. Stonham (CSO); Col R. C. Middleton OBE (Col AQ); Brig R. M. Jerram MBE (CRAC); Maj-Gen M. J. H. Walsh DSO; Brig B. W. Davis OBE (CRA); Col B. H. C. Emsden (Col GS); Col J. R. M. Hill OBE (CRE); Lt-Col P. B. Evans RCT (CRCT); Lt-Col R. Benson MBE RAPC (Staff Pmr); Rev J. W. Bell RAChD (DACG).
Not present in the photograph: Lt-Col D. F. Mallam MBE, AAC (CO 3 Regt AAC); Lt-Col R. M. G. Briggs REME (CREME); Maj D. N. D. Nicol SG (GSO2 Ops/SD); Maj M. J. G. Gregson RM (GSO2 Trg/Air); Maj R. P. D. Brook RRF (GSO3 Trg A); Capt A. E. Richards APTC (DOPT); Maj G. H. Duckett RH (SCQ Man); Maj R. P. Murphy Queens (DAQMG Qtg); Capt P. M. Eliott-Lockhart 14/20H (GSO3 Ops RAC); Maj D. D. Campbell RA (DAIO); Maj G. D. B. Thatcher RA (IGRA); Capt P. E. Piggott RA (TIG); Capt V. G. Iwanek RE (GSO3 RE); Maj F. R. Fletcher R Signals (GSO2 Sigs); Capt G. E. Rawlins R Signals (SO3 Tfc); Capt R. P. M. Rendall RCT (Adjt Tp Capt R. W. Riley REME (EME Tpt); Maj M. B. Heugh RAMC (DADMS); Maj M. D. Hogg RAOC (2IC Ord); Maj D. St J. Eve RAOC (DADOS Ops).

```
P R 011025Z AUG
FM UKLF                    HQ 3rd DIV
TO 3 DIV
BT                           1 AUG 1977
UNCLAS
DIG KNT
FROM COMMANDER IN CHIEF FOR GENERAL OFFICER COMMANDING CMM AND
ALL RANKS CMM THE THIRD DIVISION PD SADLY TODAY THE THIRD
DIVISION RELINQUISHES ITS ROLE WITH UKLF AND WILL START
PREPARING FOR ITS NEW ROLE AS THE THIRD ARMOURED DIVISION UNDER
COMMAND BAOR PD SINCE ITS FORMATION IN 1809 DURING THE PENINSULA
CAMPAIGN CMM THE DIVISION HAS HAD A VERY DISTINGUISHED RECORD
HAVING SERVED THROUGHOUT BOTH WORLD WARS AND IN LATER YEARS
IN PALESTINE CMM EGYPT CMM CYPRUS AND SUEZ PD MORE RECENTLY IT
HAS BEEN RESPONSIBLE FOR SUPPLYING TROOPS IN SUPPORT OF
OPERATIONS IN CYPRUS CMM NORTHERN IRELAND AND BELIZE PD THE
WEALTH AND DIVERSITY OF TALENT WITHIN THE DIVISION HAS
ENABLED IT TO ACQUIT ITSELF WITH GREAT SUCCESS WHEREVER IT HAS
BEEN PD YOU HAVE ALL SERVED UKLF SUPREMELY WELL CMM AND HAVE
AT ALL TIMES UPHELD THE HIGHEST TRADITIONS OF THE SERVICE PD


PAGE 2 RBDNPC 016 UNCLAS
IT ONLY REMAINS FOR ME TO WISH YOU ALL GOOD FORTUNE IN THE
FUTURE PD MY THANKS AND VERY BEST WISHES TO YOU ALL
BT
```

Left: Farewell signal from the C-in-C, Headquarters United Kingdom Land Forces, received by 3rd Division on 1 August 1977, the date that the Division became non-operational in UK pending reformation in BAOR.

Brigades become 8 and 7 Field Forces respectively, and in the case of 24 Brigade, disband. These fundamental measures had to be put into effect at a time when the Division was working hard to improve its individual and unit training standards, while 'routine' Northern Ireland commitments continued, while the capability of reacting to emergencies remained — two examples being the threatened strike in Ulster in May, and the crisis in Belize in July 1977 — and finally, while retraining of the Headquarters for its new role in BAOR was getting under way. It was a period of intense activity for every soldier and officer in the Division.

The first formation to leave the Division was 24 Brigade which on 30 July 1976 at Topcliffe, Yorks, held a memorable Farewell Parade, taken by the CGS, General Sir Peter Hunt, as his last official function before retiring from the Army. All who took part or were fortunate enough to witness this parade will never forget the manner in which the 'Guards', provided by all units of 24 Brigade, marched away into the distance led by their commander, Brigadier John Southgate.

5 Airportable Brigade, commanded by Brigadier Robert MacGregor-Oakford, left the Division on 1 April 1977 and immediately assumed the title of 8 Field Force. In a simple ceremony the C-in-C United Kingdom Land Forces, General Sir Edwin Bramall — a former Commander of 5 Brigade — recalled the distinguished service of the brigade, and its links with 3rd Division that started in 1815 on the fields of Quatre Bras and Waterloo.

As this book goes to print only 19 Airportable Brigade retains its title; it left the Division on 1 August 1977 and will become 7 Field Force on 1 April 1978. With the exception of a gap of only 18 months in 1959-1960, the 'Black Panther' Brigade served in 3 Div continuously since 1951. To mark their farewell, Brigadier Dick Vincent presented a pair of etched glass decanters to the GOC on 29 July 1977.

In recent years these three fine Brigades have truly reflected the flexible, airmobile, 'go anywhere, do anything' 3rd Division spirit.

The 5 Brigade sign is an adaption of the 'Crossed Keys' of 2nd Division, which the Brigade formed part of for many years. When the Brigade became independent in 1958 this association was commemorated by the retention of one key, while a bayonet was substituted for the other. This device, together with the figure 5, is set on a red background.

The 19 Brigade sign, designed in 1957 by the DAA&QMG, Major F. W. E. Fursdon RE, is that of the head of a Black Panther, eyes glinting, set within a red triangle. The Black Panther represents Alertness, while the triangle commemorates the long association with 3rd Division.

The 24 Brigade sign consists of red Griffon's Wings on a blue background. The design was taken from the personal crest of Brigadier Frederick Browning DSO, who commanded the Brigade in North Africa in 1941.

Postscript
Major – General M. J. H. Walsh, DSO

Soon after being told that I had been selected to command 3rd Division, well aware of my good fortune, I searched military libraries and museums for as much information as I could muster about my new command. Surprisingly, I discovered that no complete divisional history had ever been written nor for that matter had any book been published covering the history of any of the regular divisions which had been formed in the Peninsula a hundred and sixty-eight years ago. I hope that this book *Iron Division* will to some extent fill the gap in the history of our Army.

One of the first things that I soon discovered was the strong feeling of affection for our divisional sign, both by those who serve today and, in particular, by those who fought during World War II. The old 'Red and Black Triangles', whilst, as a sign, may not be as well known to the general public as the 'Desert Rat' or 'Pegasus', means a great deal to many and underlines the essential unity of the 3rd Division.

The history of a division is of necessity the history of its combatant troops. It is they who do the actual fighting, repel or destroy the enemy, capture ground, cross rivers, occupy towns or storm fortresses. It is they alone who finally win or lose the day. It is therefore very right and proper that they should be praised and rewarded for their

Below: At a luncheon given by HQ 38 Group at RAF Upavon on 28 July 1977, Major-General Michael Walsh presented to Air Vice Marshal Peter Williamson a Waterford Glass Rose Bowl to commemorate the 17 years association of the Group with 3rd Division./*By courtesy of* The Daily Telegraph

Below right: The Rose Bowl./*Litho Section, 38 Group RAF*

labours. However, we all know that their efforts would come to nought without the help of the supporting arms — the artillery and engineers, and the signals, without whom no commands would be issued and no reports received. Also, as a former Colonel AQ of a Division I am more conscious than most of the importance of the Logistic Services whose support is absolutely essential for a division to function correctly in battle. To these Supporting Arms and Services our apologies for not covering fully the great contribution they make. They have earned our heartfelt gratitude and will continue to do so in the years ahead.

I would like to thank most sincerely Colonel Robin McNish, our author, for taking on so successfully the writing of this book. He has gone to great pains to produce a factually correct history of the 3rd Division whilst, at the same time, making it alive and interesting reading. I would also like to express my appreciation to the Commander in Chief United Kingdom Land Forces, General Sir Edwin Bramall, and his staff at Wilton for their excellent support and backing.

As I write this final page the Advance Party of the Divisional Headquarters and Signal Regiment is due to leave for Germany. Next week they will be followed by a number of my staff. By the end of the year we will be established as the 3rd Armoured Division with our Headquarters in Soest. The Division looks forward to this new challenge, to taking under command many distinguished units and some who are to be formed for the first time. To those we leave behind in England, to our former Brigades, to 38 Group Royal Air Force — in the history of joint service relationships surely there has never been a stronger bond of friendship and co-operation — and to our many friends at Wilton, Colchester, Tidworth and Bulford we wish good fortune.

NATO has ensured that there has been peace in Europe for the past thirty years. If the 3rd Armoured Division, as part of the 1st British Corps and Northern Army Group assists NATO in maintaining that peace then we will have achieved our aim. This is the seventh time in the history of the 3rd Division that we have been deployed to Europe, for many 7 is a lucky number.

Michael Walsh.

Bulford
11 September 1977

PRESENTED TO 38 GROUP ROYAL AIR FORCE
BY THE 3rd DIVISION
TO COMMEMORATE OUR LONG
AND HAPPY ASSOCIATION
IN THE STRATEGIC RESERVE
AND UK MOBILE FORCE
1960–1977

Montgomery Window

The Memorial Window to Field Marshal The Viscount Montgomery of Alamein KG, GCB, DSO, DL, in the Royal Memorial Chapel, Sandhurst.

The Memorial Windows to Field Marshals have been designed and executed by Mr Lawrence Lee who writes: 'The general design follows the heraldic pattern established in the Alanbrooke window, the first of the series to be commissioned, the main feature being full armorial bearings set against an architectural frame within which is a colour, or colours, appropriate to the memorial in question. Below the arms appear relevant badges or awards while such other emblems of personal significance are placed at the top or bottom of the frame'.

The background colour to this window is the maroon of the Parachute Regiment and the badge is that of the Royal Warwickshire Regiment, into which Lord Montgomery was commissioned. At the base are the Signs of the 3rd Division, 21st Army Group, and Supreme Headquarters Allied Forces Europe. Surmounting the frame is the Sign of the Eighth Army, combined with the badge of the Royal Tank Regiment.

The Window was dedicated on Sunday 30 October 1977, by the Chaplain General, The Venerable Archdeacon Mallett QHC, AKC. The Sermon was given by Field Marshal Lord Harding of Petherton, and the Field Marshals who attended the service included Lord Carver, GOC 3rd Division 1962-1964.

The window was photographed for this work by Bernard Fowler of Camberley, and reproduced by kind permission of the Royal Memorial Chapel Council.

Commanders of the 3rd Division

Commanders of the 3rd Division, 1809 to 1977

Major-General J. Mackenzie (Killed in Action)	1809
Major-General R. Crawfurd	1809
Lieutenant-General Thomas Picton (Wounded in Action 1812)	1810
Lieutenant-General Sir Edward Packenham (Acting)	1812
Lieutenant-General Sir Thomas Picton KCB	1813
Major-General The Hon Charles Colville (Acting)	1813
Lieutenant-General Sir Charles Alten (Wounded in Action)	1815
Lieutenant-General Sir Richard England GCB	1854
Lieutenant-General Sir William Eyre KCB	1855
Lieutenant-General Sir William Gatacre KCB, DSO	1899
Lieutenant-General Sir Herbert Chermside GCMG, CB	1900
Major-General Sir Bruce Hamilton KCB	1902
Major-General W. E. Franklyn CB	1907
Major-General Sir Henry Rawlinson Bt CVO, CB	1910
Major-General H. I. W. Hamilton CVO, CB, DSO (Killed in Action)	1914
Major-General C. J. Mackenzie CB (Invalided)	1914
Brigadier-General F. D. V. Wing CB (Acting)	1914
Major-General J. A. L. Haldane CB, DSO	1914
Major-General C. J. Deverell CB	1916
Major-General Sir Robert Whigham KCB, KCMG, DSO	1919
Major-General Sir William Heneker KCB, KCMG, DSO	1922
Major-General Sir John Burnett Stuart KBE, CB, CMG, DSO	1926
Major-General H. H. S. Knox CB, DSO	1930
Major-General W. W. Pitt Taylor CB, CMG, DSO	1932
Major-General R. G. Finlayson CB, CMG, DSO	1934
Major-General C. P. Heywood CB, CMG, DSO	1936
Major-General D. K. Bernard CB, CMG, DSO	1936
Major-General B. L. Montgomery DSO	1939
Major-General J. A. H. Gammell CB, DSO, MC	1940
Major-General E. C. Hayes	1941
Major-General W. H. C. Ramsden CB, CBE, DSO, MC	1942
Major-General T. G. Rennie CB, CBE, DSO (Wounded in Action 1944)	1943
Brigadier E. E. E. Cass CBE, DSO, MC (Acting)	1944
Major-General L. G. Whistler CB, DSO	1944
Major-General J. B. Churcher DSO	1946
Major-General G. N. Wood CB, CBE, DSO, MC	1947
Major-General Sir Hugh Stockwell KBE, CB, DSO	1951
Major-General J. H. N. Poett CB, DSO	1952
Major-General J. B. Churcher CB, DSO	1954
Major-General G. C. Gordon-Lennox CB, CVO, DSO	1957
Major-General C. H. P. Harington CB, CBE, DSO, MC	1959
Major-General V. W. Street CMG, CBE, DSO, MC (Invalided 1962)	1961
Brigadier J. K. Greenwood OBE (Acting)	1962
Major-General R. M. P. Carver CB, CBE, DSO, MC	1962
Major-General C. H. Blacker OBE, MC	1964
Major-General A. J. Deane-Drummond DSO, MC	1966
Major-General T. D. H. McMeekin OBE	1968
Major-General G. C. A. Gilbert MC	1970
Major-General R. E. Worsley OBE	1972
Major-General R. M. Carnegie OBE	1974
Major-General M. J. H. Walsh DSO	1976

Left: Field Marshal Lord Montgomery inspects a Guard of Honour from the 2nd Battalion, Royal Warwickshire Regiment, on the occasion of his visit to 3rd Division at Ismailia, October 1946. To Montgomery's left rear is Brigadier Robert Bray, commanding 7 Brigade.
/ Major J. F. Ainsworth

Awards of the Victoria Cross

Awards of the Victoria Cross to members of the 3rd Division

Name and Unit	Date of Action	Place
Pte T. Grady, 4th Regiment	18 October 1854	Sebastopol
C Sgt McWhiney, 44th Regiment	26 October 1854-18 June 1855	Sebastopol
Lt W. H. S. Nickerson RAMC (att Mounted Infantry)	20 April 1900	Wakkerstroom, South Africa
Cpl H. C. Beet, 1st Sherwood Foresters	22 April 1900	Wakkerstroom, South Africa
Lt M. J. Dease, 4th Royal Fusiliers	23 August 1914	Mons
Pte S. F. Godley, 4th Royal Fusiliers	23 August 1914	Mons
L Cpl C. A. Jarvis, 57 Fd Coy, RE	23 August 1914	Mons
Capt T. Wright, 3 Div Engineers	23 August-14 September 1914	Mons/Retreat from Mons
Cpl E. Garforth, 15th Hussars	23 August-3 September 1914	Mons/Retreat from Mons
Lt C. G. Martin, 56 Fd Coy RE	12 March 1915	Spanbroek Molen, Flanders
Capt E. N. Mellish, RAChD, (att 4th Royal Fusiliers)	27-30 March 1916	St Eloi, Flanders
Cpl S. Bates, 1st Royal Norfolk	11 August 1944	Sourdevalle, Normandy
Pte J. Stokes, 2nd KSLI	1 March 1945	Kervenheim, Rhineland

Infantry Regimental Titles

During the period covered by this history, Infantry Regiments of the Line have undergone a series of reorganisations which have led to many changes in title.

Prior to 1872 Regiments were 'Numbered', although many had already adopted unofficial county titles. In 1872 County Titles were officially adopted under the Cardwell reforms, and many of the old numbered regiments were linked in pairs under the new titles.

Defence reductions in the 1950s and 1960s have resulted in many Regiments being amalgamated (marked A in the table below) or joined together to form 'Large Regiments' (marked L). Thus few of the old Regimental Titles that won undying glory in two World Wars now remain.

The following simplified table is designed to help the reader trace the Ancestors and Descendants of the Line Regiments named in this history:

Pre-1872 Numbers	Post-1872 Titles	1977 Titles	
1st	The Royal Scots	The Royal Scots	
2nd	The Queen's Royal Regiment (West Surrey)	The Queen's Regiment	L
3rd	The Buffs (The Royal East Kent Regiment)	The Queen's Regiment	L
4th	The King's Own Royal Regiment (Lancaster)	The King's Own Royal Border Regiment	A
5th	The Royal Northumberland Fusiliers	The Royal Regiment of Fusiliers	L
6th	The Royal Warwickshire Regiment	The Royal Regiment of Fusiliers	L
7th	The Royal Fusiliers (City of London Regiment)	The Royal Regiment of Fusiliers	L
8th	The King's Regiment (Liverpool)	The King's Regiment	A
9th	The Royal Norfolk Regiment	The Royal Anglian Regiment	L
10th	The Royal Lincolnshire Regiment	The Royal Anglian Regiment	L
11th	The Devonshire Regiment	The Devonshire & Dorset Regiment	A
12th	The Suffolk Regiment	The Royal Anglian Regiment	L
13th	The Somerset Light Infantry	The Light Infantry	L
14th	The West Yorkshire Regiment	The Prince of Wales's Own Regiment of Yorkshire	A
15th	The East Yorkshire Regiment	The Prince of Wales's Own Regiment of Yorkshire	A
16th	The Bedfordshire & Hertfordshire Regiment	The Royal Anglian Regiment	L
17th	The Royal Leicestershire Regiment	The Royal Anglian Regiment	L
18th	The Royal Irish Regiment	Disbanded 1922	
19th	The Green Howards (Alexandra, Princess of Wales's Own Yorkshire Regiment)	The Green Howards (Alexandra, Princess of Wales's Own Yorkshire Regiment)	
20th	The Lancashire Fusiliers	The Royal Regiment of Fusiliers	L
21st	The Royal Scots Fusiliers	The Royal Highland Fusiliers (Princess Margaret's Own Glasgow and Ayrshire Regiment)	A
22nd	The Cheshire Regiment	The Cheshire Regiment	
23rd	The Royal Welch Fusiliers	The Royal Welch Fusiliers	
24th	The South Wales Borderers	The Royal Regiment of Wales	A
25th	The King's Own Scottish Borderers	The King's Own Scottish Borderers	
26th and 90th	The Cameronians (Scottish Rifles)	Disbanded 1968	
27th and 108th	The Royal Inniskilling Fusiliers	The Royal Irish Rangers	L
28th and 61st	The Gloucestershire Regiment	The Gloucestershire Regiment	
29th and 36th	The Worcestershire Regiment	The Worcestershire & Sherwood Foresters Regiment	A
30th and 59th	The East Lancashire Regiment	The Queen's Lancashire Regiment	A
31st and 70th	The East Surrey Regiment	The Queen's Regiment	L
32nd and 46th	The Duke of Cornwall's Light Infantry	The Light Infantry	L
33rd and 76th	The Duke of Wellington's Regiment (West Riding)	The Duke of Wellington's Regiment (West Riding)	
34th and 55th	The Border Regiment	The King's Own Royal Border Regiment	A
35th and 107th	The Royal Sussex Regiment	The Queen's Regiment	L
37th and 67th	The Royal Hampshire Regiment	The Royal Hampshire Regiment	
38th and 80th	The South Staffordshire Regiment	The Staffordshire Regiment	A
39th and 54th	The Dorset Regiment	The Devonshire & Dorset Regiment	A
40th and 82nd	The South Lancashire Regiment	The Queen's Lancashire Regiment	A
41st and 69th	The Welch Regiment	The Royal Regiment of Wales	A
42nd and 73rd	The Black Watch (Royal Highland Regiment)	The Black Watch (Royal Highland Regiment)	
43rd and 52nd	The Oxfordshire & Buckinghamshire Light Infantry	The Royal Green Jackets	L
44th and 56th	The Essex Regiment	The Royal Anglian Regiment	L
45th and 95th	The Sherwood Foresters (Nottinghamshire & Derbyshire Regiment)	The Worcestershire & Sherwood Foresters Regiment	A
47th and 81st	The Loyal Regiment (North Lancashire)	The Queen's Lancashire Regiment	A
48th and 58th	The Northamptonshire Regiment	The Royal Anglian Regiment	L
49th and 66th	The Royal Berkshire Regiment	The Duke of Edinburgh's Royal Regiment (Berkshire & Wiltshire)	A
50th and 97th	The Queen's Own Royal West Kent Regiment	The Queen's Regiment	L
51st and 105th	The King's Own Yorkshire Light Infantry	The Light Infantry	L
53rd and 85th	The King's Shropshire Light Infantry	The Light Infantry	L
57th and 77th	The Middlesex Regiment	The Queen's Regiment	L
60th	The King's Royal Rifle Corps	The Royal Green Jackets	L
62nd and 99th	The Wiltshire Regiment	The Duke of Edinburgh's Royal Regiment (Berkshire & Wiltshire)	A
63rd and 96th	The Manchester Regiment	The King's Regiment	A
64th and 98th	The North Staffordshire Regiment	The Staffordshire Regiment	A
65th and 84th	The York and Lancaster Regiment	Disbanded 1968	
68th and 106th	The Durham Light Infantry	The Light Infantry	L

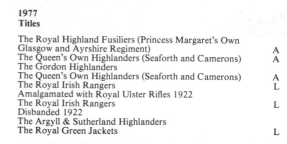

Pre-1872 Numbers	Post-1872 Titles	1977 Titles	
71st and 74th	The Highland Light Infantry	The Royal Highland Fusiliers (Princess Margaret's Own Glasgow and Ayrshire Regiment)	A
72nd and 78th	The Seaforth Highlanders	The Queen's Own Highlanders (Seaforth and Camerons)	A
75th and 92nd	The Gordon Highlanders	The Gordon Highlanders	
79th	The Queen's Own Cameron Highlanders	The Queen's Own Highlanders (Seaforth and Camerons)	A
83rd	The Royal Ulster Rifles	The Royal Irish Rangers	L
86th	The Royal Irish Rifles	Amalgamated with Royal Ulster Rifles 1922	
87th and 89th	The Royal Irish Fusiliers	The Royal Irish Rangers	L
88th	The Connaught Rangers	Disbanded 1922	
91st and 93rd	The Argyll & Sutherland Highlanders	The Argyll & Sutherland Highlanders	
Unnumbered	The Rifle Brigade	The Royal Green Jackets	L

Above: An indomitable fighting spirit inspired every soldier who wore the Three Black Triangles. A rifle section of the 1st Bn, Royal Norfolk Regiment, after the capture of Venrai, October 1944.
/Imperial War Museum

Index

H21 027 942 5

A CHARGE
IS MADE FOR
REMOVED OR
DAMAGED
LABELS.

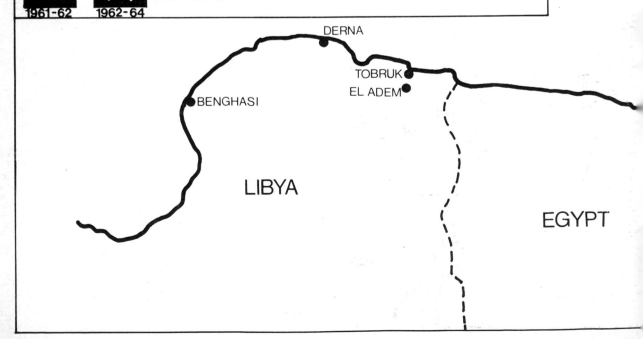

BRIGADES OF THE 3rd DIVISION 1951–1977
PERIODS SERVED UNDER COMMAND

	1 GUARDS BRIGADE	1956–1960
	2 BRIGADE	1959–1966
	5 BRIGADE	1964–1977
	16 PARACHUTE BRIGADE	1952–1954 1964–1970
	19 BRIGADE	1951–1959 1960–1977
	24 BRIGADE	1968–1976
	29 BRIGADE	1954–1958
	32 GUARDS BRIGADE	1951–1953
	39 BRIGADE	1951–1953
	51 BRIGADE	1960–1964

1961-62   1962-64

DERNA

TOBRUK
EL ADEM

BENGHASI

LIBYA

EGYPT